THE
INEVITABLE

THE
INEVITABLE

CONTEMPORARY

WRITERS

CONFRONT

DEATH

EDITED BY DAVID SHIELDS
AND BRADFORD MORROW

WITH AN INTRODUCTION BY THE EDITORS

W. W. NORTON & COMPANY
NEW YORK • LONDON

Since the copyright page cannot legibly accommodate
all the copyright notices, page 331 constitutes an extension
of the copyright page.

For information about special discounts for bulk
purchases, please contact W. W. Norton Special Sales at
specialsales@wwnorton.com or 800-233-4830

Manufacturing by Courier Westford
Book design by JAM Design
Production manager: Devon Zahn

Library of Congress Cataloging-in-Publication Data

The inevitable : contemporary writers confront death /
edited by David Shields and Bradford Morrow ; with an
introduction by the editors. — 1st ed.
       p. cm.
Includes bibliographical references.
ISBN 978-0-393-33936-9 (pbk.)
1. Authors, American—20th century—Biography.
2. Authors, American—20th century—Psychology.
3. Death—Psychological aspects. 4. Fear of death.
I. Shields, David, 1956– II. Morrow, Bradford, 1951–
PS129.I64 2011
810.9'3548—dc22

                                   2010043479

W. W. Norton & Company, Inc.
500 Fifth Avenue, New York, N.Y. 10110
www.wwnorton.com

W. W. Norton & Company Ltd.
Castle House, 75/76 Wells Street, London W1T 3QT

1 2 3 4 5 6 7 8 9 0

CONTENTS

INTRODUCTION

DAVID SHIELDS AND
BRADFORD MORROW

Birth is not inevitable. Life certainly isn't. The sole inevitability of existence, the only absolute consequence of being alive, is death. As Jamaica Kincaid succinctly put it, "Inevitable to life is death and not inevitable to death is life." Or, in J. M. Coetzee's words, "That, finally, is all it means to be alive: to be able to die." Whereas once one could frame mortality within the faithful ideology of an afterlife, now many can no longer speak with assurance about the immortality of the soul, the timelessness of art, the consolation of philosophy, or the everlasting reach of heaven. Where does this leave us? How do we face death? What is death and how does it touch upon life?

In posing these questions to twenty contemporary writers, we understood we were asking them to speak about the unspeakable, envision the unseeable. From their brave and eloquent responses, grieving and dancing in the face of the abyss, grew the organizing principle of the book: here is an early-twenty-first-century attempt to look at death from distinctly different points of view, by writers who see death as a brute biological fact that does not necessarily guarantee some passageway to eternal peace or punishment. And while this gathering may center on death, it is ultimately about the existential fact of our ineffable selves, our mortal bodies, death's fragile "other half": life itself.

Family naturally serves as a touchstone in many of these essays. David Gates's "Deathwatch" is ostensibly an evocation of the deaths of his mother, his stepmother, and especially his father, but it is at least as much a searing self-portrait of a dead man walking: "I can't make sense of this story, but I see now that it's been the only one I've ever told." In a similar way, Robert Clark makes both a literal and a figurative search for his dead sister, Charles Dickens's childhood home, and the religious ecstasy of Thomas Aquinas even as he searches for the past, the sources of his art, and the ground of his faith that consists of searching, yearning, and missing: "I would like . . . God to make me present to Himself, and to her [his sister], and to everything I thought was lost or missing." After her husband's unexpected death, Joyce Carol Oates is forced to work through the acutely painful process of suddenly being a widow, alone in a house filled with the memories and artifacts of a decades-long marriage. In "The Siege," she confronts the loneliness and guilt of the survivor, while learning how to get through days and nights irrevocably altered by death.

Several essays eulogize mothers in particular; in our beginning is our end. The first half of Kyoko Mori's "Between the Forest and the Well" evokes her mother's suicide and evolves into a necessary meditation about the author herself, alone and childless, thinking about death. "Sometime in my forties," she writes, "I came to admit the truth: the main problem with death isn't dying but being dead. Much as I'm afraid of the process, the result is unimaginably worse. . . . I am afraid of death because I believe in nothing." And yet Mori's conclusion is stunning, invigorating: "My decision-making practice is the opposite of memento mori. . . . I try to choose as though I would have to live forever with the consequences, not as though I might die tomorrow. . . . In my reverse memento mori, I've learned to cheat death, if only in imagination and metaphor." In "A Solemn Pleasure," Melissa Pritchard evokes imagery of landscapes and graveyards far from home while addressing the recent death and cremation of her mother. "She was ash in my home now," Pritchard writes, "powdered and tamped into a hideous shoe-polish-brown box, weighing little more than a feather." Kevin Baker's "Invitation to the Dance" describes the process by which he finds out that his mother has Huntington's disease and then that he has inherited the gene for the disease: "I thought about how giddy I would have been feeling if the results had been negative. I felt like blurting out the news to anyone I encountered, I just found out I will get a fatal disease. But I didn't. . . . What I really wanted was to live like I always did, taking little care of myself, wasting time worrying over politics, or how the Yankees were doing, or even the banality of other people's opinions. . . . I wanted my trivialities."

Many of these essays, such as Jonathan Safran Foer's and Christopher Sorrentino's, are highly pointillistic—death as content apparently pushing form toward a sort of scattering. In "A Primer for the Punctuation of Heart Disease," Foer proposes a new way of punctuating dialogue to denote unspoken aspects and meanings in conversations within a family that has suffered forty-two heart attacks, while examining the family legacy marked by tragic losses in the concentration camps of World War II. In Sorrentino's essay, the author makes an argument that digital proliferation—the attempt to leave a record of ourselves not so much in art as in various web presences—

avails not as far as death is concerned. "Public mourning says, *I am sad*," he writes. "*Now show me the film*." Having made this case, he proceeds to offer a moving tribute to his recently deceased father, the writer Gilbert Sorrentino, weaving polemical with personal thoughts.

Several essays resolve the issue of the difficulty of writing about death by coming at the subject from several angles simultaneously, working toward the subject of death through collage or in triptychs. (Why triptychs? Birth, life, death.) Diane Ackerman mourns the loss of a beloved friend in an intimate, moving passage that floats between two linguistic flights touching upon mortality and eternity. Greg Bottoms's "Grace Street" is a gracefully understated triptych as well: three apparently unconnected scenes, all death-haunted, from his life fifteen years ago, when he was living in a down-and-out section of Richmond. In "Cézanne's Colors," Brenda Hillman writes about the deaths of three loved ones in an essay that gestures more overtly toward the mystical than most of the other essays in the book do: "The diagnosis for everyone is death, yet even in times of thinking about the afterlife, I've thought of being part of an endless system of metaphors." Imagining consciousness as being like a bursting-with-life park near her house, in which the cycle of life and death endlessly flow, she concludes that existing knowingly within that vivid world is sufficient.

By contrast, Lance Olsen's "Lessness"—a collage of personal anecdotes, quotations, and aphorisms—evokes the irony of humankind's condition and the ways in which our "deepest need is to be free of the anxiety of death and annihilation; but it is life itself which awakens it, and so we must shrink from being fully alive." His essay is also full of gallows humor: "My wife's grandmother refused to be buried, insisting on being entombed in a mausoleum instead because, she said, she didn't want to get dirty." Robin Hemley, in his "Field Notes for the Graveyard Enthusiast," offers yet another response to the inevitable by developing a taxonomy of known and unknown graveyards, but the taxonomy dissolves. All the dead become anonymous in time, he concludes, embracing the eventual disappearance of every individual: "My gravestone will be blank."

These essays display a remarkable range of differing approaches. Sallie Tisdale, in her entomologically inspired "The Sutra of Maggots and Blowflies," uses the dipteran order of insects as a metaphor for death, evoking the transience of their brief adult lives and the repulsion and attraction she feels toward them. She talks about "decay as a kind of perfect" and wants to be able to stare at death without succumbing to it— being "in the fire" and still living one's life. Margo Jefferson reverses the trajectory of the metaphor. In "Death Wish in Negroland," she investigates the suicidal tendencies of the black bourgeoisie as an emblem of deeply haunted and conflicted desires: "I'd call it the guilty confusion of those who were raised to defiantly accept their entitlement, to be more than survivors, to be victors who knew that victory was as much a threat as failure . . . ." Peter Straub, in "Inside Story," shares with us one of his most cherished and defining secret childhood moments, a near-fatal accident that colored his entire life as a writer and a man, the roiling depths of which come into focus on his analyst's couch. Lynne Tillman's "The Final Plot" is an unblinking meditation on language and death. She addresses the subject from the point of view that death is the one subject no writer can address autobiographically, that the experience is nourished by the deaths of others, concluding, "Of death, mortals are absolutely ignorant. The dead, fortunately, are beyond caring." In "Bijou," Mark Doty describes a 1972 art porn movie of that same title, remembers a 1980s

East Village sex club, and meditates on the deathly cloud of AIDS that emerged during that era, seeing sex as a kind of affirmation of death. In "What Will Survive of Us," Geoff Dyer discusses the worldwide phenomenon of ghost bikes—bicycles painted white and placed at the scenes of fatal bike accidents to memorialize those who died—seeing them as a creative, moving improvement on the shabbiness of the more grandiose memorial art of officialdom. Finally we're all just trying to figure out how to say good-bye.

The concluding essay, Annie Dillard's brief but haunting "This Is the Life," asks: if there is no transcendental meaning, and we know we are mortal, how do we construct a life with value? "You have seen an ordinary bit of what is real," she writes, "the infinite fabric of time that eternity shoots through, and time's soft-skinned people working and dying under slowly shifting stars. Then what?" Here is the very question every writer in this anthology pursues.

David Foster Wallace, who so often set forth the most difficult questions, said, "You don't have to think very hard to realize that our dread of both relationships and loneliness, both of which are sub-dreads of our dread of being trapped inside a self (a psychic self, not just a physical self), has to do with angst about death, the recognition that I'm going to die, and die very much alone, and the rest of the world is going to go merrily on without me. I'm not sure I could give you a steeple-fingered theoretical justification, but I strongly suspect a big part of [a writer's] job is to aggravate this sense of entrapment and loneliness and death in people, to move people to countenance it, since any possible human redemption requires us first to face what's dreadful, what we want to deny." This anthology is an overt attempt to do exactly what Wallace called for.

THE
INEVITABLE

DAVID GATES

DEATHWATCH

My mother died alone, except for whatever staff members might have been around, at the rehabilitation center to which she'd been taken after her second stroke. The first had paralyzed half her body and affected her speech; I couldn't tell if she was still the same person inside and I didn't know how to ask her.

For seven years, my father brought her everywhere in her wheelchair. She had random attacks of weeping, and he couldn't leave her alone without her panicking; he bought walkie-talkies so he could mow the lawn or do a little work in his machine shop in the basement. Could I have given so much of myself to someone? I hoped I would never have to. In all those years, I didn't do much to relieve him, I never asked him what it was like for him.

I have a picture of my mother in her twenties. No wonder he wanted her. I would have. If that's Oedipal, fine: I've spent so long keeping my distance. When I knew her, she was overweight and, I suspect, her postpartum depression never lifted. She was forty when I was born, married for eighteen years, and had thought she could never have a child. The name they gave me meant "beloved." But an in-the-flesh infant, and then a one-year-old, and then a two-year-old and so on, must often have overwhelmed her. Like me, she lived in her own mind: people remember visiting my parents and having my mother pick up a book after a few minutes of chitchat. I'll never know what happened between us when it was just me and her, but I had shut her out before my first surviving memory. Like me, she was angry: my first wife claimed that her habit of shaking her finger had killed one of our houseplants.

The last time I saw my mother, she was in the rehab unit, after her second stroke, and her ruination made it hard for me to look at her. I remember her saying the word "foursquare": out of nowhere but not out of context. The antique, perhaps biblical, word meant steadfast, with a shade of defiance. I knew she could never recover. Did she know, too? My father might have had the answer, but I never asked him about that either.

The year after she died, my father married a woman named Leah. This was in 1985, and he'd been a husband since 1929. Leah had grown up in northern Vermont, and still had a strong accent after years of living in Hartford, Connecticut, raising five children by herself while working as a waitress in a diner. When she met Gene Gates, she was living in senior citizens' housing a couple of towns away; she told me later about his sneaking out of her place, at four in the morning, in his stocking feet. He was seventy-five and she was seventy-four. He told one of Leah's sons that he felt sixteen.

They wished for twenty good years together, and got twenty-one. They lived in a town of three hundred people in northwestern Massachusetts; they'd get into the car in the morning, and by nightfall they might find themselves in Virginia, in Ohio, in Canada. Leah always kept a suitcase packed.

When macular degeneration made it impossible for my father to drive—she didn't drive, and I never asked either of them why—they would sit at breakfast and plan where they *would* go that day if they could.

At ninety-four, my father could have passed for a man in his late sixties. William Howard Taft was president when he was born, and he could remember the Armistice that ended the First World War: the man who ran the local cider mill celebrated by giving all the kids in the one-room school free cider. The year before he died, I drove him on some errand, and as we turned back onto his road again, he looked out the window at the familiar blurs and said, "Well, back in the 'hood."

He'd begun working at sixteen: car mechanic, machinist, and then—when his company discovered he was a genius—a designer of electric timing devices. He told me once that he sometimes wished he'd misspent his youth the way I had. He taught me my first chords on the ukulele. He was only in his forties when rock and roll took over American music, but it never made sense to him. Several times I took him to hear Ralph Stanley, about whom I'd written a magazine profile. One day during his last year, I had him in the car, softened him up with a Merle Haggard CD, then asked if he wanted to try Bob Dylan. He listened closely to a couple of the quieter tracks from *Modern Times*, and pronounced the songs "crazy." He didn't seem to mean this as a criticism: crazy was beyond him, but he knew by now it was a recognized genre.

Once when he was ninety or ninety-one, I brought him to hear my band play a contra dance in the West Village. Afterward, he had smart advice about my rhythm guitar–playing—the running bass notes, he said, worked better than the sock chords—and he drank Manhattans and joked around with a table of women in their twenties at Café Loup. Until he died, one of them kept asking me about him, and he kept asking me about her. After his death, a writer friend of mine, with whom my father and I once had a quick beer, talked to me about him for longer than the time he'd spent with us—about the way he'd used language, about the way he'd carried himself. My friend said, "He was a *man*."

Driving had been one of his keenest pleasures; finally—to his relief, I think—his eye doctor ratted him out to the DMV; after he died, I found out that he'd been using Leah to navigate. He loved fixing up antique cars—which had been new cars when he was young. After he retired, in 1972, he restored at least twenty—many just car-shaped pieces of rust he rebuilt with salvaged metal and a welding torch. Now, he had almost no eyesight and both his big hands were permanently numb from carpal tunnel, probably from gripping steering wheels since the 1920s. Simply to drive a screw now took him five minutes. But if he couldn't see to work, he could listen to audiobooks: mostly history and politics. He had at least as much contempt as I did for George W. Bush. When he had to give up his license—what was he, ninety?—someone drove him to Wal-Mart and he bought a bicycle.

A few months before he died, he felt his way down to his shop and somehow made an aluminum bracket, with perfect right angles, so Leah could hang a telephone from the table next to her recliner. His last piece of work was a foot-tall Christmas tree to give a friend, made out of red and green pipe cleaners. It took him three days.

During his last year, I made the four-hour drive from New York more and more often, though not as often as I might have. I bought his last car, a blue-green Chevrolet Venture, so he wouldn't have to keep paying the insurance, and left it at his house so people could drive him and Leah here and there. It was the first time since he was sixteen that he hadn't *owned a car*. I hoped he couldn't see the New York license plates.

In mid-September, an EMS team took him to the hospital with severe pains in his back and abdomen. The doctors couldn't figure out what was wrong and released him. In a few days, he was back riding his bicycle down the long driveway to the mailbox and back. One afternoon in October, he helped me haul and stack firewood that I'd cut and split. I worried that I was allowing him to work too hard, but I knew how much he wanted to do it—and who was I to "allow" my father to do things? He said he wanted to try to make it to one hundred.

A week before Christmas, I called the house and Leah told me he was in pain again. Had I done this to him with the wood? She said he'd been weeping. By the time I got there, the pain had settled down, and it cheered him up to see me. It always did. I drove back down to the city late that night; I had to lecture the next day on Donald Barthelme's *The Dead Father*.

Every Christmas Eve, my father and I would sit up and watch *The Man Who Came to Dinner*. We both knew it word for word, and these days it was the one movie he could listen to and imagine all the visuals. But this Christmas Eve, he and Leah went to bed after dinner. I stayed up, drank more of the Jack Daniel's I always kept under the kitchen counter next to his Canadian whiskey, and played Spider Solitaire on my laptop. I'd been in a pit for over a year, and I'd just gone back on antidepressants. Sometime after midnight, half asleep, I thought

I heard him come out to the living room and try sleeping in his chair. I didn't get up to sit with him.

Leah woke me up early Christmas morning: Gene wanted to go to the hospital. They gave him an enema and a CAT scan. They found nothing and released him. He had a bad night, then an okay day, then a much worse night. Advil no longer touched his pain.

I drove him back to his doctor. Still nothing. That night he vomited, then dragged himself from the bathroom to the bedroom to the reclining chair, trying to get comfortable enough to sleep. He wound up in the kitchen, on a plain chair, with a pillow on the table. He refused to go back to the hospital for more useless tests. Could he be dying? Of course not. From what? He began spitting up clear, stringy phlegm. Leah and I told him he had to go back in. He didn't put up a fight.

In the hospital, I sat by his bed as he dozed. When I saw his eyes close, I'd read another few pages of *Mansfield Park*. A tall, alarmingly beautiful nurse—at this point, I was still taking notice—came into his room and gave him intravenous antibiotics "for the pneumonia that you have." Pneumonia! So *that* was it. Dangerous at his age, but not the worst.

The next morning, a nurse told me he'd slept badly, and when I sat down by him and touched his forehead, he said he was surprised he'd woken up at all. He fell asleep again, and I sat out by the nurses' station where I could see to read. I didn't care whether or not *I* woke up tomorrow. The new antidepressant hadn't yet taken hold, except that when I'd tried to get out of bed that morning, I'd moved my arm and saw glowing blue trails following it, like animated radio waves in an old cartoon. A demented woman, about my age, in hospital johnny and pigtails, was circling the nurse's station on a walker, singing and gabbling to herself: "Bless mother dear, a heartache in sugar."

The next day, he had the chills and the shakes, and was coughing up phlegm; I kept pulling long strings of it, clear and viscous, out of his mouth, winding it around a Kleenex the way you twirl spaghetti on a fork. I sat by his bed, and when he went to sleep, I worried that I would never have a real home: I'd lived in twenty rented apartments in twenty-five years. My third wife and I had bought a co-op, then sold it within two years, when our marriage ended. He woke up, and I put cold wet washcloth after cold wet washcloth to his face.

And now it was the last day of the year. A week ago, on Christmas Eve, I'd mixed a Manhattan for him, poured myself some Jack Daniel's, and we'd clinked glasses. This morning I couldn't make out what he was saying to me—ah, he wanted his hearing aids. I found them in an I Can't Believe It's Not Butter tub on his bed table; I knew by now how to put them in. He was in pain and the God-damned doctor hadn't come. It was seven-thirty in the morning. "If I'm going to kick the bucket," he said, "I want to do it at home."

But how could I give up on him? Just bring him home to die without even a diagnosis? This could be something treatable. He'd already had blood tests, X-rays, and CAT scans: this left only an MRI. But today was a Saturday, and the people trained to run the machine weren't here on Saturdays. And tomorrow was not only a Sunday, but New Year's Day. And Monday was the legal holiday. I accepted all this without an argument or a plea for special treatment and told my father it would be "just" another couple of days. (Out of the five he would have left.) He rolled his head on the pillow. But what could he do?

I'd always called my father at midnight New Year's Eve, if I wasn't there myself, and he always stayed up waiting. I told him I was going back up to the house to nap and would come back to see in the new year with him. I considered mixing just enough of a Manhattan to go in a pill vial, but I was afraid it might kill him. I passed out on the couch, slept through the alarm, and drove seventy on the two-lane road to the hospital. I got there ten minutes after the ball had dropped. My father woke up when I touched him, opened his eyes, smiled—it may have been his last smile—and thanked me for driving all that way down. I considered pretending it was a minute before midnight; he wouldn't have known. But I couldn't do that to him. Or to myself.

Then, on the morning of New Year's Day, his pain was gone. They'd stopped the morphine and the nurses were giving him only antianxiety meds they called "happy pills." His stubble was a week old, and I went out to a Walgreens and bought shaving cream and a red Gillette Mach 3 razor. I wanted it for myself; I've got it now. As I shaved him, I saw that his face had just the same problem zones as mine: especially the corners of the mouth, where you have to stick your tongue behind the lip to get at those pesky hairs. We agreed that this was a pain in the ass.

That afternoon, I got the diagnosis: congestive heart failure. He would live, at most, another six months. I forgot that this didn't account for the pain in his back and abdomen.

I arranged for home hospice care: no more ambulance rides, no more tests or treatments, and morphine FedExed to the door. They scheduled the MRI for Tuesday—this was Sunday—they would get a hospital bed delivered to his house and he could come home for the rest of his life.

My father's room had four beds with sliding curtains around them. Across from us lay a skeleton of an old man, mouth gaping. I pulled our curtain. Why should I have to look at some *dying person*? My father was eating again, so I ordered his dinner: tilapia, mashed potatoes, carrots, and orange sherbet. We'd gotten used to my feeding him. But he could stomach only the sherbet. He'd been warned off dairy products back when they'd had some theory or other about his digestion. But was there any point in denying him *anything* anymore? Still, I wanted him to have those six months, so I rationed out his sherbet when he had four days to live.

On Monday, the official holiday, the minister who'd been visiting the house for the past couple of years came by—neither my father nor Leah went to church—and asked me about my father's religious beliefs. He and I had never talked about it, but I'd assumed deist—a generically benevolent God who minded His business and let you mind yours—and I was to the left of there. The minister was a no-man-comes-to-the-Father-but-through-Me guy, but he knew not to push. I would have let him in if my father hadn't been sleeping.

They moved another new patient in: this one kept thrashing around and setting off his bed alarm. Poor bastard was probably dying too, like the skeleton guy. I took my father's hearing aids out so it would drive only one of us crazy. Late that afternoon, he woke up begging for "a happy pill, a sleeping pill, dope, anything." I got a nurse, who gave him an Ativan: I guessed this was the happy pill. He woke up an hour later and asked me for—and it took several repetitions for me to understand him—a fan to cool his face. I fanned him with a student's short story I'd been editing, then applied cold, wet washcloths until he slept again.

Tuesday went just as they'd promised: the last doctor's exam, the meeting with the discharge planner, the MRI at two-thirty in the afternoon. He cried out when they eased him onto the machine, and I held his hand for as long as I could reach it as he moved farther and farther inside the tunnel, its roof inches above his forehead. I swore to him that this was the last of it. I would get him home tonight. But now the doctors wanted to keep him until tomorrow, to wait for the test results. Tonight, I said. He's ninety-four years old, you're not going to operate on him. Tell me on the phone.

I drove up ahead of the ambulance, moved the couch to the other side of the living room, and rolled the hospital bed over away from the door and the cold air. It faced the picture window he'd put in when he'd built this house: it looked out on the old apple tree, and gentle Mount Adams in the distance. Not that he could see it now. When they brought him in, I told him he was home and he nodded.

The woman for whom my father had made the Christmas tree stayed with us that night. She'd cared for old and dying people before, and we had Ativan and Oxycodone, which had been holding him. In the morning, FedEx would be there with the morphine. Our friend took the couch, and I settled on the floor with a blanket and a pillow, between the couch and his bed.

Within minutes he woke up, in pain and panic. And now we found he couldn't swallow the pills anymore, so we put them on a spoon in applesauce, but even so they wouldn't kick in for so long, and he was moaning and crying out, he was incontinent, he was bleeding into the white sheets from his penis and his anus. We were afraid we'd overdose him, but eventually we got enough Oxycodone into him so he dozed between attacks of pain. Eventually, morning got there. FedEx got there. The hospice nurse got there. I went into the bedroom, closed the door and fell into sleep. People who knew what the hell they were doing could take this over for a while.

The doctor's call woke me up. The MRI had solved the mystery. Liver cancer. It was a matter of days. Maybe only hours.

He was still in pain, and when the nurses left us alone, I squirted dropper after dropper of liquid morphine into the back of his mouth. At first he'd recoiled from the nasty taste; now he was sucking on the dropper. I had been made to understand that *I* was in charge of giving it to him, and I also understood where that conversation was not permitted to be going. Strange to find yourself in a place you'd read so much about: like *you* suddenly at the summit of Mount Everest. But where was the supposed moral dilemma? I would keep giving him morphine until his pain stopped, one way or the other. And when it did stop, and I looked down at my father, sleeping, breathing comfortably, it was equally clear that his life wasn't mine to take. What thoughts, memories, emotions might he be having? What last things might he be working out far within himself? I had hired a registered nurse I'd never met to stay the night. She took the couch, I took the floor again. She smelled.

My father spent most of his last day on earth sleeping. Sometimes he'd respond to a word or a touch. He had gone too deep to need the morphine anymore. Friends and nurses were there. The minister was there. I didn't want to be there. Around three in the afternoon, I had the hospice phone in an additional prescription: we'd run low, and although he might never need morphine again, I remembered that first night home. Someone else could have gone, but I made the hour-and-a-half round trip down to CVS and back myself. And as soon as I walked into the house, he began to die, as if he had waited for me. No. He had waited for me.

Leah sat at his right side, I sat at his left. I held his hand, veins the size of pencils, scarred from all his years of work; his hands had always been bigger than mine would ever be. She held his other hand. We told him it was all right to go. I caressed his forehead, I kissed him. I told him I loved him and that he had been a wonderful father to me. I wept, though I tried to hide it: I didn't want him to feel wrong about going. His breaths became quieter, fainter, farther apart. We all watched for each new breath, and at some point we understood that another would not come. Everyone in the room but me had seen someone die before, but all of us kept looking at him and at each other. Now? Now? He stayed peaceful, beautiful, for a long time. Then I turned away for a second, looked again, and there lay a corpse. My father wasn't in it. How could any power ever have made this thing walk, talk, be a person? Later, when the man from the funeral home got there, I took the legs while he took the shoulders and helped him get it onto the stretcher, into the zipper bag and out to his SUV.

While waiting for him to get here, someone put a blanket over the body and somebody else heated up a pot of goulash— only in typing the word do I see the pun. We ate, we passed around the Jack Daniel's, we told stories about Gene and laughed. I wanted Leah to see the living room the way it had been when she came out of the bedroom in the morning. (After that night, she never slept in their king-sized bed again.) The undertaker helped me get the hospital bed out of the house. I moved the couch back where it belonged, lay down, and went to sleep where my father had died.

Fourteen months later, the same supply company moved another hospital bed into the same spot. I had thought Leah could have a few more good years. She'd had congestive heart failure before my father, but lately she'd been using less oxygen. She wanted to be with Gene, in an old-school, nondenominational heaven. But you could see she enjoyed running her household, seeing her friends, going out to breakfast or lunch. Someone gave her the *Pretty Good Joke Book*, from *A Prairie Home Companion*, and she retold the jokes so badly you had to love her.

In the fall, though, she started getting rushed to the hospital more often, and now her kidneys had begun to fail. Either that or her heart, her doctor said, would take her within six months. We called hospice. She'd had a long life, ending with those twenty, twenty-one good years. She told me she was content to go any day, and also content to have another day. The fluid in her lungs made it hard to breathe when she lay down, so she spent most of her last few months, waking and sleeping, in her recliner. *This isn't living*, she would say. But she had too much heart to be querulous, and liked people too much to drive them away. She still collected jokes—especially the obscene and the scatological—friends still visited daily, and young women came to her for advice. One of the nurses, a divorcée in her late forties, heard so much about those twenty good years that she made up her mind to marry the man who'd been asking her to take the chance again.

Leah had worked so hard to bring me and my father closer that we didn't come to know and to love each other until that year after my father died. In the summer and fall, I was coming up, at least for a couple of hours, most weekends. We began by talking about the man we loved: who else did either of us have anymore? We talked politics—she hated Bush too—about exes—we'd both lived wilder lives than my father—and about her death and mine. In her last weeks, I moved into the house with her and her friend Shirley, who'd been her live-in care-taker and companion for months.

She went from Vicodin to Ativan, Oxycontin, and Oxyco-done, and then we added morphine. It was trade-named Roxonol, and I couldn't stop the inane associations: "Rox-anne," Roxy Music, Rosanne Cash. When I had a few min-utes, I worked on my students' fiction. One wrote about an old woman, dying, comatose, and incontinent, who had to be moved and turned to prevent bedsores, and I was able to pro-vide the student with the term I'd just learned: drawsheet. Sometimes I failed to get the dropper far enough into her mouth, and later I'd find a green skin of Roxonol on the inside of her lip. Once she said to me, "I hope you'll have somebody to take care of *you*." It wasn't looking like it. But life was long. Wasn't it?

The day came when Shirley and I tried to help her over to the commode and found her legs no longer worked. Then the day they catheterized her. The day she could no longer swallow pills and I started grinding up Ativan, mixing it in a spoon with water and drawing it up into the dropper. The day they brought in the I.V. morphine pump: it had a red button marked DOSE, which we pushed every half-hour, to supplement the steady drip; Shirley and I took shifts, 24/7. The day came when we began pushing it every fifteen minutes. The day came when I shut the bedroom door and called the funeral home to give them a heads-up.

"I've got plenty," Leah said.

"Plenty of what?" I said.

"I don't know."

I said the obvious, the cheesy, and the true thing: "You have plenty of people who love you."

We hired people to come in. One woman brought along a thick album holding photos of her own paintings, which she said would be a good distraction for us: one was titled *Asshole* and had flames spiraling out of a solid black circle. I didn't let her come back. But another woman, an ex-minister, loved line-dancing, and when Leah was sleeping, she'd practice her steps to music from my laptop: "You Win Again" by Jerry Lee Lewis, "That's the Way Love Goes" by Merle Haggard, "The Jezebel Spirit" by David Byrne and Brian Eno. Still another liked to talk books and was a cousin of Susan Cheever's.

We stopped trying to turn Leah in bed because she shrieked in pain even when we nudged her. I stepped up the morphine: this wasn't about healing and recovery. She couldn't drink anymore, so we swabbed her mouth with sugar-cube-sized sponges on sticks, dipped in water and smeared with a mint-flavored mouth moisturizer. She hardly moved anymore, but she would close her lips around them. I worked on a student's story that began, "When you are dying, I tell Neil, it is like driving south up a mountain." I changed "it is" to "it's," then realized she needed that formal tone. I was also rereading *Martin Chuzzlewit*, in which a miser son schemes to poison his miser father to get the inheritance early. I was going to inherit this house and what remained of the money, which dwindled each day. I worried that people would think I was the wrong one to be in charge of the morphine.

I got so used to her lying there, to moistening her mouth and pressing the red button, that I thought we might just stay like this. The urine bag had stopped filling days ago, yet her breathing didn't weaken. And then one day it did, and she began to die that evening, right around the time my father had died, with most of the same people around her. One of her sons and one of her daughters held her hands. I kissed her and put a hand on her forehead. I couldn't, in conscience, assure her that Gene was waiting—he was or he wasn't, and she'd know any minute—but I told her it was all right to let go, and that I loved her.

She began that loud, harsh, ragged breathing called the death rattle. When it stopped, I thought that she had settled back into soft, nearly undetectable breaths, as my father had done. "She's still with us," I said to a nurse. "Do you agree?" The nurse said yes; apparently she thought I meant this in a mystical sense. I kept watching Leah: I had seen what a corpse was; this wasn't it. Based on the nurse's authority and my own experience, I assured people that she hadn't died yet. Yet they were beginning to get up, saying good-bye, driving away. It seemed odd that not even her own son and daughter were going to see this through to the end, but I understood: they'd gotten the idea, they'd been there for her when it counted, and they each had a long drive home. I didn't get it for an hour and a half, when a friend came over to close the open mouth and the jaw wouldn't move.

My mother's, father's, and stepmother's bodies are buried together in the hill town where they lived, their names and dates all on the same stone. If I want my own twenty good years, I'd better get cracking, as my mother used to say. But maybe I'm somewhere in the middle of them now, and these are what good years *are*. The meds are still working, and I look forward to seeing the blue trails.

I've got Gene's voice on a cassette tape, which I've never played. Once, after his eyesight was shot, he'd complained of having nothing to do, and I suggested he talk into a tape recorder about his life; I would transcribe it. I put off listening to it, then weeks went by and then it was shamefully late, so just never mentioned it again. I'm afraid to listen now: I might hear something I should have addressed. Wasn't there enough of that already?

I have dreams in which he and Leah recover completely, and dreams in which being dead is only like being of a different race. I'm always having the impulse to call him up and talk over the news: I hate that the world is leaving him farther and farther behind. Or to remind him to get to his radio because WAMC's Sunday afternoon bluegrass show is on *right now*. And I've had one dream in which my mother's face hovered in black and white close-up: she was so beautiful again. I thought she wanted us to understand each other.

After Gene died, Leah believed he was somewhere helping us. She heard his voice, saying he was waiting for her. Once she saw him sitting on the couch—*just as clear as I see you now*. She hurried to put her arms around him and they went right through and she began weeping. She said it wasn't a dream.

After Leah died, the friend for whom Gene made the pipe-cleaner Christmas tree told me she'd been going through their house—*my* house—trying to price their belongings for a yard sale. She said, "Gene and Leah, you have to help me out," and she heard Gene say, "Leah's busy right now, but I'll help you." She'd talked with him before: once he'd told her to tell *me* to check into any suspicious moles that might appear on my back.

Why hadn't he spoken to me directly? Well, why hadn't I spoken to him directly? Or to my mother? Thirty years after she died, I found out that as a young woman she'd been a fan of Django Reinhardt and the Hot Club of France. Why had I never known? Then again, why had she never told me?

Not long ago, my cell phone rang and a man said, "Hey! How are you?" And I said, "Ah, I'm fine. Look, this is embarrassing, but who *is* this?" The display had said UNKNOWN I.D. "*You* know," the man said. We went around and around like this. Then the man said exactly what *he* always used to say when he called me: "It's your dad." It wasn't my father's voice.

Having watched that before-and-after on his deathbed, I'm satisfied that there's such a thing as the spirit. I was with Leah and our friend on that. But I know my father well enough to know he wouldn't do parlor tricks from beyond the grave. And he wouldn't give me more weirdness than I could handle, since he knows me too. What's between him and me, in both senses of "between," and between me and my mother, will be here as long as I'm here, and after that it's nobody's business forever. I can't make sense of this story, but I see now it's been the only one I've ever told.

KYOKI MORI

BETWEEN THE FOREST AND THE WELL: NOTES ON DEATH

On the summer night I realized that I too would die, my mother had left the windows open to let out the heat. Waking up to the cooler air streaming into my room, I was astonished by how puny my arm looked in the light from the street. My elbow stuck out from under the covers like a ridiculous chicken bone. My body wasn't sturdy enough to last forever. Someday, my arm—and the rest of me too—would disappear from this world. The curtains stirred in front of the windows—in, out, in, out—as though the room were struggling to catch its breath. I was eight years old. I knew my ancestors had lived and died; that's how I came to be born. Now I understood what this had meant all along: sooner or later, it would be my turn to die. I pulled the covers over my head and hugged my knees to my chest, but there was no hiding from death. I thought I would never again be able to sleep. But before long, it was morning and my mother was shaking me awake. I had drifted off because I didn't really believe I would die, at least not anytime soon.

It's amazing I didn't contemplate my death earlier and more

often. All through my childhood in Japan, death was everywhere, openly feared. You did not put four cookies or apple slices on a plate at teatime because that number, pronounced *shi,* was a homonym of death. The hotels in Kobe, my hometown, did not have a fourth floor. My mother cautioned me never to pick up someone else's comb, not for reasons of hygiene but for those of luck. The word for "comb," *kushi,* also meant "painful death." If I touched a stranger's *kushi* to my hair, I might die in their stead. At night, we had to be careful not to sleep with our heads pointed north, like corpses laid out for funerals. My mother got upset if my brother and I ever stuck our chopsticks in our rice bowls and left them there: that was how rice was served to our dead ancestors at the Buddhist altar—the living should always pick up their chopsticks and put them neatly on the table.

My mother's mother, Fuku, came from a line of women famous for their longevity. Fuku's grandmother, mother, aunts, and great-aunts had all lived to be over ninety. Fuku often scolded me for being a picky eater. "You won't live long eating like that," she sighed. To her, longevity was an accomplishment— something you earned by living right—and she had the backing of history. On our field trips to the temples, shrines, castles, or museums in Kyoto and Nara, my classmates and I viewed the centuries-old scrolls and tapestries depicting the lives of emperors, shoguns, and religious sages. The decorative frames around the pictures had motifs of pine trees, phoenixes, sea turtles, beetles, and other symbols of longevity. If living long was a wise man's reward and virtue, then dying young wasn't just a misfortune or disappointment. In fearing death, we feared moral failure.

But in the legends from the same feudal past made into TV

movies, small bands of brave samurai warriors stormed the huge castles of their powerful enemies. Hopelessly outnumbered, our heroes—some of them only thirteen or fourteen—charged into the paths of arrows and spears with their swords raised high. Everyone died, of course. Or they won the battle but were sentenced to death afterward. Allowed to sit together one final time in their ceremonial white kimonos, they committed seppuku while their friends and families wept. The beauty of their courage was compared to that of cherry blossoms—a handful of luminous petals shedding together in the sun.

Dying gloriously, with honor, was a group activity. A virtuous death did not come to a man or a woman acting alone. When my mother chose death over her unhappy marriage, she was painfully aware of the longevity of her maternal line. At forty-one, she wasn't even halfway through her expected life span. She imagined fifty more years of crying every night, of burdening my brother and me with her unhappiness, and decided we would get over her death soon enough. My father considered her suicide so shameful that he bribed the police and the newspapers to report the cause of her death as an accidental gas leak. My brother and I were forbidden to talk about her or visit her family. My brother was eight; I was twelve. He obeyed and I didn't.

My only brush with death, so far, occurred when I was ten. My mother and I were swimming at a beach resort on the Japan Sea coast. One minute, we were riding the waves and laughing, and the next minute, I was alone in the water, struggling to stay afloat. The beach looked farther away than the longest distance—fifty meters—I'd ever swum in a pool. A blue swell, like a sand dune made of water, separated me from my mother. All the other swimmers—mothers, children, a few fathers—were clustered in the knee-deep water near the beach. When I tried to stand up to catch my breath, my legs slid sideways, a big wave went over my head, and I crashed into an underwater sandstorm. I came up just in time to get pounded down again. Then my mother was treading water beside me, telling me something I couldn't hear. I propelled myself toward her and clasped my arms around her neck. As another wave crested over us, I held on to her with all my strength.

When we resurfaced, my arms and legs tangled around her neck and waist, my mother was coughing. "You have to let go," she gasped. "Otherwise, we'll both drown."

Until the day she died alone, two years later, she would praise me for loosening my grip before the next wave came and trying to float on my own. The tide was carrying us away from the beach and stirring up a fierce undertow. Though my mother was a strong swimmer, even for her it was already too late to swim back. Between us and the open sea, there was a spit of land jutting out into the water. If we stopped fighting the waves, my mother saw, we could swim to the rocks on its edge. "Look," she said, treading water and pointing behind us. "That's where we have to go." I didn't have time to worry about how we were turning our backs to the beach and swimming farther into the sea. I reached forward and pushed the water behind me. I was going to have to haul my way out of the killing waves, my legs churning their own undertow. My mother had placed herself between me and the open sea where we would surely die. She was swimming slower so I could keep pace. Before anyone on the shore realized we were in danger, we reached the rocks and climbed out of the water. From there, we were able to walk back to the beach. The year before, a man fishing at night had drowned in the same undertow, but we didn't know till we were safely back in our hotel.

That was the last summer before my mother started crying every night. My father had been unfaithful to her throughout their marriage, but she was sure she had made her peace with his long absences, the late-night phone calls from his girl-friends, the lies he told and those he didn't bother to tell. She had my brother and me, her parents and brothers: all of us, she believed, needed her. Until she turned forty, my mother was a woman who feared death rather than desiring it. Caught in an undertow, she did not assume that only one of us could survive.

I left Japan eight years after her suicide and spent my twenties and thirties in small midwestern towns, first going to school and then teaching. My adult American life did not cause me to contemplate death very often. Especially in Green Bay, Wis-consin, where I eventually settled with a tenured job at a small liberal arts college, not a whole lot happened to prevent anyone from reaching their maximum life expectancy. Just once, I spun my car in a snowstorm, but the road was—typically—empty. When I hit the guardrail and stopped, the radio was still playing the same song and the car was dented but drivable. Keeping that car, with its rear-wheel drive, was perhaps the only death-defying choice I ever made.

Unlike some of my friends, I wasn't attracted to danger. In our last year of graduate school, when four of my classmates

signed up for an afternoon-long skydiving orientation that cul-
minated in jumping out of a tiny plane over a cornfield, I only
went to watch. The plane circled the cornfield for nearly thirty
minutes to get up to the right altitude. There was no way I
could have sat through that flight, much less walked out and
jumped. I did not take up rock climbing, white-water kayak-
ing, or downhill skiing. I ran on the sidewalk, cycled on bike
trails, and swam in the pool at the Y. True, no sport was completely safe. The first month I lived in Green Bay, a bowler
returning from the local lanes was killed when a drunk woman
rear-ended his car, causing his custom-made ball to launch
itself from the backseat and hit him in the head. After that, I
was careful to put anything heavy—for instance, my Smith-
Corona typewriter—on the floor underneath my passenger
seat, not next to me. My car was a two-seater, so no baggage
could possibly clobber me from behind.

The most dangerous contact sport, of course, was marriage. My mother wouldn't have killed herself if she hadn't
married my father. When Japanese couples of my parents' generation divorced, the woman lost everything. My father would
have sent her home to her parents, married one of his girl-
friends, and started a new life. He would have kept all his
money, my brother—his son and heir—and even me. We
wouldn't have been allowed to write, call, or visit our mother
till we were fully grown. Dying was the only way my mother
could leave her marriage and not suffer years of shame and
disgrace. In the months leading up to her suicide, she had
often reminded me of our near-drowning in the Japan Sea.
"Remember how you let go?" she asked. "I'm so proud of you
for not being afraid, for wanting to live."

To cling to someone was to be a coward or worse, to die. I

only married after making sure I didn't need a husband to support me or make me happy. I had a teaching job and a writing career; I kept my own friends, my own name, my own money. If my husband hadn't been an honest and loyal person utterly unlike my father, maybe it wouldn't have taken me thirteen years to wonder why I was married at all. If I was happiest alone, why was I living with another person? I couldn't come up with a good answer. Instead, I started questioning the peace I'd made with having settled in Green Bay, my husband's hometown, where people stared at me and complimented my English and treated me like a foreigner. After our divorce, I moved one thousand miles to a big city on the East Coast. At forty-two, a year older than my mother had ever been, I was trying to be reborn without having to die.

I'm fifty-one this year, so no one would be surprised to hear that all my grandparents and both my parents are dead. My grandmother, Fuku, managed alone in her house till she was ninety-four. Though she died in a nursing home, she was only there for a week, as a temporary patient. She'd hoped to recover from her pneumonia in time to attend my cousin Akira's wedding and move back home. Like all the women in her family, she ended up a widow, but my grandfather, Takeo, didn't die young either. He was in his mid-eighties when he had a heart attack, which was what killed my paternal grandfather too, at around the same age. My father and his sister both succumbed to cancer in their sixties, just like their mother before I was old enough to remember her. My father outlived his father by less than two months.

I spent a weekend with Fuku on my first return to Japan as an adult. At our parting, when she suggested we might not meet again, I laughed. "You used to say that when I was a kid," I told her. "My mother, brother, and I would be leaving your house after our summer visit and you would get all teary and predict you might not be around to welcome us the following summer. That used to upset me, until I realized you said the same thing every year. I don't believe you anymore." I don't know how long I thought she would live. She was ninety-two that summer. I didn't plan to be back in Japan again anytime soon. I had stayed away already for thirteen years. Of course, she was right: that was our last visit.

My doctor in Green Bay once told me about a new patient of hers who had answered the usual screening questions about family history with, "Don't worry, Doc, people in my family all died from natural causes." When she explained that those were the causes she was particularly interested in, the man looked baffled.

The deaths in my family had seemed unreal or irrelevant to me—I had assumed—because my father, his father, Fuku, and Takeo all died after I'd left the country. I wasn't close to my father or his father anyway. Though I longed for Fuku and Takeo in my teens, their house was a long day's trip away, so I only managed to see them twice, in secret, after my mother's death. Once I was in the States and had no intention of going back to Japan, everyone in my family belonged only to the past. It didn't matter whom I loved or didn't, who had died and who was still alive. Long before they died, Fuku and Takeo were as unreachable as my mother, and my father and his father might as well have been strangers. But that isn't why their dying didn't make me contemplate my own mortality. No

matter how close you were to someone or how much you identified with them, other people's deaths are nothing like the
possibility of your own. Losing someone and ceasing to exist
are two separate problems. We experience loss often enough,
many of us from an early age; however painful grief is, it's
something we already know. Our own death—not the process
but the result—is the one thing we can never experience,
know, or understand.

I used to claim that I was afraid of dying and not of death.
It was the process I dreaded, not the result. I didn't want to
suffer pain, look ugly, or feel panicked and helpless. I hoped
not to undergo a long, drawn-out illness like cancer because
then I would have to think about my death for months, be
required to read confusing medical pamphlets, and make
"informed decisions," only to delay the inevitable. I wouldn't
mind being dead, I insisted, if I could die suddenly, unexpectedly, painlessly, and (perhaps most important) unknowingly
from a heart attack or a tree falling on my car. Or in my sleep
in very old age.

One of my childhood friends had a grandmother who wor-
shiped a Shinto god with an onomatopoeic name. If this god,
Pokuri-san, decided to accept the offerings she'd been making
every morning with oranges, flowers, and prayers, then one
day, when she was old but still healthy, she would be doing
something she enjoyed, like walking across the street to meet a
friend at a tea shop, and in the midst of it, she would die
instantly from a heart attack. One second, she'd be waving to
her friend waiting under the tea shop's pretty awning, and the
next second, *Pokuri* (or *Pow!*), she'd fall over dead—no time for
panic, dread, or pain.

I still hope that I can die without suffering too, but I

wouldn't waste my time praying to the god of easy death. Sometime in my forties, I came to admit the truth: the main problem with death isn't dying but being dead. Much as I'm afraid of the process, the result is unimaginably worse.

My grandmother believed that when we die, we will join the spirits of our ancestors, whom she called *hotoke-sama* (the honorable Buddha spirit) or *gosenzo-sama* (the honorable ancestors); she pictured us sitting on a pure white cloud in Buddhist heaven and watching over our descendants. Other people's grandparents prayed to various popular Shinto gods besides Pokuri-san: the kitchen god, the money god, the matchmaking god, the traffic-safety god, the education-excellence god. All of these gods were once mortal men and women; because they were especially virtuous, a more important god (just who this was, I was never sure) granted them life after death and power to hear people's prayers. Christians believed in eternal life too. At the private school I attended, which had been founded in the 1860s by an American missionary woman, I memorized Bible verses, sang Methodist hymns, and wrote essays about spirituality in two languages and won awards for my performance. In the end, none of this religious exposure or training *took*. I am afraid of death because I believe in nothing.

Or, more accurately, I am afraid of death because I cannot fully believe or disbelieve the conflicting stories. If I could just accept one—we cease to exist and become nothing, we join the ancestors, some people are turned into gods (but probably not us), or we wait for Christ to resurrect some of us and condemn others to hell—then I could make my peace with the inevitable (nothing) or proclaim my faith before it's too late to enter heaven instead of hell. Believing is the safer bet. If faith allowed me to die without fear but death proved to be an eternity of no existence, I wouldn't be around to regret my choice. That would be better than ending up in hell for having failed to believe in the right religion.

But what is the right religion, and how can I pursue any faith when my only motive is the fear of death? It wasn't always this way. As a teenager, I loved the gospel story about Peter walking on the water with Jesus until he became afraid and began to sink, or the one about the disciples meeting the resurrected Christ and recognizing him only when he sat down to break bread with them. I liked Jesus the best when he was feeding the multitude or weeping over his friend Lazarus's death, not when he refused to see his mother, brothers, and sisters who'd come to hear his sermon or when he told Martha, the busy hostess, that her sister had chosen better by sitting at his feet and listening to his stories. For a few years, between fourteen and seventeen, I believed he was real—still alive among us, as my teachers said—because no dead person, I was sure, could inspire such strong admiration and irritation at once.

By the time I went to college, though, I knew that Jesus was real in the same way as Hamlet, Jane Eyre, Jay Gatsby, Holden Caulfield, or the Makioka Sisters. I'm not saying he was fake or insubstantial. I was beginning to understand life through the lens of literature, not the other way around. Jesus and a host of other characters from books enabled me to read the people I met and analyze the complications I made with them. The characters influenced my decisions and shaped my

life, but they won't change my death. When I die, I must part
with all the people I loved—even those who have spent centuries inside books and attained their eternal life. They will live
on, but I won't.

Those of us who don't believe in eternal life can still attain
substitute or metaphorical immortality by leaving a legacy. My
brother, our cousin Kazumi, and I, however, are the last of our
family on my father's side, with no children to carry on our
name. I don't expect many people to be reading my books after
my death, and I haven't worked hard enough for any cause to
make a lasting difference. The closest I get to vicarious immortality is through nature. I take some comfort in thinking that
even after I cease to exist, the natural world I was once a part
of will cycle on with its seasons, with the flowers, grasses, and
trees being reborn every spring. But I grew up in the 1960s and
1970s under the threat of worldwide nuclear annihilation, only
to enter my middle age with the polar ice caps melting. The
possibility of the world renewing itself forever, even if that
made any difference to me after I'm dead, isn't one I can take
for granted.

When I'm feeling optimistic, though, I do entertain the
notion that some part of me might survive my body's demise.
This undying essence would no longer be female, Japanese, five
feet two inches, or any particular age, but even without a body,
I imagine myself as a runner, the one consistent thing I was in
life. In kindergarten and the first grade, I loved the ten-meter
sprint, the air rushing past me as I hurled myself toward the
white finish-line tape that touched my white gym shirt and

floated around me. My first long run was in the third grade, when our physical education teacher took the sixty of us from our big combined class to the city cemetery two miles up the hill, lined us up at the gate with our backs to the garden of granite, and told us to run back to the school ground. The exhilaration of that long downhill sprint—seeing the cream-colored roof of the school building and realizing I was in the first pack of kids to be finishing—stayed with me through the 1,000-meter runs I did on our high school's track team, the 10k's and half-marathons I competed in during my twenties and thirties, and the 5-mile run that is still the most important part of my day. If I could outlast my body and become a spirit, I would pump my air legs and air arms to sprint up and down the hill between the cemetery and my grade school and all the other hills I've ever trained on. In death, I want to be air moving through air—nothing through nothing—forever changing and unchanged.

Everything we say about death is actually about life. I like to imagine being dead as an endless run because I've always felt the most alive while running. My grandmother, who valued family above all else, longed to be reunited with her ancestors and descendants through Buddha. To her, death was a huge family gathering with plenty of food. Every morning while alive, she prayed to the family dead at the Buddhist altar by offering them tea, rice, beans, vegetables, and fruits; then she went to the kitchen to cook breakfast for her children and grandchildren. In death as in life, she wanted to be inside that same cycle of comfort and respect.

My ex-husband, Chuck, hated finishing any projects, especially those he enjoyed. In college, he declared a new major every couple of years, always thrilled with his choice until he got close to fulfilling his requirement. He took ten years to complete his B.S., and when we divorced, he was enrolled in his third master's program as a no-degree candidate. It's no surprise, then, that he believed in reincarnation. His ideal death was an opportunity to start over indefinitely.

The hell we fear too is a metaphor for what we abhor in life. Mine would be an eternity stuck inside a small, dark coffin, unable to move, isolated from everything and everyone. The scrolls showing the Buddhist hell, where gaunt, starving souls wandered through a horrific landscape, didn't scare me quite so much even as a child. At least in that version, you were allowed to move around, you had multitudes of other sinners with whom to bemoan your fate, and the mountain of needles and the sea of blood looked spectacular, if not inviting.

Unfortunately for all these fantasies, death begins where pictures and words stop. It's the one thing we'll never be able to describe, even with our most oblique metaphors. No wonder all the heroes in Shakespeare had such long speeches as they were dying. It was their last opportunity to understand in words who they were and what they had loved and desired in life.

My last name, which means "forest" in Japanese, is "death" in Latin, as in memento mori—the medieval monks' practice of meditating on death to understand the need for salvation and enlightenment. In the name's original language too, a forest implied darkness and danger. To a Japanese rice farmer, any land covered with trees was a wilderness, a place far away from home. My ancestors would have shared Robert Frost's view of the snowy woods as lovely, dark, and deep—a place to admire from a safe distance. For my father's family, their very name reminded them of what to avoid or outwit. My mother's maiden name, by contrast, was Nagai, which meant "eternal wellspring." The village her ancestors came from was called Tai, "rice paddies and a well"—all that a farmer needed for sustenance.

To contemplate death is to balance myself between the two families that made me, to straddle the contradictions of my heritage and upbringing. While my mother rejected her legacy of longevity and died young by choice, my father died, still relatively young, from a disease he never expected to get. He had always assumed that his mother's cancer was caused by her having been in Hiroshima at the time of the atomic bomb, when he himself was safely away at college in Kyoto. People in the Mori family were not the contemplative memento mori types anyway. In the middle of the heart attack that would kill him before the day was over, my paternal grandfather asked my aunt to call an ambulance and then went back to his room to put on his best suit; he came out all dressed up and sat down in his formal drawing room to wait, but when the paramedics arrived, ten minutes later, he was back in his room changing into his golf shirt and sporty khaki pants—he'd decided that casual attire was more appropriate for a medical emergency. He wasn't trying to meet his death with dignity. As he did throughout his life, my grandfather was thinking first and foremost about his appearance.

Even the irreligious among us often practice a secular version of memento mori to evaluate the choices we've made in life. If we knew we were going to die in ten years, would we still be

working the job we have today, living in the same house or
city, married to the same person? What if we were going to die
in five years, one year, six months, three days, or a few hours?
What would we do differently? Surely my grandfather wouldn't
have answered this question by saying that he would change his
clothes twice. But how do we know that the choice we imagine making under the pressure of death is more true or noble?
The one time I was about to die, I only wanted to avoid death
and continue to live. I didn't let go of my mother in that undertow in the Japan Sea because it was the right thing to do or
because I was brave. All my action proved was that I wanted to
live, not how or at what cost. In this, I was more like my
father's family than my mother's.

Memento mori didn't help my mother, who imagined death
and chose *it* instead of finding a way to live as though she might
die any day and therefore had nothing to lose. The latter would
have meant leaving her marriage, going to stay with her parents, and holding on to some small hope, at least, that her parents would love and console her while she endured her disgrace
or that my brother and I would come to her when we were old
enough to leave our father's house. Even if we didn't, she wasn't
going to lose us any more in life than she did in death, but my
mother wasn't thinking of those chances. She chose the pure
certainty of death over the banal compromises of life.

Because I've lived most of my life in the shadow of her suicide, I don't think of death—imagined or real—as the truth
serum that would reveal our best, most honest intentions. My
decision-making practice is the opposite of memento mori.
Faced with a big career change, moral dilemma, or romantic
prospect, I try to choose as though I would have to live forever
with the consequences, not as though I might die tomorrow.

Living to see the result of my potential mistake is just as sobering a thought as the possibility of dying with regrets, but as long as I'm alive, I can rescind, modify, or transform even the worst choices I've made. In my reverse memento mori, I've learned to cheat death, if only in imagination and metaphor.

Death means having no more thoughts to understand or express in words. How can I imagine not having words when that very imagining must occur in words as long as I am alive?

ROBERT CLARK

BAYHAM STREET

I had a sister whom I hardly knew, whose existence I might doubt entirely if it were not for some photographs that show us together. I can see her, you might say, in my mind's eye, but only in one dimension: I'm not sure I can say what she "was like," how her features, bearing, and voice seemed in their entirety. Up to a point, I might have been able to piece her together—to imagine, if not a story, at least a character—through the photographs. But a photograph is no more than a refraction in a moment that nothing other than a lens ever saw, scarcely a pinprick in the fabric that veils a life. A photograph seems to contain and to mean much more than that, but perhaps what it does most of all is to induce longing, a hunger for everything—the day and the persons and the place—that it does not contain and which is irretrievably lost to us.

So sensing, perhaps, that it was a dead end, that it would end in bafflement and frustration, I didn't pursue the trail of this sister I'd scarcely even met—I haven't even bothered to mention her name, Patty—but someone sent me another photograph. When my grandparents' house was cleared out, their books were donated to the local library and, sifting through the cartons, a librarian found a photo album. She knew my name and sent it to me.

It was a tiny thing, the pages just big enough to hold one small photo each of me, my siblings, and cousins. It had belonged to my grandmother, and I'd seen pretty much every photo in it, these having been widely circulated among the family; every photo but one, that of a little girl, perhaps four years old, in a green dress on a red sofa against a green wall.

She has a fierce look, of insouciance and even defiance. Her arms are crossed in a kind of resigned impatience. She could not care less and yet she insists that you pay attention to her. I thought I knew who it was—the album contained nothing but my grandmother's grandchildren—but the little girl's demeanor threw me off. This child wasn't anything like what I had understood or had remembered Patty to be.

I sent the picture to my other sister, who's five years older than I and was two years Patty's senior. She didn't recall seeing it before, but she confirmed that it was our sister: Patty, who had been diagnosed as mentally retarded when she was two; confined to an institution; who was put (unlike me and my sister) in my father's custody when my parents divorced; who subsequently developed into a child with normal psychological and cognitive functioning; and who died—by then a bright and vivacious young woman—in a head-on collision during her second year of college.

Her transformation had been dramatic, even miraculous, and no one ever explained quite how it came about. There'd been a psychiatrist in Boston, a Dr. Fleming, but beyond the fact that someone had done some sort of therapy with Patty, the secret, as the cliché says, died with her. But by all reports she was someone else entirely as an infant and small child or, rather, she was almost no one at all. I was an infant then, but my sister remembers Patty's visits home from the institution. She wanted to play with Patty the way a big sister should play with her little sister. But Patty wouldn't play. She sat. Or sat and stared. Sometimes she said strange or incomprehensible things. She said "kalifidos," by which my sister eventually figured out she meant "cowboy."

Other people had reported similar things: she was slow, vacant, abstracted. And there were other photos that seemed to corroborate that view. In her baby pictures, she's doughy, ill defined, never quite roused from sleep. In a later photo, she's about two, and she's standing in front of a mirror trying to comb her hair. She's smiling avidly, as if she's amusing herself by combing the hair of this *other* child, the one she sees in the mirror. Either way, she's been photographed unawares—unlike any of her other childhood photos—and, also uniquely, she's smiling. She thinks she's alone, just her and perhaps this other little girl who lives in the mirror. And so she is happy.

That photo was taken on one of Patty's visits home from her institution. My mother and father were still living together, although their marriage was disintegrating. And perhaps Patty—the shame and worry and disappointment of her—was a factor, a shadow cast over their happiness, a vacuum that deprived them of oxygen, that caused the flame between them to die. In any case, it was said that my mother couldn't cope with Patty or, for that matter, very much else.

In fact, the most specific explanation any of us ever heard for Patty's condition had to do with my mother, with something she had done or failed to do for this daughter of hers. Part of the vagueness and mystery surrounding the matter attaches to the fact that none of us is quite sure with whom the story originated. But the gist of it was that my mother had caused Patty to withdraw, to hide or disappear, to annihilate herself.

There's one more photo that perhaps bears out something like this. She's looking at the camera, or at a person near the camera. Her mouth is slightly open, the upper lip just arched upward as though she's about to speak or is beginning to register some surprise. As in the other photos, she's wearing a smocked dress, and here she has a little purse slung over her shoulder. But this grown-up accessory doesn't delight her as the comb did in the other photograph: it looks like it's been pasted on her. Alongside the purse, her arm is stretched out, underside up, as though someone's about to draw blood from it. You come to her eyes last, despite the fact that they're dark, shiny, perhaps terrified. They're plangent, but somehow lack the capacity or will to cry. They're bright but stony, anthracite, obsidian. She's terrified of death or, rather, she's as afraid of dying as she is of living.

I first heard the idea that my mother was the author of Patty's condition when I was perhaps thirteen. Just then, I'd been reading Freud—more accurately, popularizations of Freud—and it seemed quite reasonable to me that a mother might do this to a child, or wish to (and in the Freudian cosmology wishing and doing were much the same thing): it was within a mother's powers of oppression and repression, active or passive, to crush a child or cause her to disappear into herself.

Anyway, it went without saying in the years between, say, 1955 and 1965, that it was at least in large part my mother's fault, and that she would, of course, herself appreciate this fact—she'd majored in child psychology in college—and be ashamed of it. Even without knowing quite why and how, she'd victimized this little girl, and she'd driven her husband away, or he'd left in disgust.

But that is not what struck me in the photograph I'd been sent. Far from being diffident or passive, Patty is intense, maybe even angry. She dominates the frame that encloses her and the colors that ought to subsume her. Her presence is such that she might almost come out of the photograph, thrust herself before you, and spit "kalifidos" in your face.

But, as someone pointed out right away, more than anything, she looks like me, like a shard of my family, like all of us who survived her, who persisted here after she was gone.

I received that photo in the mail perhaps three years ago, and although I felt the imposition, the demand it seemed to make every time I looked at it, I did nothing about it. My other sister, however, was going to pursue the matter: she, after all, had known Patty. She lived in Massachusetts, where Patty had spent most of her life, and she would look into her case. I, meanwhile, was chasing down other things, all of them missing or lost. I went to Bayham Street instead.

Charles Dickens lived on Bayham Street, Camden Town, London, in 1822, age ten, in a house of yellow brick. And there, staring out the window of "the little back garret," commenced the worst period of his life. On account of his family's penury, he was pulled out of school and put to work ten hours a day in a blacking factory under Hungerford Bridge. His father was thrown into the debtors' prison at Marshalsea. Charles lived on Bayham Street scarcely a year—his family moved constantly in order to evade their creditors—but it was the first place he lived in London and in some ways the last; in his imagination, he seemed to inhabit it for the rest of his days.

It was definitively the house of the Cratchits in *A Christmas Carol* and of Mr. Micawber in *David Copperfield*. The view from the garret window of the dome of St. Paul's shrouded in smoke and fog is surely Pip's first vision of London in *Great Expectations*. And it was, for me, the first source of Little Dorrit's view from Southwark Bridge, the panorama she would carry with her to Italy. I felt that in that garret, ashamed, oppressed by his child labor, and half-orphaned, that Dickens took his emptiness, the void that he might have become, and began to make it into art. I wanted to see where this had happened, to see what traces of it might still persist.

I went to London three times over the next two years and on each trip I went to Bayham Street. It's an ugly, straight swatch of row houses, flats, and public housing projects running south from Camden Town Underground station. The first time, I walked down one side of Bayham Street to its terminus at Crowndale Road—perhaps three-quarters of a mile—and back up the other side, looking for the blue plaque that marks buildings with historical and literary associations in London. But there were no plaques on Bayham Street. It seemed impossible that any place in London connected with Dickens wasn't marked in this fashion, least of all his first boyhood home in the city. Perhaps I'd made a mistake about the name of the street.

At home I rechecked the address, and when I returned to London six months later, I brought the house number with me. I now knew the address was 16 Bayham Street. But though there were dozens of small brick houses of early nineteenth century vintage, none of them corresponded to that address. So there was no number 16 and no blue plaque either. It occurred to me that perhaps the house had stood on the site of one of the vast blocks of public housing flats—built, it seemed, in the 1960s or '70s—at the south end of the street, and that in their construction the houses, the address, and the blue plaque might have vanished. Perhaps I was the only person who had any interest in finding or seeing the house; perhaps I was the only person who understood how important that place had been. And in this thought I took a sort of melancholy pride. But either way, I had to accept that neither the house nor the place where it stood seemed to exist.

The next time I came to London, in the spring of 2005, I had no plans to visit Bayham Street. I'd spent the previous five days in Germany walking for six hours a day, and thanks to a pair of ill-fitting shoes, my feet were almost bloody with abrasions and blisters. I was stopping in London for twenty hours to catch my breath and wait until my flight home left the next day.

That next morning, I went to Gower Street in Bloomsbury to shop for books. The Dickenses had lived on Gower Street after vacating 16 Bayham Street, after Charles's father had been sent to Marshalsea. I wasn't moved by this fact—I think I'd forgotten it just then—but by a sense almost of dereliction, of having left undone something that ought to be done. So, with a plane to catch in a little over two hours, I took the tube to Camden Town.

I walked quickly over to Bayham Street and started down the west side, no number 16 and no blue plaques visible anywhere. In the distance, I could see the end of the street at Crowndale Road, and I asked myself if I was really going to walk the whole way down; if I really needed to make this pointless trek in its entirety a third time. I had a plane to catch and a ten-hour flight to endure. So I compromised. I walked another block to where the modern housing projects began—the point beyond which there were no nineteenth-century buildings—and crossed over to the east side of the street. I swear I surveyed every façade of every house between there and the Underground station, but I found nothing at all.

I went back to my hotel, got my bag, and rode the train to the airport. I was angry that I'd wasted yet more of my limited time abroad on Bayham Street, but at the same time I felt a kind of guilt, a sense that if I had only tried harder or looked more carefully I would have found Dickens's house. And as stupid and futile as I knew the impulse was, there was no other solution to my disappointment—to ease the longing, to complete the quest—than to go back to Bayham Street another time on another trip.

I was disappointed even before I'd gotten to London. I'd been in Italy for six weeks and then in Germany for a few days afterward. I'd gone to Germany specifically to visit Dresden and then Weimar. From the reading I'd done and the music I listened to, it came to seem to me that for 150 years—from the late eighteenth century through the first third of the twentieth—Germany possessed perhaps the most brilliant philosophic, scientific, and creative minds in the Western world. Then, in scarcely a decade, it descended into the deepest barbarity humankind has ever known. This is a now commonplace observation. It wasn't entirely clear to me whether it described a paradox or a necessary relation, an inevitability, but I wanted to see the evidence for it for myself.

For me Weimar and Dresden represented the poles of that history. Bucolic, cobbled, park-like Weimar was the home of

Goethe and the Romantic movement, Germany's intellectual and literary heart, and the site of the foundation of its last democratic government before Hitler. Dresden, the Baroque capital of the kingdom of Saxony, had once been called "Florence on the Elbe." It was a center of German music and opera and an artists' colony that sheltered Schumann, Wagner, Ibsen, Caspar David Friedrich, and Dostoevsky. Its museums were the best in Germany and contained, among other masterpieces, Raphael's *Sistine Madonna*, the painting the nineteenth century considered the most beautiful art work in the world. In the final months of World War II, Dresden and perhaps 50,000 of its inhabitants were incinerated in a firestorm of Allied bombing, the greatest conflagration in the western theater of the war. Whether portrayed as an act of slaughter and destruction unjustified by any military need or as a well-deserved retribution for the Nazi horrors, the annihilation of Dresden seemed to me to mark the final extinction of the German genius and civilization born at Weimar.

In Dresden, I'd checked into a postmodern edifice called the art'otel. My room was elegantly spare, decorated in black, gray, and blond wood. It overlooked the city soccer stadium, the assembly point over which the British bombers fanned out on their incendiary runs sixty years before. You would not know that from looking at it, or by turning in the opposite direction, to the southeast, where the bombs fell. Excepting the city's reconstructed Baroque churches and palaces, most of the buildings in Dresden were erected after 1950. The more appealing among them are in the mode of the art'otel, but the majority are examples of Soviet Modernism from the era of the German Democratic Republic. The rubble and ruins have been completely vanquished, but a vista of empty form imposed on a waste ground—the ash meadow, the field sown with salt—stands in their place.

But it was ruins, or the remnants of them, I had come to see. I wanted to see cinders and scorched bricks, a Baroque statue, perhaps decapitated or armless, tilted at an impossible angle but still standing on a darkling field of debris, a waft of phosphorous on the air. I wanted, if not the dead themselves, the places in which they died, the stage upon which their holocaust had been acted out.

There is a host of stories about the horror of the firestorm and its aftermath that might drive anyone, man or child, mad, unspeakable things that might turn you to stone were you to see them: cellars, for example, packed with asphyxiated, bloated corpses of mothers and children, inside which recovery workers could scarcely keep their footing on account of the carpet of maggots covering the floors. During the bombing, Dresdeners instinctively took shelter there, but the updraft of the firestorm outside literally sucked the oxygen from the basements.

The air temperature rose into the hundreds of degrees. Many people fled to the bank of the Elbe and immersed themselves in the water. Others tried to evade the heat by hiding in water tanks and fountains. But as the air temperature increased, the water in the fountains heated as well. Those who sheltered in them were boiled alive and then the water itself evaporated, leaving their corpses beached in the empty pools.

There is a photograph I came across that illustrates this phenomenon, and while I found it moving—it shows that there was literally nowhere to go, no escape from the firestorm— I suppose it also exercised a morbid fascination upon me. The fountain was in the Altmarkt or close by it, and I spent some hours scouring the area looking for it in the same hopeful and frustrated manner I'd searched Bayham Street, and to no more avail.

All that, seemingly every trace, has been erased. The past has been carted away, leveled, and paved over. It was not simply that there was no sign of the past—no ruins or reminders—but that even the presence of the past had been obliterated: even the absence of what once was had been taken away. The past is, of course, dead, but here it had apparently never lived.

The Dresdeners of today are proud of their city, of its flawless replication of historic buildings and the cutting-edge architecture of its new ones. But for me, the excision of the past seemed to spill over into the present. The present, too, felt empty. That evening, my feet sore from the day's futile reconnaissance, I ate alone in my hotel's chic dining room. For whatever reason—a lack of out-of-town visitors or locals accustomed to dining out—the room seemed a stylish void, its grey walls too grey, the light a little too stark. The waiter stood nervously behind the bar or disappeared into the shelter of the kitchen. Music—the forlorn ranting of Leonard Cohen—echoed from the sound system. I felt lonely and grieving. I missed my family. I missed everyone I'd ever known, or known of.

The next morning, I went to see the *Sistine Madonna*, the painting that transfixed the nineteenth century, the golden age of the annihilated Germany that once existed nowhere as much as in Dresden. It had preoccupied the people who preoccupied me: for Ruskin, it was the beginning of the end of art, the triumph of the artificial and the artificer over Gothic faith and naturalism manifested by the anonymous craftsman, but for Dostoevsky it represented the stunning intersection of the numinous and beautiful. It had been secreted underground outside the city and had survived the firestorm.

I hoped to either love it as much as Dostoevsky or disdain it as had Ruskin, or at least try to see some of what the past—the dead of 150 years ago—had seen in it. If nothing else, unlike Dresden, it was present, intact. There's a round banquette placed just in front of the painting, and you can sit before it as before a fire or an altar. So I did.

You know it, this painting. Or rather you at least know *them*: the indolent and resigned putti at the bottom of the frame. To us, that tranche of the *Sistine Madonna* is almost an artwork in its own right and—to judge by its constant reproduction on calendars, posters, and consumer whatnot—as much a talisman of art in the late twentieth and early twenty-first centuries as the entire painting was in the nineteenth. And what makes this image iconic for us is the obvious fact that these angels are a couple of comedians, wiseacres, and ironists. The curtains on either side of the frame have been pulled back to reveal Mary, her baby, and their papal attendants. It's—if you will—*The Madonna Show* and those little guys are the stagehands. They're not impressed, they've seen it before, and they're waiting for it to be over. These putti are cute but knowing, even hip. In their recognizance of what's happening, they're recognizably us, of our time.

Of course, they're really of Raphael's time, but perhaps their seeming membership in ours reveals something about the nature of a work of art: its capacity to project a presence—a transcendent yet objective being—independent of any epoch, including its own. Or perhaps it merely allows for interpretations—projections that come from us rather than the artwork—that our subjective circumstances incline us to make. At any rate, these putti seem themselves to be offering an interpretation of what's going on above them, a sardonic or at least comic commentary on the picture they're a part of.

You might say that what the putti—these moderns with wings—are commenting on is precisely what the nineteenth century loved about this painting: its notion of beauty as spectacle, as a parting of the curtains to reveal a view of the divine, of heaven. The Madonna and her attendants are standing on clouds, and they too are a little vaporous, particularly the Madonna herself, whose tender beauty is somehow unboundaried, as though diffusing the light she contains. In truth, she was, to me, a little vague, not quite present. But the nineteenth century loved words like "diaphanous" and "effusion" and perhaps it loved this painting for so embodying them. For me, however, the Madonna's compassion and illumination did not so much shine as leak from her, puddling in a watery sweetness. In our time, at least, Rothko's layered nimbuses, his lozenges of fulminating color, may seem deeper and truer, may better signify the transcendent.

For all that, she seemed to me the first emphatically real historic presence I'd encountered in Dresden. She wasn't a replica, a reproduction, or a symbol of something missing or lost. But she also wasn't particular to this place. She could project herself—her facticity as art—anywhere. But I had come here to find genuine traces of something I felt I needed to comprehend, markers that were more than symbols or plaques or monuments. I wanted, if not the flames of the firestorm, a whiff of their smoke, a sign of their onetime presence here.

I ate a delicious piece of lemon cake in the reconstructed Baroque café near the reconstructed opera house on whose site Wagner and Richard Strauss had premiered their works. I began walking back to the art'otel and it was snowing, turning darker and colder. The weather was coming in from the north and the east, from Poland and Russia, from the taiga and the steppes, the deep primal backyard—the shadow self, perhaps—Germany had so many times tried to enslave or destroy.

The avenue that led back to the hotel cut through what had been the royal precincts of the electors of Saxony, the princes who had made this place "Florence on the Elbe." Along one side were several office and apartment blocks from the GDR and along the other, stretching at least one block, was a vacant lot, a thicket of trees, brush, and abandoned refuse and junk. At its far corner, jutting out from the tangle of bare trees and shrubs, huddled in the east wind and its scattershot of snow, stood the façade of what once must have been a small but imposing building.

As I came closer, I saw there was an inscription over the portal in the center cut in early-nineteenth-century characters. It said ORANGERIE. The gateway was barricaded and braced with wood, as were the windows and the doors to either side. The stone was covered in places with graffiti and posters, and otherwise cracked, pocked, and stained. It might have been due to weathering, subsidence, and vandalism, but also, given its placement directly on the bombers' track, from heat, flame, and shrapnel.

When the building was intact, it must have had an ornate glass carapace beneath which orange and lemon trees were cultivated. Among them, in the custom of the time, the elector and his court might have taken tea and imagined themselves on the Bay of Naples. Now the building was pathetic twice over, once as an architectural folly consecrated to growing oranges where oranges could not grow and now as the shabby remnant of a once great but now deposed kingdom and culture. The portal was like the curtain of the *Sistine Madonna*, 150 years ago opening onto an ersatz Eden, and today, as the gelid wind blew in from the east, onto a GDR barricade with an overgrown lot behind it.

It was too cold to linger, too cold in fact to go out for the rest of the day, and I was catching a train to Weimar the next morning. But in the night, I realized that the Orangerie was what I had come to Dresden to see, or that it was going to be the best I could do, a real sign, a ruined but intact presence of the firestorm and the world it had incinerated. In the morning, on the way to the station, I lugged my bag to the curb opposite and took a picture. The snow had turned to sleet and most of what had fallen yesterday was melting beneath a southwest wind, from the direction of Weimar and of Naples.

Weimar was, on its face, everything that Dresden failed to be. There were old burghers' houses, venerable squares, church-yards flocked by birds, and a long park that wended along the river to Goethe's summer cottage, which even empty suggested the presence of children, of little girls in pinafores and smocked dresses in some eternal golden past. But most of all there was the light, on that day blue and gold, and you might well imagine why Goethe had become fascinated by optics and the science of color; why, it was said, his last words on his deathbed were "*mehr licht*"—more light.

The town is built less of stone or brick than plaster and wood, and the predominant colors are pine green, a pale butter-yellow, and a deep amber, the hue of the German dying fall, a register removed from the olive, lemon, and russet of

Italy. Goethe was, of course, the original northern European Italophile, the author of the verses Schubert set to music in praise of Italy as the antidote to Romantic longing and melancholy.

As the cradle of German Romanticism, Weimar has, of course, a magnificent cemetery, a rolling cavern of conifers and vines. But then perhaps Weimar itself is one vast graveyard that we amicably share with benign ghosts, its muses and geniuses, the dead with whom—having not been annihilated by history and its fires—we live in a parallel dimension, just adjoining theirs.

I got lost in the cemetery and I didn't mind at all. I couldn't find my way out to the southeast exit I believed ought to lead to Nietzsche's house. At last I found a gate that gave onto a street of nineteenth-century houses, the Victorian suburbs of Weimar. Nietzsche's house—or rather his sister's house where, frail and demented, he spent the last thirteen years of life—lay somewhere nearby. I found it on a busy road descending a hill, a garden sloping away from one side of it. It was a boxy, mansard-roofed house, its volume restricted as though by a corset. There was a fussy conservatory porch on one side of it, and I supposed Nietzsche must have been wheeled out here most days to take a little sun. I supposed he stared out into the garden, dozed and muttered to himself, and drooled.

It's a mediocre house of brick, the epitome of the upright bourgeois contentment that Nietzsche held in deepest contempt. Like Goethe, he'd taken shelter in Italy. He wrote his last book, *Ecce Homo*, in Turin, and then he went mad and finished up in this faux villa. If there is any mercy, he never knew where he was. It seemed that the spirit of German genius I'd sought in Dresden was born perhaps three-quarters of a mile away at Goethe's house and had died here.

I'd come to Germany from Italy myself. Before Dresden, I spent two months in Umbria, writing and teaching American undergraduates. The town was called Orvieto, and it is famous for a crisp white wine and for its Duomo, which contains frescoes by Fra Angelico and Signorelli. It's a big church for such a small town, owing to two facts: that, on a high and secure plateau not far from Rome, the medieval popes frequently took refuge here; and also that it was the locus of the miracle of Bolsena, the event that put the important feast of Corpus Christi on the church calendar.

The miracle takes the substance and form of many such stories—apocryphal hokum frothed up into transcendent epiphany—and goes like this: It seems that a German priest, Peter of Prague, stopped at Bolsena to say his daily mass en route to Rome. He was a good and pious priest, but one who found it difficult to believe that Christ was actually present in the consecrated Host. On that day, however, as he said the words of the Consecration, blood began to seep from the Host, to trickle over his hands, to drip onto the altar and the corporal. The priest immediately went to Orvieto, where the pope was then in residence, and the authenticity of the miracle was confirmed. The feast was officially instituted a year later.

I don't know how much this would have normally interested me: I am reserved and a bit cerebral in my Catholicism, and I find myself a little embarrassed by devotions of a too sweaty and visceral sort, those involving relics, flaming hearts, tears, and, as here, blood. But in the miracle of Bolsena, there was one more key figure besides Peter of Prague and Pope Urban IV: Thomas Aquinas. Thomas is, of course, *the* great Catholic theologian, utterly devout but rigorously intellectual. He marshaled, as much as anyone ever has, the reasons one ought to believe—the logic and system of God and his creation—and he has deepened, insofar as I understand him, my admittedly shallow faith. He's also "difficult" in the contemporary sense and, in my considerable vainglory, I like the feeling of belonging to the elite who try to take him on.

So I was intrigued to discover that Thomas had been involved in the affair of Bolsena; that he'd been in Orvieto at the time in 1263 and Urban had put him on the case, so to speak, as both an investigator of the miracle and the author of the liturgy in which the feast day was to be formalized. On further investigation, I learned that Thomas's residence in Orvieto was not half a block from the apartment I was living in. Like Bayham Street and the hotels in Rome and Naples my grandfather had stayed in a hundred years ago that I'd also been trying to locate, this was a search, both archeological and intellectual, I had to undertake.

Thomas's home in Orvieto was on the present-day Piazza XXIX Novembre, where my son had been playing soccer every day with the neighborhood kids. The piazza was dominated by a 1930s-era building used as a military barracks, but in one corner stood the church of San Domenico. I'd been looking at it as I oversaw Andrew's play in the center of the square. On its flank, adjacent to the barracks, the exterior wall of the nave showed signs of what once must have been another wing of the building just as tall as the rest of the church: the shadow of an enormous arch, of buttresses removed, of truncated columns, of an open space now sealed with stone. I spent some time trying to figure out what this signified. I went inside the church, both at mass (the parish was one of the most vibrant of the town) and afterward, and what I saw inside was as confusing as the outside: columns with one side stripped away as though by a cleaver, and others whose feet didn't align with their trunks or that terminated halfway up the wall for no reason. More happily, there were also some signs of Thomas here: a patch of thirteenth-century fresco and, more substantially, an oak box said to contain the chair in which he wrote, taught, and prayed.

In those two materials, the wood and the paint on the wall, Thomas was, I felt, still vaguely present in the church of San Domenico, although perhaps only he could tell you precisely to what extent and in what manner. Thomas's great preoccupation was the relation between the seen and the unseen, between things and their sources, between their material substance and the form in which they appear, contained in the flux of time and space. In this, he was attempting to fit the philosophical realism of Aristotle (whose writings had just been rediscovered by medievals) to Christian theology and revelation. You might say he was trying to square matter with spirit, no easy task, then or now.

Thomas was particularly well suited to investigate the miracle at Bolsena. What had transpired with Peter of Prague represented a momentary tear in the veil separating the physical and spiritual aspects of the sacrament of the Eucharist. One definition of a sacrament is "an outward and visible sign of an inward and invisible grace," but in this case the unseen—the actual transformation of bread and wine into Christ's body and blood—had become utterly tangible.

Admittedly, this notion of the "real presence" is one of the more difficult—not to say, for some, incredible—doctrines of the Church. Christians intuited it from Christ's words at the Last Supper ("This is my body"), but it was Thomas, with help from Aristotle, who worked out its underlying logic. Things, according to Aristotle, consist of substances and "accidents," their essential matter and the visible form in which that matter manifests itself. For example, you might say that ice, liquid water, and vapor are all accidents of the substance H_2O. In the mass, the substances of bread and wine are transformed into Christ's body and blood while retaining their original outward accidents.

This is still a miracle—it transcends what seem to us the laws of science—but there's a kind of wholehearted optimism in Thomas's thought: created things are both real and good rather than defective or false. Thomas insisted on not only the real presence of the Eucharist but the real presence of objects and persons and therefore of their value, their worthiness to be attended and loved. For Thomas, Peter of Prague's inability to believe in the real presence was a refusal to see the reality of the real at its most profound, the indwelling of God in His creation.

To me, in Orvieto, it also seemed that Thomas must be insisting on his own presence—signs of himself—here and now that I might see. But I couldn't puzzle out the church of San Domenico, still less locate the place where Thomas had done his writing and thinking. Yet it was that trace of his presence that I really wanted to find. Meanwhile, I'd gone down to Rome to visit the Ambasciatori Palace Hotel, where my grandfather had lodged some dozen times in the 1920s and 1930s.

The Ambasciatori had been remodeled three or four times since then, most recently in the nineties, "*nel rispetto dell'originaria fisionomia degli ambienti"*—in keeping with the original appearance of the surroundings. But other than the grand staircase in the lobby, which might have contained some elements from eighty years ago, it seemed that not a single surface present in my grandfather's time had survived.

In 1934 he'd brought my father with him here as a young adolescent. Apparently, my father had not been impressed by the Ambasciatori Palace either. In a letter home on hotel stationery, he only complained that "I don't like speagete" and that "I never can understand what they are talking about when they try to tell us what there is to eat." He also wrote that he hoped to see Mussolini "some day when he comes out of his house," although I never knew if this wish was granted. He can't understand the things he wants to know. He can't see what he wants to see. He's unmistakably my father, and Patty's father too.

That same year, Mussolini had been at work in Orvieto, and what he did there had a bearing on the Piazza XXIX Novembre and the church of San Domenico. As in other such regimes, the Italian fascists promoted "physical culture"—a cult of the body founded on notions of the Italian nation and race—and they wanted to establish an "Accademia Femminile di Educazione Fisica," a woman's athletic academy. The chosen location was Orvieto, and the building then occupying the prospective construction site was the church of San Domenico and its cloister.

I'd learned this after my return from Rome and the Ambasciatori. Our apartment was in a palazzo belonging to an elderly couple who were natives of Orvieto. Signora Petinelli was an elegant woman in her late sixties, a skilled cook and a font of Orvietan history and culture going back to the Middle Ages. Her husband, *"il dottore,"* was a nattily dressed retired surgeon and art connoisseur who, that autumn, recited Catullus in Latin as he gave me a flu shot.

They knew all about San Domenico and the Accademia Femminile: It had all happened while they were children living in this neighborhood. A controversial project at the time, it pitted civic boosters who welcomed the largesse from Rome against preservationists and the clergy and congregation of San Domenico. The fascists and the boosters won out, of course, but, in a sop to the parish, a portion of the church was allowed to stand. The entire nave—the church's larger, main axis in which the congregation sat—was demolished and the transept—the church's shorter, smaller crossing axis—was transformed into a nave with a new altar at one end. The truncated pillars I'd seen inside and outside were the scars from the amputation of the original nave.

Until then San Domenico had consisted not only of the church but of gardens, a dormitory, a cloister, and a refectory where the brothers—among them Thomas—worked, ate, and slept. All that was gone, save for the rump of the transept. It did not seem enough, not as much as I wanted of Thomas's residual presence, of real signs of the reality of the great architect of realism, of the real presence.·

Any Orvietan over the age of sixty-five could probably have told me what I'd wanted to know. But I didn't speak Italian well enough to form the question or, without several slow repetitions, to understand the answer. More crucially, I felt driven—perhaps almost to the point of obsession—to use only the evidence of my own eyes, however uninformed my capacity to perceive the reality of the things I was looking at. I was twice blind, both to words and to the realities of things seen and unseen.

Sigmund Freud, I later learned, had also been to Orvieto. In fact, he based the first chapter of one of his key works, *The Psychopathology of Everyday Life*, on an incident connected to Orvieto's Duomo, the great church raised in response to the revelation of the real presence to Peter of Prague. On a train, Freud wanted to talk about the frescoes in the Duomo, but he could not for the life of him recall the name of one of their two principal creators—Signorelli—despite having seen them on several visits. Analyzing this inexplicable lapse of memory, Freud recollected that just prior to his attempt to talk about the frescoes, he had been preoccupied with the suicide of one of his patients whose problems Freud traced to "an incurable sexual disturbance," undoubtedly homosexuality. He decided that the troubling nature of these thoughts—of sexuality and death—had caused him to forget the name of Signorelli, and upon this incident Freud subsequently formulated one of his principal discoveries, repression.

The notion that wishes, intentions, and purposes run deep within us like underground rivers is key to Freud's view of the soul. We both know and do not know what we are doing, and repression is the device whereby we square that contradiction. It's what enabled that unknown diagnostician in the 1950s to conclude that my mother might both want to drive Patty mad—withdrawing her love in such a way that Patty in turn withdrew herself entirely from the world—and yet feel she would never, ever want to do such a thing to her child; that her maternal love was double-edged, that its presence was a kind of void into which Patty might fall and disappear, consumed.

That is Freud in extreme form, Freud forgetting Signorelli's name almost as if he wished the Duomo frescoes destroyed. For me, in Orvieto, I can't say that I in some way avoided the facts

I thought I wanted to know. But I would say that my own pre-occupations and needs prevented me from finding what I sought, from hearing and seeing what was before me, from translating the words and images correctly. Sometimes things may indeed look or sound absurd but still in fact represent the truth. Sometimes "kalifidos" does mean "cowboy."

To find what I wanted to find, I needed help, and Signora Petinelli gave it to me. Presence doesn't always make itself present simply because we desire it to be. And perhaps the presence we seek—however sure we are that it is other persons and things, the presence of the past—is actually our own presence, the reality of ourselves standing in relation to all reality, to the real presence. Maybe I needed Bayham Street, Dresden, Weimar, and Rome for that purpose, and now Orvieto too.

I'd been a little dejected by the discovery of the almost total destruction of signs of Thomas Aquinas in Orvieto. Then, in scarcely an aside, Signora Petinelli mentioned there was a little more, "*poche piccole tracce*"—a few small traces—inside the academy, now the military barracks into which the priory had originally extended. She would try to get me inside: she knew people, calls could be made.

A few days later, Signora Petinelli knocked on our apartment door. Was I ready to go? She had talked to the *commandante*. We could come if we went right now. She and I walked down the block and across the Piazza XXIX Novembre. Buttons were pushed, speakerphones addressed, and buzzers sounded. The metal gates swung open. A young officer escorted us through a vestibule and through a second gate.

We were outside again, in a vast courtyard enclosed by walls in the same Mussolini-Modernist style as the façade, an arena in which I supposed the flower of fascist womanhood performed their calisthenics. But on one wall, along the bottom, something entirely different stood out in relief: an arcade—a series of open arches separated by Romanesque columns atop a wide level balustrade—of dark amber stone. It was a section of cloister, cut off above and on both sides and incorporated into the fourth fascist wall, left intact on an architect's whim or in a perverse attempt at recycling or cost control or maybe because of some inchoate sense that, yes, the Accademia Femminile di Educazione Fisica ought to contain a little fragment of San Domenico.

"It's thirteenth century," Signora Petinelli said with confidence. That meant this was Thomas's cloister, that he would have worked and written here; would have paced circuits through this corridor and around the other three sides—now vanished—of the cloister.

Signora Petinelli was talking rapidly in Italian about Thomas and the priory, apparently for the officer's benefit. Most of what she was saying was going past me. I thought the officer could not possibly know who she was talking about or take any interest in it, but it seemed that he did. He nodded assent or expressed surprise with genuine enthusiasm and curiosity. Or so it seemed to me, since he spoke English even more poorly than I spoke Italian.

As Signora Petinelli continued recounting the history of the priory, Corpus Christi, the real presence, and this *fratre*, *scrittore*, and *grande filosofo* who had lived just here three-quarters of a millennium ago, I simply stood looking at the stratum of cloister frozen in Mussolini's wall. This, somehow, was the trace of Thomas I had been after, the real presence of him, caught unmistakably here. And to record and mark it—just to make sure of what I was seeing—I wanted to take a picture.

As soon as I lifted my camera, the officer raised his hand and gestured an emphatic no. Signora Petinelli protested that surely there was no harm in photographing an old section of wall. But it was absolutely forbidden, the officer said apologetically. No photography whatsoever was permitted in a military installation. He turned to me and spoke half in Italian, half in English. Surely I understood the reasons, after "*il undici Settembre.*" "All this must stay . . . lost, secret," he said.

So there could be no photo. I would have to accept what I had seen on faith, to keep it present before my eyes through trust and hope. Once past the gate, I did take a picture of the children—Andrew's soccer friends—on the piazza, and they, present there, will have to stand as the outward sign of what is inside, of what Thomas and his God are making real, putting us in the presence of, realizing in and through us.

When I came back from Italy, Weimar, Dresden, and London, I hoped there might be some word about my sister Patty. We'd tracked down her psychiatrist, Dr. Fleming, who had apparently effected or at least witnessed her transformation. But we were too late. After a distinguished career at Massachusetts General, Children's Hospital, the Judge Baker Clinic, Children's Center, and Harvard Medical School, she'd died four years before at the age of eighty-nine.

We'd also tried to locate Patty's medical records. Someone in our family had dimly remembered that there was supposed to have been a case history published that was based on her. The name had been changed, but we would surely recognize her by the details. I went to the medical school library near my home and scavenged the indexes and databases. I found two articles by Dr. Fleming, one on a medication used in the treatment of schizophrenia, the other on the families of juvenile offenders. Neither had anything to do with Patty.

The hunt for medical records continued. All the institutions Patty's doctor had been associated with were helpful, but one by one they reported they had found nothing. Perhaps Dr. Fleming had treated Patty as a private patient, in which case a relative might know the location of her papers. But Dr. Fleming had left no survivors, and it seemed unlikely that files and paperwork from forty years past would have survived her.

So my family and I are left where we began, with the vague impressions and hunches of people now dead that we heard speak long ago, of whom our own memories have begun to fade. My mother too is gone. She spent the last year of her life in a nursing home, all the day lying flat on her back with her hands folded over her stomach, staring at the ceiling and now and again dozing off. She'd laid herself out like a corpse. When she did die, without so much as a gasp, just before dawn on a morning in March, it took the nurse and orderly some time to realize she'd undergone any alteration at all.

I wish I'd asked her about Patty. But neither I nor my other sister had ever devised a way to bring up the subject without it leading to a discussion of Patty's specific pathology and thence, inevitably, to my mother's part in it; to her role as the "rejecting" or "emotionally absent" mother who induced "infantile schizophrenia" in her child as surely as if she'd throttled her or scalded her with boiling water. Looked upon now from an age less certain of Freud's intuitions on repression and unconscious wishes—of the inexplicable absence in the mind of a name connected to a fresco cycle in a church in Orvieto—it seems a little too dramatic, too determined to find the fatal deeds and outsized personalities of the Greek tragedies Freud loved in a smallish mock-Tudor bungalow in the Midwest of the early 1950s. I suppose that in practical terms it's also a calumny on my mother that provides an answer to the mystery of Patty at the cost of raising, for me, an unacceptable question.

So, barring that explanation, here is what I know about Patty: She was born, she vanished into a state a little like autism or retardation or catatonia, she reemerged as a person pretty much like anyone else, and then she died. She was not here, then she was here, and then she was gone again: absence, presence, absence. Or so it seems.

I wonder about the moment she died, the cars hurtling toward one another, fusing, separating, and coming to rest, steaming, burning, exhausted. After the alarm, the terror, perhaps the flare of images as every instant of her life—the secret, hidden parts none of us ever saw—passed through her mind's eye, what happened, where was she? As the impact came, as she dove into the firestorm, through that veil that hung before her like the windshield toward which the oncoming car was pressing, did she disappear? Did her soul and the soul of the old woman in the other vehicle wheel past one another, above the smoldering thicket of the wreck? When did she leave the scene? When was she no longer present there or in any other place to which we, the living, can go?

Thomas said that the soul is "substantial form," an immaterial matter that shapes and integrates all the parts and aspects of the human person. A person is not a person without a soul or without a body, and it is the presence of this substantial form that makes a body a person rather than a corpse. I am not sure I know what Thomas meant by this, although I am sure he did.

I wonder if it was necessary that every trace of life—like the cooling metal of the engine and the condensation of radiator water on the asphalt—be stopped and still before her soul could take its leave. So perhaps she lingered in that place long after the state troopers arrived and the spinning red and blue lights were extinguished and the ambulances departed with their cargo.

I don't know. I can't see any sign of it. The picture of the soul—the psyche—I grew up with is closer to Freud's than Thomas's, a chasm of fractured strata through which one descends into ever-deepening and incomprehensible darkness, far from any unifying form, still less the presence of its creator. But faith—my faith and Thomas's—the one that I attempt to maintain a grasp upon despite the evidence of so much of my senses, the glaring absences that seem so often to make proofs, says it is otherwise: that Patty is present to God and God is present to her, not by signs or traces, through memory or hope, but in fact, in full view. I would like, as Thomas described, God to make me present to Himself, and to her, and to every-thing I thought was lost or missing.

I don't, of course, know how or if that will happen. I may go back to Bayham Street. After I came home, after it was clear there were no records, no signs or explanations of Patty—after I learned she might have been as imaginary or as real as Little Dorrit—I found out that Bayham Street had been renumbered late in the nineteenth century. Number 16 is now number 141. There is also, somewhere, a plaque, and I found a picture—a little hazy and ill-focused—of it. It isn't blue at all. I am look-ing for the boy in the garret looking out onto the fulminating world, calculating how he might make his way in it, how he could leave a mark upon it that someone much later, someone like me, might find.

SALLIE TISDALE

THE SUTRA OF
MAGGOTS AND BLOWFLIES

The great entomologist Jean-Henri Fabre covered his desk with the carcasses of birds and snakes, opened the window, and waited.

He didn't have to wait long.

From the time I was quite young, I loved cold-blooded creatures. I had to be taught not to pick things up in the woods: to me it was all good, all worth examination, from beetles to mushrooms to toads. I was stealthy, and in the thistle-ridden fields near my house, I caught many blue-belly lizards to keep as pets. My father built a cage for them, a wonderful wood-and-screen contraption that smelled of pine and grass and reptile. I kept garter snakes and frogs and chameleons too. Once, someone gave me a baby alligator. I had several praying mantises, and built them elaborate branch houses in the cage and fed them crickets. I don't know where this came from, my appetite for the alien; it feels like an old question, long and mysterious.

My study of living things, part inquiry and part the urge to possess, became inevitably a study of predation and decay. I had to feed my pets, and most preferred live food. The mantises always died, their seasons short. The chameleons died, too delicate for my care. The alligator died. I tried to embalm it, with limited success—just good enough for an excellent presentation at "Show and Tell." When one of my turtles died, my brother and I buried it in my mother's rose bed to see if we could get an empty turtle shell, which would be quite a good thing to have. When we dug it up a few weeks later, there was almost nothing left—an outcome I had not anticipated, and one which left me with a strange, disturbed feeling. The earth was more fierce than I had guessed.

In time, I became specifically interested in human bodies, how they worked and how they got sick and what they looked like when they died. This did not pacify my mother, who worried aloud about my ghoulish preoccupations. I did enjoy the distress I could cause by something as simple as bringing an embalmed baby alligator to school in a jar. But I was also—and for a long time I could not have explained why it was of a piece with my impassioned studies—exquisitely sensitive to the world's harsh rules. I regretted each cricket. An animal dead by the side of the road could bring me to tears, and I cried for each dead lizard, each mantis. A triad, each leg bearing weight: sensitivity, love, and logic. The weight on each leg shifts over time: Now, a penetrating awareness of the cruelty seemingly built into the world's bones. Now, a colder logic, an awareness of the forces that balance systems at the cost of individuals. At times, in brief pure blinks of my mind's eye, a love painful in its intensity, an unalloyed love. I love the tender, pale blossoms opening now on the cherry tree in my yard, the sudden pound of lush raindrops from the empty sky: each thing I see is a luminous form in a sparkling world. Such love is a kind of grace; enshrined in it, all is right with the world. It is a little touch of madness, this kind of love—raw and driving.

Some years ago, I began to study the small things in the forest that I didn't understand, moving from the lovely and lethal amanita mushrooms to the stony, invincible lichens to the water skippers coasting lightly across the little creeks. I began to study insects especially and then flies in particular.

Flies are so present and innumerable that it is hard to see their presence clearly, hard to believe in their measure. There are around 120,000 species of flies, depending on who's counting, and they have many names: bee flies, cactus flies, papaya flies, warble flies, brine flies, nimble flies, biting midges, green midges, gall midges, mountain midges, dixid midges, solitary midges, net-winged midges, phantom midges, so called because the larvae are transparent and seem to disappear in water. Studying flies, my head begins to spin with suborders and divisions, tribes and clades, and the wild implications of the Latin names: Psychodidae and Sarcophagidae and *Calliphora vomitoria*.

The order Diptera is old, as are most insects; it was well established by the Jurassic Era, 210 million years ago.* (Unlike all other insects, flies do not have four wings. Diptera comes

---

* We are one kingdom with flies: Animali, and then we diverge. (You can remember the taxonomic series of kingdom, phylum, class, order, family, genera, species with an appropriate mnemonic: *Keep Pots Clean; Our Food Gets Spoiled.*) Flies are found in the phylum Arthropoda: exoskeletons, jointed legs, and segmented bodies, a group that includes crabs, centipedes, and spiders as well. The flies are in the subphylum Mandibulata, which means mandibles on the second segment past the mouth opening, and just imagine that. We are not in Kansas anymore. Class Insecta means a body is divided into head, abdomen, and thorax. The insects from here on out—beetles, fleas, ants, scorpions, walking sticks, and many other types—are entirely separate orders.

from the word *di* for two and *ptera* for wings.) Fly biology is a vast and changing field. New species and subspecies of flies are always being discovered. Familiar species are found in new locations; variants between species are analyzed in new or more subtle ways, and so the taxonomic distinctions between flies are always being revised. But in the general term, flies are defined by their single set of wings, legless larvae, and mouth parts designed for biting, sucking, or lapping.

Inside these templates of order, there is stupefying variation. They are divided into families, genera, and species by the varied location of veins in the wings, their color, body size, types of mouthparts, the number of stages of larval development, the type and separation of eyes, antennal structure, the arrangement and number of bristles on the body, the length of the legs, and habitat—differences controversial and infinitesimally detailed.

We often know them as the most common and familiar things, as single things: individual flies rescued or swatted, struggling in webs, crawling dizzily across cold windowpanes on a milky October day. One finds flies in odd places, but so often they are not a surprise even in surprising locations—in the laundry basket or buzzing inside the medicine cabinet, or caught unaware in the wash water. Almost every fly you catch in your house will be a housefly, one of the family Muscidae, chubby and vigilant flies that can birth a dozen generations every summer. (House flies are found in virtually every place on earth save for Antarctica and a few isolated islets.)

Sometimes we know them as plagues: I've been battered by biting flies in forests, near mangroves, and in sand, flies the size of pinheads so thick I couldn't walk twenty feet without getting a crop of angry red bites on every inch of exposed skin.

These are the ones we call punkies or gnats or no-see-ums, the fly family known as Ceratopogonidae. There are more than 4,000 species of them—tiny, almost invisible flies with stinging bites, inexplicable dots of pain.

The *Encyclopedia Britannica* says simply, "It is not possible to discuss all dipteran habitats." Flies live in the air and the soil and under water and inside the stems and leaves of plants. They live high in the mountains, in sand and snow, tide pools and lakes, sulfur springs and salt lagoons. The brine fly lives in the thermal springs of Yellowstone at temperatures up to 43 degrees Celsius. There are flies in the volcanic hot springs of Iceland and New Zealand living at even higher temperatures. Certain flies handle extreme cold easily too, blessed with a kind of anti-freeze and other strange gifts. The wingless snow fly lives underground in burrows, and wanders across the white fields during the day—wee black spots walking briskly along in the afternoon. The Himalayan glacier midge prefers temperatures around the freezing point, but has been seen active at −16 degrees Celsius. (When placed in a hand, it becomes agitated and then faints from heat.) One carnivorous fly lays its eggs in pools of seeping petroleum, where the larvae live until maturity. One wingless fly lives inside spiders. Certain flies can live in vinegar. There are flies munching contentedly on spoiled vegetables. When we eat them by accident, they just ride the peristaltic wave on through, exiting in our feces and moving along.

The single pair of wings that is crucial to the identity of flies may be very small or startlingly large or vestigial, may lay open or closed, look scaly, milky, beribboned with black veins, smoky or transparent. Instead of a second set of wings, flies have small bony structures called halteres. They are mobile gyroscopes for flight, beating in time but out of sync with the wings, twisting with every change of direction to keep the fly from tumbling. Most are astonishing flyers, able to move in three dimensions at speeds hard to measure. Some can hover motionless and fly backward or forward or sideways like helicopters. (Flower flies, which look alarmingly like wasps but are harmless, will hover in front of your face, appearing to gaze directly into your eyes.) Midges beat their wings more than a thousand times per second; this is too fast for nerve impulses and instead involves a mysterious muscular trigger effect. A fruit fly can stay aloft for an entire afternoon, burning 10 percent of its body weight every hour. There are clumsy flies: The march fly travels laboriously only a few feet off the ground, and so is continuous fodder for car radiators; march flies are often seen banging into people and bushes, and even the walls of buildings. Soldier flies can fly, but don't very often; they sit for long periods of time on leaves or flowers. Other species prefer to walk or run, sometimes on the surface of water; the louse fly, often wingless, walks sideways, like a crab.

British poet John Clare wrote of flies that "they look like things of mind or fairies." There are flies so small they can barely be seen by human eyes, others as wide and long as a man's hand. Their bodies may be lime-green or shiny blue, glowing black, metallic or dull yellow, pearly white, leathery, variegated in browns, matted with dust. A few are flecked with iridescent gold and silver. They are squat or slender or wasp-waisted. Their legs may be very long and fine or stubby, delicate as a web or stout and strong. Fly genitalia, one text notes, are "extremely polymorphous." Some flies have beards or even furry coats made of bristles; others seem hairless. The hover flies mimic bees and wasps, growing yellow-brown bristly hair like the fur of a bumblebee or striped like yellow jackets. The tangle-veined fly, which is parasitic on grasshoppers, has a loud, beelike buzz. A fly's antennae may be akin to knobs or threads or whips or feathers or pencillike brushes. Insects do not breathe, exactly; they perform gas exchange in a different way from mammals, through tubes called spiracles. Their larvae breathe in many ways, through gills and snorkels, or by taking up the oxygen stored in plant roots and stems. Spiracles show up just about anywhere: beside the head, in the belly, in a maggot's anus.

What great variety they have! When Augustine argued that the fly is also made by God, he spoke of "such towering magnitude in this tininess." The family Nycteribiidae, the bat ticks, are true flies but look like spiders without heads. They live only in the fur of bats, sucking bat blood, hanging on with claws. Exposed, the stunted bugs run rapidly across the bat's fur before disappearing underneath. But the family Tipulidae, the crane flies, fill your palm. They look like giant tapered mosquitoes, with very long, slender, spiderlike legs, three eyes, big veiny wings that may span three inches. They do not bite. These are the ballerinas of the flies, delicate and graceful. Male crane flies form mating swarms that dance above treetops at sundown, or flow over pastures in a cloud, pushed by the breeze.

So one fly seeks light and heat; another avoids both. One is a vegetarian—another a terror. They flit like tiny shadows in the night skies, crawl across the windowpane and out of the drain and into the garbage and into our eyes. Sometimes flies migrate out to sea far from anything human, flitting across the white-capped waves of the ever-moving sea for miles, for days. The fly is grotesque and frail and lovely and vigorous, quivering, shivering, lapping, flitting, jerking, sucking, panting:

theirs is an exotic genius, a design of brilliant simplicity and bewildering complexity at once.

I study flies; I am stunned by them. I love them, with a fleeting love—with the triad: love, logic, sensitivity. Did you notice how calmly I noted that there is a fly which lives inside spiders? Another that is parasitic on grasshoppers? This is a humming, buzzing world; we live in the midst of the ceaseless murmur of lives, a world of strange things whispering the poems of old Buddhas. The world's constant rustling is like the rubbing of velvet between distracted fingers; it can drive one mad. Beside the cherry tree, under that bright sky, lives the sheep bot fly. It enters a sheep's nostrils, where it gives birth to live young. The maggots crawl up the nasal passages into the sinuses, where they feed until they are grown—a process that lasts nearly a year. The sheep's nose runs with pus; it shakes its head at this odd itch, shakes and rubs its nose into the ground, grits its teeth, jumps about, growing ever weaker. The condition is called the blind staggers. One day the sheep gives a great sneeze, and out shoot mature sheep bot flies. They are ready to mate, and make more babies.

It is right here with flies that I face a direct and potent challenge: What do I really believe? What do I believe about beauty and the ultimate goodness of this world?

Jean-Henri Fabre lays out his corpses by the open window. A few days later, he writes, "Let us overcome our repugnance and give a glance inside." Then he lifts the bodies, counting the flies that have come, the eggs they lay, the larvae that form "a surging mass of swarming sterns and pointed heads, which emerge, wriggle and dive in again. It suggests a seething billow." He adds, as an aside, "It turns one's stomach." He examines and measures and counts, and then gently places a few

hundred eggs in a test tube with a piece of meat squeezed dry.
A few days later, he pours off the liquescent remnants of the
once-hard flesh, which "flows in every direction like an icicle
placed before the fire." He measures it, and keeps careful notes.

"It is horrible," he adds, "most horrible."

I have been a Buddhist for more than twenty-five years,
since I was a young woman. My avid urge to understand bodies didn't stop at the bodies themselves; I sought for a way to
think about the fact of life, the deepest query. Buddhism in its
heart is an answer to our questions about suffering and loss, a
response to the inexplicable; it is a way to live with life. Its
explanations, its particular vocabulary and shorthand, its gentle pressures—they have been with me throughout my adult
life; they are part of my language, my thought, my view. Buddhism saved my life and controlled it; it has been liberation and
censure at once.

Buddhism is blunt about suffering, its causes and its cures.
The Buddha taught that nothing is permanent. He taught this
in a great many ways, but most of what he said came down to
this: Things change. Change hurts; change cannot be avoided.
"All compounded things are subject to dissolution"—this formula is basic Buddhist doctrine, it is pounded into us by the
canon, by the masters, by our daily lives. It means all things are
compounded and will dissolve, which means I am compounded
and I will dissolve. This is not something I readily accept, and
yet I am continually bombarded with the evidence. I longed to
know this, this fact of life, this answer—that we are put together
from other things and will be taken apart and those other
things and those things we become will in turn be taken apart
and built anew—that there is nothing known that escapes this
fate. When one of his disciples struggled with lust or felt pride

in his youth or strength, the Buddha recommended that the follower go to the charnel ground, and meditate on a corpse—on its blossoming into something new.

We feel pain because things change. We feel joy for the same reason. But suffering is not simply pain: It is our peculiar punishment that we know things change and we want this to be otherwise. We want to hang on to what is going away, keep our conditions as they are, people as they are, ourselves as we are. In Buddhist terms, this is variously called thirst or desire or attachment or clinging. It means that we hold on to the hope that something will remain, even as it all slides away like sand in running water, like water from our hands. Knowing the answer does not stop the question from being asked.

Desire is not always about holding something close; it has a shadow, the urge to push things away. Buddhists usually call this aversion—the desire for the extinction of something, for separation from it. The original Pali word for aversion, *dosa,* is various and shaded, translated sometimes as anger or hatred, sometimes as denial, as projection, aggression, repulsion, and now and then as disgust or revulsion or distortion. Aversion has as much force and fascination as the positive desires we know. It may be simply a reflexive flinch, a ducking for cover; it may be much stronger. Like desire, aversion is a many-colored thing, flavored by circumstances. It is a kind of clinging—clinging to the hope of *something other than this.*

When I began to study flies, I couldn't seem to stop. Fabre wrote, "To know their habits long haunted my mind." I think of the violence with which we describe such prurient obsessions—we say we cannot tear our eyes away. My eyes are glued to flies and it is as though they are stitched open against my will. I feel revulsion, I flinch, I turn away, I duck for cover.

I get squeamish, which is a rare feeling for me. But I also feel curiosity and admiration and a kind of awe. The buzz of a fly's blurred wings is one of the myriad ways the world speaks to us; it is one of the ways speech is freed from our ideas. I feel that if I could listen, if I could just listen without reacting, without judgment or preference or opinion—without reaching for a dream of how things might be otherwise—there is something I would understand that I have yet to know.

Compassion in all its flavors is woven through the enormous canon of Buddhist thought. Its root meaning is "to suffer with." We are able to feel compassion toward those beings who look like us and those with whom we are most familiar. (These are not the same thing; dissimilar creatures can be deeply familiar, as we know from our time spent with dogs, with horses—even lizards.) At what point do we extend this circle past what is known, past what looks like us? At what point do we suffer with what is completely strange? And how far must that circle extend before it includes the sheep bot fly?

This mix of push and pull I feel when I look at insects is akin to the way the tongue longs for an acquired taste. The first time one tastes certain complex flavors, they are unpleasant, even offensive. But in time it is that very flavor, its complexity— the bitterness or acidity mingling with other layers—that brings you back. Whether it is wine or chili powder or natto— a Japanese delicacy of soybeans bound into a sticky, cobwebbed mold—one returns in part because of the difficulty. We are sharply, pleasantly excited by the nearness of rejection, by skirting along the edge of things, the dank and sour things that instinct reads as dangerous. These shadings of flavor ever so briefly evoke poison and rot—the urine scent of beer, the lingering oily bitterness of coffee, the rank tang of certain cheeses (and I will return to cheese; it factors here). There is a brief shrinking away, perhaps very brief, miniscule, but there nonetheless.

This is a little bit of what I feel toward flies. Let us give a glance inside—a glance, a gasp, a shiver, the briefest reactivity: and then another look, a bit sideways though it may be, and then another. Then there follows the need to look: interest turning into inquiry into passion: the desire to know, to see, and something more, something crucial—the need to bear it, to be able to bear it, to be able to look as closely and thoroughly as I can.

Flies have long been considered the shells and familiars of gods, witches, and demons. They are associated with reincarnation, immortality, and sorcery. They are so unutterably strange, all swarming and speed and single-mindedness, and they cannot be avoided. I really mean that; we eat flies every day.* The FDA permits thirty-five fruit-fly eggs in every eight

---

* Consider the cheese skipper, a kind of black fly found all over the world. They are so called in part because they skip, or leap, when disturbed; they curl up, grabbing the tail with the hooked mouth, tense, and then let go—springing like a coil, fast and hard. Cheese skippers are attracted to meat, cheese, and corpses, which develop a cheesy smell at a certain stage when butyric acid is present. Their family name, Piophilia, means milk-loving. The larvae can be eaten accidentally, and may survive ingestion and burrow into the gut. One imagines the little thing shrugging its non-existent shoulders and changing course. When the larvae infest a hard cheese like pecorino, they decompose the fats until the cheese turns creamy and pink, at which point the Italians call it casu marzu, "rotten cheese." Gourmets like it, and will blend casu marzu into a paste to spread on bread. Most people try to remove the maggots first. Selling this cheese is illegal in Italy, because even shredded maggot parts are dangerous—all those hooks. But not everyone does this. Some consider the maggots part of the delicacy—an aphrodisiac, or a peculiarly nutritious food.

ounces of golden raisins; up to twenty maggots "of any size" in a hundred grams of canned mushrooms, and a fair number of both eggs and maggots in tomato products. Last night's mushroom pizza? A womb of flies.

Flies sense the world in every way, its faintest textures: miniscule currents of shifting air, the vibration of a bird's approaching wings, the scent of decaying flowers or a mouse's corpse a half-mile away. Some flies have a complex and unique ear, a flexible tympanal membrane in a complex structure behind the neck. A few parasitic flies listen for the distinct sound of their selected prey; one imagines a head carefully cocked.

They taste and smell in ways far more subtle than ours. There is no profound difference between the two senses, anyway; both are a way of identifying chemicals, defining them, discriminating. They sense the sex pheromones released so hopefully by their prey, and follow; they smell the prey's feces, its breath, or the small damage done by other hunting insects. Biting flies are sensitive to stress chemicals, including the higher levels of carbon dioxide emitted when mammals exert themselves. The black flies respond directly to the scent of human sweat. Many flies have taste and smell receptors on their complex mouthparts, their antennae, the delicate legs and fine-clawed feet. Walking, they sample the coming meal; instantly, the proboscis unwinds. Flies are sensitive to minute differences in the world's chemistry, and its surprising similarities: one of the parasitic Lucilia flies is attracted, according to one text, to "wild parsnips and fresh meat." One molecule attracts the male to the female, another causes the male's ritual courtship flight; a third causes the female to relax and hold still. Their world is a superdimensional pheromonal architecture, a mingled and vaporous mist multiplied by sight and sound and space.

Consider the compound eye, common to all insects, variously evolved in flies. A fly's eyes may be huge: the eyes of horse flies are bulging black caps filling the face. Other flies may have tiny eyes, and some flies have no eyes at all. (The pyrgotid flies have strangely shaped heads that protrude in *front* of their eyes, an evolutionary development hard to comprehend.) The eye may be flat or bulging, round or triangular in shape, shining like a jewel. A deer fly's eyes are brightly colored, green or gold with patterns and zigzags. Tachinid flies have reddish eyes; dance flies have orange ones. Each facet of a compound eye is held at a unique angle, independent of all the others. They are capable of differentiating between the wavelengths of light and can distinguish the angle at which sunlight falls, allowing them to navigate off the surface of water. A fly has a thousand eyes, four thousand eyes, side by side without gap. The fly cannot focus on a single form, but sees each form from many angles at once. Each single thing is multiplied, the object broken like a mirror into shards, into shocks of light, and remade like water into a single lake, a prism, a drop of dew.

Flies eat blood and meat and feces and other insects and each other, but also pollen, nectar, algae, decaying seaweed and fungi. Bulb-fly maggots are tiny dilettantes, seeking only the inner tissue of hyacinth, tulip, narcissus, and lily bulbs. Fruit-fly maggots are picky: one species eats walnut husks, another eats cherries. Pomace flies live on rotting fruit, but they don't eat the fruit; they eat the yeast that grows on rotting fruit. (This is a brief world indeed; a new generation is born every ten days or so.)

Flies bite, suck, slice, lap. Bee lice live in the mouth of bees, eating nectar. Stiletto-fly larvae sometimes live in wool blankets and decaying wood. Among the black flies, which plague cattle, each species specializes in a cow part—one sucks blood from cows' bellies, one from cows' ears, and so on. The flat-footed flies, which run in a zigzag pattern across plants, include a variety called smoke flies; they are attracted to fires and eat the burned wood afterward. Eye gnats are drawn to tears, sweat flies to sweat, face flies to eyes and noses.

Flies hurt us, but only in passing; sleeping sickness, malaria, yellow fever, river blindness: mere accidents. The sheep bot fly can live in many places, including human eyes if eyes are more convenient than the sheep—but it prefers the sheep. We are simply more food, more warm and meaty beings among endless beings. But what food!—palaces of muscle and blood, rich and fertile fields.

I read otherwise sober and mechanical descriptions of flies and trip over the anthropomorphic complaint. Both Pliny and Plutarch complained that flies were impossible to train and domesticate. Among modern thinkers, one fly is "good" and the other is "bad," one is a "pest" and another a "bane" and another a "benefit." The tachinid flies are parasitic on destructive caterpillars and snipe flies eat aphids, so they are described with kind words. Their predation does us good, but all predation does something good and not just the predator. Predation makes way. It makes room.

Even entomologists hate flies, on principle. Edwin Way Teale, who wrote of the natural world his entire life with reverence and cheer, hated the housefly. He obsessed over the number and variety of bacteria, fungus, viruses, and parasites they carried from place to place, and finally seems to have simply flung his hands into the air and given up, declaring the housefly "an insect villain with hardly a drop of redeeming virtue." Leland Howard, a United States Department of Agriculture entomologist, wrote an encyclopedic account of insects in 1904 that is still quoted today. He called the harmless salt-water flies "sordid little flies," and the wingless bird tick "apparently too lazy to fly." Of the bluebottle, which sometimes has parasitic mites, he wrote, "It is comforting to think that the house-fly has these parasites which torment him so. Such retribution is just."

Humans are a nightmare; we tear the earth apart. We trepan mountains and pour them into rivers, take the soil apart down to its atoms, sully the sea, shred our world like giant pigs rutting after truffles. We poison our nest and each other and ourselves. We eat everything, simply everything, but we turn away from flies.

The circles of compassion can suddenly expand. Federico García Lorca wrote that he rescued flies caught at a window; they reminded him of "people / in chains." And of course I've done the same, I often do—catch flies and crickets and spiders and let them go, careful of their frailty. This brief moment of the widening circle—it is easily challenged by the maggot, by the swarm. The larvae of the fungus gnat sometimes travel in great masses, for reasons no one can guess— huge groups called worm snakes piled several deep, squirming along about an inch a minute. I know why Beelzebub is Lord of the Flies; is there any other god who would slouch so towards Bethlehem?

I long sometimes for a compound eye. It is a tenet of my religious practice, an ever-present thorn, to remember that my point of view, that any point of view, is merely a point. My eyes cannot see a landscape, let alone a world. But how we judge things has everything to do with where we stand. Can I learn to see a form from many angles at once? Can I see other beings, this moment, my mistakes, my words, like this? Can I know multiplicity as a single thing?

So many flies: Mydas flies, sewage flies, robust bot flies, gout flies, scavenger flies, snipe flies. Big-headed flies, thick-headed flies, picture-winged flies, stilt-legged flies, spear-winged flies, banana-stalk flies, flower-loving flies, stalk-eyed flies, flat-footed flies, pointed-winged flies, hump-backed flies.

The literature of Zen Buddhism is thick with nature—nature images, metaphors, puzzles and questions, but mostly the calm and serene inhuman world of clouds, seeds, spring shoots, meadow grasses, and ponds, the moon and the mountain and the wave and the plum blossom. (Kobayashi Issa, an eighteenth-century Buddhist haiku master, wrote: "Where there are humans / there are flies / and Buddhas." But he is talking, I think, rather more about humans than flies.) Such images are used as metaphors for all kinds of Buddhist concepts, but they are partly an effort to convey the nature of how Zen Buddhism describes reality itself, the world. Hongzhi, a great Zen master of China, described it as "sky and water merging in autumn"— a vast, shifting, unbounded world.

Central to Zen Buddhism is a belief in *busshō,* usually trans-lated from the Japanese as Buddha Nature. (In English we like to capitalize words like "buddha" and "nature," ostensibly to distinguish subtly different ideas with the same sound. Today, glancing inside the seething billow of life, it seems to me that such stylistic touches are only an impotent fist-shaking at the

greatness of what we try to say with the words. But I will follow the rule.)

Busshō is shorthand for something that requires quite a few
words to explain—or it is already one too many words for what
can't be explained in words. Buddhism is founded on the idea
that all things are impermanent, that nothing has a fixed self-
nature that passes through time unchanged. Change is not an
aspect of the matrix, but the matrix itself. It is because no one
thing is permanent that we are not separated from anything—
not bounded, not contained. All beings are constantly appearing, constantly springing into existence, hurtling out of
themselves, of what they were, what preceded. Buddha Nature
is—what? Original nature. Perfect nature—the substrate or
source of all things. But it is not God, it is not ether, it is not
simply a womb that gives birth. It is all things; it is that which
manifests as things—as the world—as people, rocks, stars,
dewdrops, flies—all beings, all forms, all existent things. All
existence.

What do I know about Buddha Nature, anyway? I can't
even tell you what it is—and Buddha Nature isn't an "it," and
it isn't really an "is," either; not a quality attached to anything
or a state of being or an ether in which things exist; Buddha
Nature as I understand it—there's that "it" again—is this, this,
this, here, this miniscule and gargantuan and muscular rela-
tional and organic now, the luminosity of the sparkling world,
the vast inevitability of loss, and not that exactly, either. I use
that phrase, Buddha Nature, even as it fills my mouth with ash,
to mean all those things and more—relation, aspects, moments,
qualities, acts, eons, and muscles—and I use it in a positive way,
with pleasure, with outright joy, to mean that all of us—those
of us who think we are something unique and those who never

think about it, and all those creatures who don't do what I might call thinking but are yet alive, and all those things we bang up against and assume aren't alive at all—are in some way kin, in some way both source and effect, eternally and continually and without hesitation, spontaneously and instantaneously and infinitely giving birth to ourselves, spilling out of nothing into nothing, with great vigor—leaping, sliding, appearing, disappearing into and out of a lack of solidness, into and out of the nonexistence of permanent nature, and that because this is the law—the muscle, the hinge—of reality—it's good. It's all right. Everything is all right.

Everything is all right. The female horse fly favors large warm-blooded animals. They see quite well and will fly around their prey just out of reach, finally biting one's back or leg. (As is true with many other biting flies, including mosquitoes, only the females bite. The males live on plant pollen and juices. It so happens as well that the males live brief lives while the females live the whole long, hot summer. The story is told that the Declaration of Independence was signed on July 4 because the horse flies in Philadelphia were intolerable that year, and the delegates called for an early vote so they could get out of town.) The "phlebotomous" insects, as they are called, have anticoagulant in their saliva; after a bite, the blood continues to run, sometimes dangerously so. (To be precise, the horse fly slices rather than bites; its mouthparts are like tiny knives.) In their turn, horse flies are eaten by robber flies, who capture them on the wing and then find a convenient twig to rest on while sucking them dry. Robber flies are sometimes called bee-killers; they prize honey bees and will watch them from the shadows while the bees gather pollen, then suddenly dart out and seize one from behind, so it can't sting. They drain the bee dry and drop its empty shell; below a familiar perch, the bodies slowly pile up.

The cluster fly lays its children inside earthworms. If you crush a cluster fly, it smells like honey.

The female thick-headed fly hangs around flowers, drinking nectar, like a bully at a bar. She waits for a bee or wasp and when one comes close, she grabs it. The bee seems not to care, does not resist, while she deposits an egg before letting go. The bee flies away, the larva hatches, and burrows within. The larva eats the bee slowly until it dies, then falls to the ground within the bee's body and burrows underground to pupate. Flies are holometabolous, meaning the young undergo a complete metamorphosis into the adult form, into a completely different form. The pupa is the quiescent phase between, and may last days or weeks or even longer. The pupae of flies are not protected by cocoons like those of butterflies; they simply harden, or build a shell from soil or spit. Some flies make a puparium from their own skin. Eat the bee, crawl underground, sleep the winter through, and emerge as a fly, seeking bees. That is the cycle, the great web of its life, round and round.

Pyrgotid flies do the same thing to May beetles, except that, instead of burrowing into the ground, they live in the empty beetle shell over the winter. Flesh flies live under the skin of a turtle and in the stomach of frogs. The sheep bot fly—I have described this creature already. But there is also a bot fly that infests rabbits, and a bot fly that lives in horses' throats, a bot fly that favors horses' noses, and another bot fly that prefers horses' tongues. There are bot flies specific to kangaroos, camels, warthogs, zebras, and elephants. The human bot fly, transmitted by mosquitoes, is cosmopolitan in its tastes; besides people, it infects dogs, cats, rabbits, horses, cattle, and sheep.

One of the drawbacks of a long Buddhist practice is that one sometimes has the urge to present one's self as more composed than one actually is. (Let's be clear here; I mean me.) Emotional equanimity is a Buddhist virtue, a reflection of one's ability to accept reality and a sign that one is not contributing to the heat of suffering in the world by resisting that reality. That this equanimity is a real thing to me, a true tranquility found through steady practice, is beside the point. My tranquility may be real, but it is not immune to conditions; it is no more permanent or unchanging than my skin. At times there is a loud voice inside me, complaining indignantly: *Explain this!*

Someone please explain this.

In my dreams, I could not make *Apocephalus pergandei*. It is named after Theodore Pergande, a renowned entomologist of the latter nineteenth century who was particularly interested in aphids and ants. He was observing carpenter ants one day when he saw the heads of the ants begin to fall off one at a time. When he investigated, he found what has become known colloquially as the ant-decapitating fly. The mature fly lays eggs on an ant's neck. The larvae hatch and then bore into the ant's head, eating it from the inside. Eating, the larva grows, slowly killing the ant, which apparently expires just as its head pops off. But as many of us wish we could do, it does not leave its childhood home behind. Instead, the little vermin remains inside for a while, and if you look closely, that is what you will see: ants' heads, walking around, filled with the children of flies.

A Buddhist practice requires rigorous self-disclosure—mostly to one's own self—and a kind of undefended willingness to be present in one's own crappy life as it is. This means noticing how often we tell lies about ourselves. I lie about many things, to myself and others. I lie about the way that triad on which I balance tilts: sensitivity, logic, love. It limps at times, or I find myself one-legged, just plain falling down. I am not always at home in this world, not always relaxed, not always in love with this great big Buddha Nature–ridden place.

The Tachinidae is one of the largest, most selective and successful fly families. "Ingenious," says one entomologist, for how they have solved the problems of their peculiar niche— "respiration in particular," since it is tricky to breathe inside things. Tachinid larvae are pure parasites, infesting virtually every kind of insect. One type lays its eggs on the leaves preferred by a certain caterpillar; the caterpillar eats the eggs, and the larvae hatch inside—born, as it were, at the buffet table. Another chooses male crickets and katydids. The female can hear the precise frequency of the male cricket chirp. (She can also hear, though the calls are many times higher, the ultrasound calls of the insectivorous bats she wants to avoid.) She follows the chirp carefully through a mechanism unlike human hearing. When she locates the host, she lays her live babies beside or on them. They burrow in and eat selectively to keep the host alive as long as possible.

Caught in a certain light, tachinid flies glow, their wings like violet veils, ovaline eyes the burnt-orange of sunset. I sit in the dark summer night, pleasantly melancholy, listening to crickets and contemplating *busshō* in a pulsing world.

I can pretend to have this settled. I can pretend to not mind. Certain gall midges are parasitic on themselves: the larvae hatch inside the mother and eat her from the inside out. I am appalled, even as I recognize the marvelous efficiency. Then I turn away from my own appalled thoughts. I am practicing acceptance. I bow. I tell myself it is a kind of compassion. It is sacrifice. (As though I understand *that* in some way.)

The horse fly bites a horse, and the blood runs, and before the wound even closes, the face fly creeps in and settles down to stay. The human bot fly captures a bloodsucker, such as a mosquito, and lays eggs on its body—just enough that the mosquito can still move freely. Then the mosquito finds a host and lands. The heat of the host causes the bot fly larvae to hatch; they slide off to the host's skin, down a follicle of hair and in, another accidental gift. The larvae live just under the skin. They form a breathing hole with their hooks, keeping it open by digging constantly. This is called myiasis, flies developing in living flesh. (Many fly families indulge; the human bot fly is just one.) The maggots live under the skin until they are about an inch long. One observer of the condition wrote that myiasis causes "intense discomfort or pain," which is not a surprise. But the maggots are never still; he adds that people also complain of "the disquieting feeling of never being alone."

A person with myiasis must be patient; it is damaging to try to remove tiny larvae. One treatment is suffocation: coating the openings with paraffin or nail polish or turpentine, or lathering on chloroform dissolved in vegetable oil. One of the most effective methods for removing them is to lay strips of raw bacon across the wound; the larvae come running. Squirming, rather, in their roiling, systaltic wave.

Oh, well—parasitism is routine in the insect world. Can we call it cruel, this life governed by instinct? Consider this: Two flies glued down by their wings to a table, for convenience. A drop of paraffin is carefully poured on their backs and then scooped out into a crater. Each fly's thorax is opened into the crater with a tiny scalpel, exposing the muscle. Saline is dropped into the craters for moisture. The flies are then rotated and joined, back to back, the paraffin gently sealed with a hot needle to form a double fly. This new kind of fly can walk, sort of, each taking a turn riding the other piggyback—or it can be neatly glued to a stick. For convenience. Now the scientist has a wonderful thing, a little monster with which to study many things: metabolism, hunger, dehydration, decay.

Explain that.

The larva grows, then settles into pupation. After time, after a mountain of time, the maggot disappears, the cask opens, and a fly emerges. It is fully mature; it will grow no more. The larvae of black flies are aquatic; the matured fly secretes a bubble of air and rises in it like an astronaut to its new life in the air, bursting out of the bubble at the surface. One observer said that a sudden hatching of black flies leaves the water "in great numbers with such force and velocity" that it seemed as though they were being "shot out of a gun." In contrast, the net-winged midge makes a submarine, a stiff case that floats to the surface, where it bursts open; the adult rises from its vessel as delicate as mist. At first it is a wrinkled and empty fly bag, without color or strength. The new being takes a great gulp of air and expands, incalculably vast and whole, the actualization of fly.

So many flies: tabinid flies, greenbottle flies, bronze dump flies, stilt-legged flies, bush flies, stable flies, louse flies, fruit flies, dung flies, rust flies, elk flies, seaweed flies, rust flies, scavenger flies, gadflies, skipper flies, soldier flies, hessian flies, Richard flies, light flies, stone flies, sand flies, grass flies, eye gnats, wood gnats. A myriad of mosquitoes.

There is something so simple and clear about the speech of flies; if I knew fly words, what would be clarified in my own?

I study how flies use the world—how they make something of it that wasn't there before. They liquefy the dead, they slurp up the world, inhaling the bodies of others. They shoot out of lakes and the ground and out of bodies, joyous, filled with air. If I believe—and today, I think I do—that every being is Buddha Nature, that there is no place Buddhas cannot or will not go, then I must give a glance inside.

I don't know what a Buddha is.

One fly, its passing hum, this we know—but they mob up, don't they, into masses of flies, into rivers and mountains of life, crawling and skipping and vibrating without rest, working at disintegration and change. Phantom midges form such enormous swarms they have been mistaken for smoke plumes, humming with such force that, in the words of one observer, they sound "like a distant waterfall."

Many fly swarms are birth explosions; others are orgies. Male dance flies join in huge mating swarms, graceful ellipses that flow up and down across meadows and gardens. They make frothy structures called nuptial balloons to carry on their abdomens for attracting females. Some species put seeds or algae in their balloons; others go straight for dead bugs—the bigger the better, as far as the female is concerned. (Female dance flies routinely eat during sex—maybe from the nuptial balloon they have accepted as part of the bargain, but often they eat another fly.) One type of dance fly uses only saliva and air, creating a lather of emptiness; as they dance, the empty bubbles glitter like lights.

Long-legged flies do their mating dance in slow motion,

their rhythms complex and mysterious; they wave black and white leg scales back and forth in front of the female like a vaudeville stripper waves her fans. Pomace flies have tufts of dark hair on their legs called sex combs, with which they hold the female still during mating. The male penetrates from behind, the female spasmodically jerking in response. Already-mated females are unreceptive; they curl their abdomens under, fly away, or kick at males.

The impregnated female seeks a nest. A few flies give live birth, and a few incubate their young. The tsetse fly, keds, and bat flies all hatch within their mother and are fed with something akin to a milk gland until they are ready to pupate, at which point they are finally expelled. But most flies lay eggs—a single egg, or hundreds, or thousands. She has a tele-scoping ovipositor, fine and small, which emerges from her abdomen and gropes its way inside—into the soft spaces, in the dark. Flies lay their eggs in the roots and stems of plants, in fruit, in the algae of a still pond, in shit, in hair and hide, in the bodies of other insects, the stomachs of cows, the dirty hunks of wool around the anus of the sheep, in the pus of an infected wound. (The preference of many carnivorous species is the corpse.) Blowflies deposit eggs in the eyes, ears, nostrils, mouth, vagina, and anus. Female flies are choosy; many have taste buds on the ovipositor to help them pick the best location—each fly to its own place. Insistent and shy, the ovipositor worms its way down: into garbage and wounds, into the rotten flecks of meat on the floor of a slaughterhouse, into stagnant water, between the membranous layers of a corpse, between fibers of living muscle, on the umbilical cord of newborn fawns—into "any convenient cavity," says the *Britannica*—and deposits tiny eggs shimmery and damp, masses of them. She is careful not to crowd them, filling first one newly made womb, and then another and another. A day later, she dies.

Horrible. Most horrible.

Larvae are the unfinished fly; they are like letters not yet making a word. Maggots are the simplest of larvae; they are the ur-fly, the refined essence of the fly, the marvelously simplified fly—its template, a profoundly primitive thing. Many maggots have no head, consisting only of a body and a mouth filled with hooks. They move by wavelets of muscular contraction and relaxation, grasping with the mouth hooks and other hooks along their sides. They can roll and spring and slide.

After they hatch, they eat and grow. This process may be slow or fast. The chironomid midge larva in West Africa grows in spurts, drying out and reviving through extreme temperature variations and waves of drought and rain. When it is almost completely desiccated, it enters into a condition called cryptobiosis—still alive but with no signs of metabolism. Sprinkled with water, it wakes up, takes a meal, and starts growing again until the next dry spell. The blue bottle fly requires an almost totally humid atmosphere—something a corpse can easily provide in most cases—and in good conditions hatches almost as soon as it is laid. They begin to eat, and never stop. I am being literal, they never stop. (Trashmen call maggots "disco rice" for the way they wiggle through the waste.) If undisturbed, a maggot will eat without ceasing until it is grown. There is a distinct advantage to maggots having anal spiracles; there is no need to stop eating in order to breathe.

Aristotle, like many others for most of history, believed that some flies "are not derived from living parentage, but are generated spontaneously . . . in decaying mud or dung; others in timber." They simply appear all at once from manure and corpses, with no sign of having been born. How else to explain this locomotion, this primordial fecundity?

Maggots can reduce the weight of a human body by 50 percent in a few weeks. In the decomposing of a body, there are several waves of insects, each colonizing in its turn in a strict sequence. The first wave is blowflies and houseflies of certain species; they begin to arrive within minutes of death. Their bodies are beautiful, glasslike in shimmering greens and blues; their eyes a deep, warm red. They glisten, tremble, and the larvae hatch and eat. They are ingenious little maggots. A dead body is in fact alive, a busy place full of activity—so much that the body seems to move of its own accord from their motion. The sound of all this movement, all this life, writes one entomologist, is "reminiscent of gently frying fat."

In time, other species of blowflies and houseflies arrive. The corpse begins to blacken, soften. (Corpses at this stage are called "wet carrion" by biologists.) The meat on which the maggots feed begins to liquefy and runs like melting butter. This is the fluid Fabre contemplated in quiet shock. "We here witness the transfusion of one animal into another," he wrote. If the maggots fail to move in time, they drown in the broth of the corpse they are eating.

By the time these larvae have fallen off into the soil to pupate, a third wave of flies arrives—fruit flies and drone flies and others, flies that prefer the liquids. Toward the end, the cheese skipper appears, drawn to the smell, and carefully cleans the bones of the remnants of tendons and connective tissue.

I contemplate my ordinary, imperfect, beloved body. I contemplate the bodies of my beloveds: individual, singular, unique, irreplaceable people, their skin and eyes and mouths and hands. I consider their skin riddled and bristling with that seething billow, I consider the digestion of their eyes and the liquefaction of those hands, my hands, my eyes—the evolution of the person into the thing, into wet carrion and eventually into a puddle, into soil, into earth, and flies. And it will come, whether I turn away or not.

We are nothing more than a collection of parts, and each part a collection of smaller parts, and smaller, the things we love and all we cherish conglomerates of tiny blocks. The blocks are built up; they will be taken apart the same way; we are nothing more. (And yet we are something more; this is one of the mysteries, I know. I cannot point to it, hold it, name it, except in the limited and awkward ways I have already tried. But there is something more, and it is the totality of this *nothing more*.)

Flies are wholehearted things, leading wholehearted lives. They understand dissolution, and by understanding I mean they live it. The parts are separated, they become something new. Pouring one's life into compoundedness without resistance, living by means of compoundedness and its subsequent falling apart—this is the wisdom of the creatures of the earth, the ones besides us, the ones who don't fight it. Because the human heart is devoted to compounded things and tries to hold them still, our hearts break. (One more thing to dissolve.) How can we know their lives? How can we understand the spongy proboscis, softly padded, with its small rasping teeth?

What better vision of the fullness of birth and the fullness of death than the maggot and the fly? A legless, headless, gill-breathing vermiform, giving way to the complete stillness of the pupa, and emerging as a land-based flyer—each stage utterly unlike the others, with nothing remaining of what was before. In their turn, maggots and flies help us along in our own fullness of birth and death, until what we were is completely changed. Decomposed, recomposed, compounded, dissolved, disappearing, reappearing—a piece from here and a fleck from there, a taste of this karma, a speck of that memory, this carbon atom, that bit of water, a little protein, a pinch of pain: until a new body and a new life is made from pieces of the past. The wee bit they claim, can you begrudge it? Dissolved, our flesh is their water, and they lap us up.

"Placed in her crucibles, animals and men, beggars and kings are one and all alike," wrote Fabre. "There you have true equality, the only equality in this world of ours: equality in the presence of the maggot." What lucky flies smelled the flowery scent of the Buddha's death, and came—flowing through the air like a river in the sky, a river of flies! What lucky maggots were born in his body, in the moist heat of the afternoon while the disciples still mourned! The maggots and blowflies are the words of the old Buddhas, singing of the vast texture of things, a lullaby of birth and death. They came and turned him into juice and soil, the Buddha flowing gloriously like cream into the ground.

After a night of more routinely menacing scenes—an insecurely locked door, a strange man in a wig—I woke in the early morning from a brief, vivid dream. There had been a series of burning rooms, and finally a room completely engulfed in flames. I saw several people walking calmly through the room, untouched, smiling. I woke as one turned and looked at me, and said, "I can't tell you how safe I feel in this house."

One of the most famous parables of Buddhism is that of the burning house. The story is told by the Buddha in the Lotus Sutra. A man's children are trapped in a burning house and won't leave when he calls them. In order to get them out, safe and free, he promises carts full of treasure, great treasure. Finally, tempted, they come out and are saved. Fire is change, loss, the impossibility of holding on; fire is also the burning, ceaseless desire we feel to hold on to that which can't be held. The house is burning, and we stupidly stand there, refusing to leave—until we are tempted by the promise of treasure—the precious jewels of the Dharma, the practice, the Buddha himself.

Bring what you will to this story, the point is to leave the house, to come out, to be free.

Right here, what do I believe? I do believe in perfection, right here—and not just perfection existing in the midst of decay, but decay as a kind of perfection. I believe in beauty, especially in the moments when one least seeks it—not just the dewdrop, the grass, but beauty in the shuffling of papers on the desk in the little cubicle thick with the snuffles of the sweaty man a few inches away. Beauty in the rattle of the bus sliding halfway into the crosswalk right beside you. Beauty in the liquid aswim with maggots. In everything, in anything. I can believe this, without in any way really understanding. Even after I have my answer, the question is always being asked.

When I begin to truly accept myself as a flit, a bubble, a pile of blocks tilting over, my precious me as a passing sigh in the oceanic cosmos of change—when I accept this moment passing completely away into the next without recourse—when I begin to accept that its very fragility and perishing nature is the beauty in life, then I begin to find safety inside a burning house. I don't need to escape if I know how to live inside it. Not needing to escape, I no longer feel tempted, no longer need promises or rewards. I just walk through it, aware of fire.

The north woods in summer smell like blackberry jam, and in the pockets of sun the tiny midges dance in the heat-sweetened air. They are drunk with it, galloping round and round as their lives leak quickly away. They are points of light in the light.

JONATHAN SAFRAN FOER

A PRIMER
FOR THE PUNCTUATION
OF HEART DISEASE

□ The "silence mark" signifies an absence of language, and there is at least one on every page of the story of my family life. Most often used in the conversations I have with my grandmother about her life in Europe during the war, and in conversations with my father about our family's history of heart disease—we have forty-one heart attacks among us, and counting—the silence mark is a staple of familial punctuation. Note the use of silence in the following brief exchange, when my father called me at college, the morning of his most recent angioplasty:

"Listen," he said, and then surrendered to a long pause, as if the pause were what I was supposed to listen to. "I'm sure everything's gonna be fine, but I just wanted to let you know—"

"I already know," I said.

"□"

"□"

"□"

"□"

"Okay," he said.

"I'll talk to you tonight," I said, and I could hear, in the receiver, my own heartbeat.

He said, "Yup."

■ The "willed silence mark" signifies an intentional silence, the conversational equivalent of building a wall over which you can't climb, through which you can't see, against which you break the bones of your hands and wrists. I often inflict willed silences upon my mother when she asks about my relationships with girls. Perhaps this is because I never have *relationships* with girls—only *relations*. It depresses me to think that I've never had sex with anyone who really loved me. Sometimes, I wonder if having sex with a girl who doesn't love me is like felling a tree, alone, in a forest: no one hears about it; it didn't happen.

?? The "insistent question mark" denotes one family member's refusal to yield to a willed silence, as in this conversation with my mother:

"Are you dating at all?"

"□"

"But you're seeing people, I'm sure. Right?"

"□"

"I don't get it. Are you ashamed of the girl? Are you ashamed of me?"

"■"

"??"

¡ As it visually suggests, the "unxclamation point" is the opposite of an exclamation point; it indicates a whisper. The best example of this usage occurred when I was a boy. My grandmother was driving me to a piano lesson, and the Volvo's wipers only moved the rain around. She turned down the volume of the second side of the seventh tape of the audio version of *Shoah*, put her hand on my cheek, and said, "I hope that you never love anyone as much as I love you¡"

Why was she whispering? We were the only ones who could hear.

¡¡ Theoretically, the "extraunxclamation points" would be used to denote twice an unxclamation point, but in practice any whisper that quiet would not be heard. I take comfort in believing that at least some of the silences in my life were really extraunxclamations.

!! The "extraexclamation points" are simply twice an exclamation point. I've never had a heated argument with any member of my family. We've never yelled at each other, or disagreed with any passion. In fact, I can't even remember a difference of opinion. There are those who would say that this is unhealthy. But, since it is the case, there exists only one instance of extraexclamation points in our family history, and they were uttered by a stranger who was vying with my father for a parking space in front of the National Zoo.

"Give it up, fucker!!" he hollered at my father, in front of my mother, my brothers, and me.

"Well, I'm sorry," my father said, pushing the bridge of his glasses up his nose, "but I think it's rather obvious that we arrived at this space first. You see, we were approaching from—"

"Give . . . it . . . up . . . fucker!!"

"Well, it's just that I think I'm in the right on this particu——"

"*Give it up, fucker!!*"

"Give it up, Dad!" I said, suffering a minor coronary event as my fingers clenched his seat's headrest.

"Je-sus!" the man yelled, pounding his fist against the outside of his car door. "Giveitupfucker!!"

Ultimately, my father gave it up, and we found a spot several blocks away. Before we got out, he pushed in the cigarette lighter, and we waited, in silence, as it got hot. When it popped out, he pushed it back in. "It's never, ever worth it," he said, turning back to us, his hand against his heart.

~ Placed at the end of a sentence, the "pedal point" signifies a thought that dissolves into a suggestive silence. The pedal point is distinguished from the ellipsis and the dash in that the thought it follows is neither incomplete nor interrupted but an outstretched hand. My younger brother uses these a lot with me, probably because he, of all the members of my family, is the one most capable of telling me what he needs to tell me without having to say it. Or, rather, he's the one whose words I'm most convinced I don't need to hear. Very often he will say, "Jonathan~" and I will say, "I know."

A few weeks ago, he was having problems with his heart. A visit to his university's health center to check out some chest pains became a trip to the emergency room became a week in the intensive-care unit. As it turns out, he's been having one long heart attack for the last six years. "It's nowhere near as bad as it sounds," the doctor told my parents, "but it's definitely something we want to take care of."

I called my brother that night and told him that he shouldn't worry. He said, "I know. But that doesn't mean there's nothing to worry about~"

"I know~" I said.

"I know~" he said.

"I~"

"I~"

"□"

Does my little brother have relationships with girls? I don't know.

↓ Another commonly employed familial punctuation mark, the "low point," is used either in place—or for accentuation at the end—of such phrases as "This is terrible," "This is irremediable," "It couldn't possibly be worse."

"It's good to have somebody, Jonathan. It's necessary."

"□"

"It pains me to think of you alone."

"■↓"

"??↓"

Interestingly, low points always come in pairs in my family. That is, the acknowledgment of whatever is terrible and irremediable becomes itself something terrible and irremediable—and often worse than the original referent. For example, my sadness makes my mother sadder than the cause of my sadness does. Of course, her sadness then makes me sad. Thus is created a "low-point chain": ↓↓↓↓↓ . . . ∞.

* The "snowflake" is used at the end of a unique familial phrase—that is, any sequence of words that has never, in the history of our family life, been assembled as such. For example, "I didn't die in the Holocaust, but all of my siblings did, so where does that leave me? *" Or, "My heart is no good, and I'm afraid of dying, and I'm also afraid of saying I love you. *"

☺ The "corroboration mark" is more or less what it looks like. But it would be a mistake to think that it simply stands in place of "He agreed," or even "Yes." Witness the subtle usage in this dialogue between my mother and my father:

"Could you add orange juice to the grocery list, but remember to get the kind with reduced acid. Also some cottage cheese. And that bacon-substitute stuff. And a few Yahrzeit candles."

"☺"

"The car needs gas. I need tampons."

"☺"

"Is Jonathan dating anyone? I'm not prying, but I'm very interested."

"☺"

My father has suffered twenty-two heart attacks—more than the rest of us combined. Once, in a moment of frankness after his nineteenth, he told me that his marriage to my mother had been successful because he had become a yes-man early on.

"We've only had one fight," he said. "It was in our first week of marriage. I realized that it's never, ever worth it."

My father and I were pulling weeds one afternoon a few weeks ago. He was disobeying his cardiologist's order not to pull weeds. The problem, the doctor says, is not the physical exertion but the emotional stress that weeding inflicts on my father. He has dreams of weeds sprouting from his body, of having to pull them, at the roots, from his chest. He has also been told not to watch Orioles games and not to think about the current administration.

As we weeded, my father made a joke about how my older brother, who, barring a fatal heart attack, was to get married in a few weeks, had already become a yes-man. Hearing this felt like having an elephant sit on my chest—my brother, whom I loved more than I loved myself, was surrendering.

"Your grandfather was a yes-man," my father added, on his knees, his fingers pushing into the earth, "and your children will be yes-men."

I've been thinking about that conversation ever since, and I've come to understand—with a straining heart—that I too am becoming a yes-man, and that, like my father's and my brother's, my surrender has little to do with the people I say yes to, or with the existence of questions at all. It has to do with a fear of dying, with rehearsal and preparation.

✂ 🕸 The "severed web" is a Barely Tolerable Substitute, whose meaning approximates "I love you" and which can be used in place of "I love you." Other Barely Tolerable Substitutes include, but are not limited to:

→|←, which approximates "I love you."

𝔭 □, which approximates "I love you."

🕯, which approximates "I love you."

×✈, which approximates "I love you."

I don't know how many Barely Tolerable Substitutes there are, but often it feels as if they were everywhere, as if everything that is spoken and done—every "Yup," "Okay," and "I already know," every weed pulled from the lawn, every sexual act—were just Barely Tolerable.

:: Unlike the colon, which is used to mark a major division in a sentence, and to indicate that what follows is an elaboration, summation, implication, etc., of what precedes, the "reversible colon" is used when what appears on either side elaborates, summates, implicates, etc., what's on the other side. In other words, the two halves of the sentence explain each other, as in the cases of "Mother::Me," and "Father::Death." Here are some examples of reversible sentences:

My eyes water when I speak about my family::I don't like to speak about my family.

I've never felt loved by anyone outside of my family::my persistent depression.

1938 to 1945::□.

Sex::yes.

My grandmother's sadness::my mother's sadness::my sadness::the sadness that will come after me.

To be Jewish::to be Jewish.

Heart disease::yes.

← Familial communication always has to do with failures to communicate. It is common that in the course of a conversation one of the participants will not hear something that the other has said. It is also quite common that one of the participants does not understand what the other has said. Somewhat less common is one participant's saying something whose words the other understands completely but whose meaning is not understood at all. This can happen with very simple sentences, like "I hope that you never love anyone as much as I love you¡"

But, in our best, least depressing moments, we *try* to understand what we have failed to understand. A "backup" is used: we start again at the beginning, replaying what was missed, making the effort to express ourselves in a different, more direct way:

"It pains me to think of you alone."

"←It pains me to think of me without any grandchildren to love."

{} A related set of marks, the "should-have brackets," signify words that were not spoken but should have been, as in this dialogue with my father:

"Are you hearing static?"

"{I'm crying into the phone.}"

"Jonathan?"

"□"

"Jonathan~"

"■"

"??"

"I::not myself~"

"{A child's sadness is a parent's sadness.}"

"{A parent's sadness is a child's sadness.}"

"←"

"I'm probably just tired¡"

"{I never told you this, because I thought it might hurt you, but in my dreams it was *you*. Not me. *You* were pulling the weeds from my chest.}"

"{I want to love and be loved.}"

"☺"

"☺"

"↓"

"↓"

"⚫"

"☺"

"□↔□↔□"

"↓"

"↓"

" ▶▶◯◀◀ "

"■+■→■"

"☺"

"👂□"

"▧ ⊠"

"◎□❖◯◆◯◯□◆⊙●"

"■"

"{I love you.}"

"{I love you, too. So much.}"

Of course, my sense of the should-have is unlikely to be the same as my brothers', or my mother's, or my father's. Sometimes—when I'm in the car, or having sex, or talking to one of them on the phone—I imagine their should-have versions. I sew them together into a new life, leaving out everything that actually happened and was said. ◆

DIANE ACKERMAN

SILENCE AND AWAKENING

I.
AND THE SILENCE THAT IS

Winter trees bring to mind eastern gods, whose many limbs curve gracefully, touching the universe in all directions. When the wind rocks their branches, a few last marcescent leaves whisper eerily. The world brims with foreign languages, spoken much as we speak—by passing air over solid forms whose various holes and flexings fine-tune the sounds. It doesn't matter whose or what's breath is used, or sometimes what liquid, since sound travels so well through water. The great Lake Cayuga, deep and soupy with life in late summer, and shaped by millennia of erosion and sediment, has its own key, and waterfowl and frogs float their calls on the water. Sounds carry over frozen water too—in the Arctic, voices can travel for a mile across hard flat snow.

A friend has invited me on a silent retreat. Relatively silent. After all, the birds would still sing and call, the leaves rustle, the cicadas scrape, the wind sough. Exclude them, leave the galaxy even, and there's still the background hiss from the Big Bang, which radio telescopes record as a sort of hoarse streaming sigh. I mean human silence, which on this retreat also includes turning off the wordless communications, what the Japanese call *haragei* (ha–ra–GAY), body language, gesture, facial expression, a telling glance.

"Soon silence will have passed into legend," sculptor Jean Arp warns in *Sacred Silence*. "Man has turned his back on silence. Day after day he invents machines and devices that increase noise and distract humanity from the essence of life, contemplation, meditation. Tooting, howling, screeching, booming, crashing, whistling, grinding, and trilling bolster his ego."

Once a year, on a changing day in April, people in Bali celebrate Nyepi (nn–YEH–pee), a national day of silence that follows the dark moon of the Spring Equinox and ushers in the Balinese New Year. On this Hindu holiday, both car and foot traffic are prohibited (except for emergency vehicles), radio and TV must play low if at all; village wardens keep people off the beaches; work, socializing, and even lovemaking stops, as a nation sits and falls silent together, for one day of introspection in an otherwise hectic year. Not only does the dawn sound different, it smells different. Without the reeking exhaust from cars and trucks masking subtler scents, the air smells naturally floral, and it's enriched by the green aromas of vine-clad forests.

During Nyepi, surrounded by the incense of wildflowers, one mulls over values, beholds the balance of nature, meditates on love, compassion, kindness, patience. Dogs bark, cicadas call shrilly, but the streets breathe a quiet rare for that clamorous island, a silence framed like a painting. Not the silence of deep space, nor the hush of a dark room, but an achieved silence, a found silence that's refined and full. The Japanese word for silence, *mokurai*, combines *moku*, silence, with *rai*, thunder, creating a sense of silence as a powerful force, a reverse thunder. One doesn't *fall* silent when tasting impermanence—the sting of everything appearing, disappearing and changing from moment to moment—but undergoes silence, creates silence, becomes silence.

There are many forms of silence: the silence after raindrops fall on the metal roof of an old corn binder pickup truck; the silence just before the word "silence," and just after; the silence of light cutting through the pool water to stencil giraffe hide onto the bottom; the silence that exists when your dead mother no longer calls your name, the silence inside manicotti-shaped sleeping bags when the sleepers have left; the silence of one's DNA when one is scattered dust; the silence of neurons sparkling in the lens of a scanning electron microscope; the silence inside the ear when a phone call ends; the silence thick with the silences of loved ones; the silence of other paths one might have taken; the silence of recluse firmaments glimpsed through a telescope; the silence between one's hands cupped in prayer; the silence that water striders leave in their wake, the silence of a yolk-yellow sun running atop the horizon at dawn; the silence that we package into seconds and minutes, the minute silence of all packages, the silence of the crying baby one never had; the silence of swimming in thick furry ocean; the silence of snow pressed against one's closed eyelids; the silence that hung in the air after you said "Will you write those thoughts down?" when what you really meant was "Will you write those down *for me*?"; the silence of the fog left by one's breath on a chilly morning; the silence of your name before you were born; the silence of slow-motion memories; the silence of quaking aspen leaves viewed through a window; the silence of wandering thistledown; the silence of igneous rock; the silence of mirrors;

the silence held by the *b* in the word "doubt"; the infinite silence reflected in all silences; the silence of an inactive volcano; the silence of the heart's stilled motor.

Death is the silence in an invisible valise carried under one arm. As we walk, an elbow leaves room for it. Through a window I see quaking aspens fidgeting silently (the glass baffles noise) in a dumb show of shivering leaves. Surely my death will dawn like that: first the aspens will flicker; then the scene will fade to black and white; leaves will spin even faster in the wind, but silently, and I will have been.

2.
MISSIVE

An ancient definition of dawn is the moment when one can recognize the face of a friend. A morning phone call delivers the news of the death of John O'Donohue, lark-tongued Celtic poet, philosopher, theologian, ex-priest, and what the Irish call an *anam cara*, a soul friend. At first my brain denies the hearsay and refuses to add it to its library of facts. In shock and disbelief, my brain trips all over itself, then I feel the sudden monstrous subtraction that comes with the death of parent, child, grandparent, sweetheart, special friend. Two and two no longer equal four, the world comes unhinged, and a draft blows through it. I may grow old enough to know many loved ones who didn't wake to see the dawn, but I feel fortunate to have had a friend as divinely articulate as John, someone so in tune with life.

He loved the *thisness* of things, as well as their poetry, and especially loved thresholds and awakenings and dawn. "If you had never been to the world and never known what dawn was,"

John once said, "you couldn't possibly imagine how the darkness breaks, how the mystery and color of a new day arrive."

"Subversive" was a perfectly odd and daring word that he favored, one that evoked an insurgency of belief, an insurrection against habitual ways of knowing, a charity of awareness, blessed by the heart's iambic, despite the ego-mad *I am*'s of everyday life. Presence mattered, perhaps more than anything, because he understood the tragedy of being absent from one's own life.

I loved John's belief in the feral soul of poetry. He found poetry a kind of attentiveness, a form of endless rebirth, a mystical path to the divine. He understood, as truly as glass understands light, the ability of poetry to heal a mutilated world. And so he practiced Dharma poetics, poetry as a vehicle of awakening.

The first Irish poem, declaimed by Amairgen in 1700 B.C., as he stepped onto shore and claimed the land for his people, presents his spiritual and supernatural heart:

> *I am the wind which breathes upon the sea,*
> *I am the wave of the ocean,*
> *I am the murmur of the billows,*
> *I am the ox of the seven combats,*
> *I am the vulture upon the rocks,*
> *I am the beam of the sun,*
> *I am the fairest of plants,*
> *I am the wild boar in valour,*
> *I am the salmon in the water,*
> *I am a lake in the plain,*
> *I am a world of knowledge,*
> *I am the point of the lance of battle,*
> *I am the God who created the fire in the head.*

"This ancient poem," John writes in *Anam Cara*, "preempts and reverses the lonely helplessness of Descartes's *'cogito ergo sum,'* I think therefore I am. For Amairgen, I am because everything else is. I am in everything and everything is in me. It is a oneness first known between mother and child."

We once spent a day coteaching a workshop called "Awakening the Senses, Romancing the Words." We focused on how the lamp of art allows one to shine light into dark corners, glimpse the intangible, spell beauty, and pan through the flow of experience for nuggets of illumination. This was a writing workshop about paying close attention to life, using poetry, story, myth, and meditation to honor the call of beauty and develop our capacity to find it in the most unexpected places.

I called him O John, and we were slated to meet at a symposium a few months from now, and again at a mindfulness retreat in late fall. I already lament those missed reunions and confluences of hearts and minds. But mainly I feel lucky to have known one of life's sublime celebrants for a few of his dawns. In the spirit of his poetic "blessings": may your mornings greet you with such a friend.

John's poetry and prose is so deliciously smeared with the senses that I can picture him now, fiercely alive with the electric fizz of being, not dead, just out of reach for a while, writing in his seaside house in Connemara, Ireland. My mind furnishes his house and places him in it, as it always has—how can he not be there now?

O John, the first light this morning that doesn't shine for you hangs on the air like old yellowed linen. Shouldn't there be scarlet banners celebrating your passionate verve? Or at least a plume of color staining the sky the way you left your imprint on everyone, reaching deep into them, finding their state of highest grace, and helping them rise to it? You knew the best one could become, the plateaus of being, and the thresholds that arise, frighten, but must be crossed to become the self one dreams. I didn't know you often, but deeply, as a pilgrim side of me.

On the last evening of your life, you slept with your fiancée, Kristine, felt saturated with joy, having spent the happiest day. You were that rare man who met the girl of his dreams and stayed happy for the rest of his life—but only a few hours remained of it. You were fifty-three, planning a marriage, picturing the faces of the children you hoped for, full of a thousand blessings. For hundreds of thousands of years, most of our time on this planet, people could expect a life span of only eighteen years: still, fifty-three seems shockingly few.

Everyone who ever spent time with you came away changed. It's not that you were nobler than other noble souls, or more devout, or kinder, or more reverent. You drank too much, were prankish, could be hilariously irreverent. But you lived your words about being present in the world, you were able to be utterly alive in an era of distractions.

Had you awakened, you would have found the sky right where you left it, the way we all do, your sweetheart beside you, nestled in the aura of romantic love with all its hallelujahs. Your future included a new collection of poetry and prose called *To Bless the Space Between Us*, and the silent blessings of all your students and readers, the newlyweds whose vows you blessed, the mourners whose loved ones you buried, the parents whose newborns you helped christen, and the flock of spiritual seekers whose hunger you fed.

We all died last night, as we do every night. Waking is always a resurrection after what might have been death. What would dawn have been like, had you awakened? It would have sung through your bones. All I can do this morning is let it sing through mine.

3.
NOTHING DOING

In a dream, I'm flying above thick heavy storm clouds at dawn into a zone of sunlight with streaks of blue sky and wispy clouds. I see a heavy blanket of cloud stretching below me, and under that all of life on earth gyrates. I feel like I'm floating through the noncorporeal mind, floating after death, away from earth, from body, from sensory awareness. After the momentary shivers and terrors comes a sense of freedom. I don't want to return to the storm. Aloft, all is white, an antarctic vista as far as I can see, white but with dimension: puffs here and there, sinkholes, hills, occasional tints of pale blue smeared across endless pastures of smooth white.

Slowly, I become aware that I am in my mother's mind as she was dying seven years ago today, in a hospital I know well, in her mind that had stopped holding on to earth and let herself float, float up through clouds beyond the body, to a realm of sky with blue striations, slowly rising and feeling no senses, no action or activity, yet an awareness of a self floating up out of the self, through the gates of the mind. As her mind began floating away beyond anything like thought, word or want, a granular white fog moved in, obscuring even the clouds.

Then I realize I am looking at the marbling of the body, the flesh and fluids, seeing from inside the tissues. Looking down, I can feel the body beneath the broken clouds of consciousness, the body with its flowing channels and pastures, its microbial cities and swamps, and dense neural pathways. Then an array of clouds obscures the body, hovering thickly in white ridges and dark grey anvils. We fly right into one surging cloud, become immersed in it, and fly out the other side. Wispier clouds swim across the emptiness like small thought fish.

Floating somewhere between the body and the mind, I spot a long waterway stretching from north to south, irrigating the lands all around it. Through a hole in the cloud floor, I see a wide winding river and miles upon miles of farm fields. Then slowly floating even higher, we enter an area of blue sky and pure yellow sunlight with stray clouds above, and curving all around the bowl of the horizon. The clouds move closer, and I climb knowing that when I pass through them I will enter pure air, pure starlight. It is not so bad parting with the earth. There is great relief.

Life is teeming, anonymous, and disposable. Some religions encourage a loss of self, in essence a glimpse of death during life, with a welcome escape from the struggles of identity. Still, I'm fearful. One is always too young and unready, too polite, too dignified for such radical decay. In this dream the sun blurs the horizon with gold, night and day meet in one quadrant of loss, an indivisible quiet. A heavy white blanket lies below and cloud banks press on the trigger points of morning. Soon we sink between layers in a white-out bleak as noon on a glacier. Finally, through a long grey coma of clouds, we descend.

I wake up slowly, consciously, trying to remember the softness of my mother's beautiful pale skin, the exact pitch of her upbeat voice, what she looked like as a slender young woman, her changing hairstyles over the years, and as many happy memories of being with her as possible. Not a lot of those memory twigs exist, unfortunately, and I could use some to nest in now. Marcia died three years after my father, Sam. A sense of mourning has been shadowing me for days, the way it sometimes does as her birthday approaches. I've no desire to visit her grave because I believe she's not really there but has rejoined pure energy, once again a shimmer of atoms at dawn. The locals don't say "passed away" but "passed," which sounds a bit more mystical, as in "passed to the other side" or "passed through the veil."

I sense her in the atomic mother-brightening dawn that's glowing chestnut with platinum geysers. I wish our time together had been more intimate, that I'd known more of her dreams and sorrows, understood her better, and that she'd felt known by me. No use fretting over lost possibilities. I hear real peace comes from loving one's fate, not just accepting it, because life is as it is and how one responds is what yields happiness or discontent. Loving your fate without trying to fix it, without asking the universe to be anything it's not, is easier to phrase than to feel, except as desire, and, ironically, the desire itself contradicts the lesson. I find it a state of grace hard to reach. Like trying to frame problems as invitations, not challenges. These fine adjustments echo through the halls of morning.

In Tibetan monasteries, one learns to practice a "death meditation" at dawn. Upon waking, instead of joining others for sitting meditation and chores, one lies in bed with eyes closed, and says to oneself: "I'm going to die tonight. What shall I do with the rest of my time?" This isn't meant to be a rare occurrence in the otherwise smoothly slathered hours of one's life, but a regular practice over months or years—because it might be true of any day, and certainly will be true one day. Cuddled up with my loving dear? Looking at photographs of my mother? Strolling down the street and feeling the sensations of being alive and in motion? Admiring the beauty of the natural world from sunrise to sunset? Writing a poem? Doing good for the loved ones and others who remain on earth? I begin to appreciate and schedule my allotted hours to what matters most, and that's a tonic to carry into waking life.

The birds start choiring early on, as if they're dragging the sun up to please the aborigines who dream it with song. A flock of starlings flies over like a pack of noisy children. Yellow-white crystals of sunrise give whatever they strike a brilliant blue luminescence, and it's as if my mother left her awe everywhere for me to find, especially today, lit by the luminol of dawn.

MELISSA PRITCHARD

A SOLEMN PLEASURE

HELEN REILLY BROWN
July 14, 1918—April 6, 2008

CLARENCE JOHN "JACK" BROWN, JR.
April 17, 1918—June 13, 2003

CREMATION
REQUIREMENTS

Cremation is performed by placing the deceased in a combustible casket or container, that in turn, is placed in a cremation chamber and subjected to intense heat/flame. Bone fragments and dust are brushed from the chamber after cremation; however, it is impossible to remove all of the cremated remains. Because some dust and residue always remain in the chamber, there may be an inadvertent or incidental commingling of residue from previous cremations. This also may occur as a result of mechanically processing cremated remains.

Cremated remains may be buried, entombed, placed in a niche, scattered over private land with permission of owner or over public property (may require permit), or remain in family's possession, usually in an urn (wood, marble or metal container).

Cremated remains should be collected upon notice of availability. The crematory authority may dispose of the remains in a legal manner 120 days after the cremation or after agreed-to pick-up date.

—*Consumer Guide to Arizona Funerals Information,*
Arizona State Board of Funeral Directors
and Embalmers

FUNERAL SERVICES FOR HELEN BROWN

CATEGORY A—SERVICES

Professional Services

Direct Cremation (Non-declinable)	$1,000.00
Cremation Fee	$300.00

Transportation

Transfer of Remains to Funeral Home—Vehicle	$350.00
Service/Utility Auto	$175.00
CATEGORY A—TOTAL	$1,825.00

CATEGORY B—MERCHANDISE

Minimum Cremation Container	$95.00
CATEGORY B—TOTAL	$95.00

CATEGORY C—CASH ADVANCES

Copies of Death Certificate	$150.00
Medical Examiner Permit	$15.00
CATEGORY C—TOTAL	$165.00

TOTAL A,B, & C	$2,085.00
Services, Merchandise and Cash Advances	
State and Local Taxes	$7.56

BALANCE DUE	$2,092.56

REQUIRED DISCLOSURES:
Direct Cremation

A direct cremation (without ceremony) includes transfer of deceased within 50 miles; basic services of Funeral Director and Staff; refrigeration (for the first 24 hours); cleansing, handling and care of unembalmed remains; dressing; use of facility and staff for private viewing by next of kin (up to ½ an hour); and transportation to crematory, crematory fee (for processing time greater than 48 hours from time of arrangement conference, excluding weekends and holidays). If you want to arrange a direct cremation, you can use an alternative container. Alternative containers encase the body and can be made of materials like fiberboard or composition materials (with or without an outside covering). The containers we provide are cardboard (with no pillow or bedding), basic container (totally combustible containers) include pillow, bedding and with or without fabric covering, hardwoods (either natural or stained finish) with crepe or velvet interior.

This package includes Paradise Memorial Crematory, Inc.'s cremation fee.

The deceased Helen Brown
Will be held at Messinger Indian School Mortuary
7601 East Indian School Road, Scottsdale Arizona
Until final disposition.

Melissa Pritchard
(Print Name of Responsible Party)
Date 4-06-08
Time 16:45

HAWTHORNDEN CASTLE
LASSWADE, MIDLOTHIAN
SCOTLAND

—Ut honesto otio quiesceret

Soon after the death of my mother, I found myself at an international writer's retreat held in a Scottish castle named Hawthornden, an hour outside of Edinburgh. A short walk from the castle, part of a 120-acre woodland estate running alongside the River North Esk, is the cave that sheltered Sir William Wallace, the Scottish hero made famous by Mel Gibson's portrayal in the film *Braveheart*. Hawthornden Castle is part ruin, a thirteenth-century medieval castle with a warren of Pictish caves below it, hand-carved of rock and said to have hidden Robert the Bruce, Bonnie Prince Charlie, and perhaps William Wallace. The habitable half of the castle was built by Sir William Drummond, Cavalier poet and friend of Ben Jonson, Michael Drayton and other literary figures of his age. Hawthornden Castle has been an International Writers' Retreat since 1985, and writers, selected several times a year for monthlong residencies, live in rooms, working behind doors marked BOSWELL, BRONTË, HERRICK, JONSON, EVELYN, SHAKESPEARE, YEATS.

In filling out my application, months before, I had whimsically requested the use of a typewriter. Because of the noise such an antiquated machine would presumably make, I was separated from the row of writer's rooms on the third floor, rooms accessed by a staircase as tightly spiraled as a nautilus shell. Instead, I was put into private quarters on the second floor reached by a short climb from the first. The name on my door was Shakespeare.

I had come to Scotland to write, but I had also come to grieve. Our culture is skittish of mourning, impatient and awkward with bereavement's uneven process. Friends had been exceptionally kind, but the overall message I had gotten from society, the environment-at-large, was make haste, move on, pay bills, earn your keep.

SHAKESPEARE. My wailing room, done in dark red, dark green, and ivory, housed a benign monster: an immense, pillared, wood-canopied bed hewn of heavy timber so old and dark it appeared black. On the headboard, formally painted in golden lettering, was the year 1651, and the initials P H and M H. Set off by hand-carved floral and geometric patterns were human figures, two male, one at each end of the headboard, and one female, in the center, her arms crossed beneath her naked breasts, fingers encircling each erect, if slightly squared, nipple.

The room had a mantled fireplace, a wardrobe and a plain desk set before a large pair of paned windows overlooking a sea of forest, an unseen river, the North Esk, rushing along below, and above, a Gainsborough sky with shifting, scudding wreaths of silver and white cloud.

For the thirty days I lived in this room, the only sounds I heard (even better when I flung the windows wide and fresh, wind-scrubbed air poured in) were birdsong—wrens, warblers, magpies, woodpeckers, kestrels, and others—the murmur of the Esk, and trees, an ancient woodland of oak, ash and elm, and hawthorn as well, tossed by an occasional tempest of wind, leaves flashing white and green, a sound like rough surf. Gentler sounds came from the kitchen, directly beneath my room, when the Scottish housekeeper, Mary, prepared hot porridge and coffee in the morning, and later in the day, as the French cook, Alex, slid dishes out of cupboards, chopped vegetables, conducted a muted clatter of pots and pans, her efforts sending the tantalizing savor of what we were to dine on that night drifting up the curved stairway. The spark of guilt I felt, being given such private, spacious quarters because of a typewriter I would end up never using, was quickly extinguished. Given my suppressed mourning, my blanketing sadness, this room, away from the rest, was perfect for sorrow.

The Reformation-era bed, the atmosphere, ascetic, no modernity beyond electric lights and decent plumbing—no e-mail or Internet, no phone, no television or radio, no cars—the quiet, the forest, the light—my books and my pens—my meals prepared (a basket of food left outside my door promptly at noon, a tea tray in the afternoon), laundry done, linens changed weekly—my only assignments to sleep, eat, walk, write (though no one ever inquired as to one's progress), and converse with four fellow writers during dinner and in the upstairs drawing room afterward, where we took up reading Thomas Hardy's *The Mayor of Casterbridge*, eager, each evening, for the self-induced tragedy of Michael Henchard—this cradled way of life, a childhood without chores, I called it, became a place where sorrow unveiled itself. A place thick with tales of Picts and Celts, Romans, Druids, fairies, Knights Templar, Grand Master Freemasons, Gypsies, and the pagan Green Man, with castles and ruins of castles, forests with paths wending along rivers, steep precipices, meadows pearled with sheep and lambs, lanes flanked by wild rose, foxglove, saxifrage, horsetail, bluebells. Ghosts presided too, lively and miasmic, haunting chapels and caves, appearing on forest footpaths and in Hawthornden Castle. Spirits disporting themselves as misty presences, as lights going on or off, doors opening and closing on their own, and once—we all saw it—a lamp flying across the drawing room. In my state of loss, I found such capricious afterlife cheering.

SHAKESPEARE. My first night, I fell into a quarter-sleep (the birds, still singing? the light, why so much?) tempered by a soft incredulity at my good fortune. My second and third and fourth nights passed in sporadic weeping, harsh bursts of grieving. Womb of my own dear self, source and friend, my petty quarrel and perpetual conflict, the one I had grown so intimate with in those final, terrible months, She was *gone*, a common word that had assumed grave, terrible, stony weight. *Gone.* Vanished. *Gone.* Invisible. *Gone.* No more. *Gone.* Incorporeal. *Gone.* Departed. *Gone.* Disappeared. Anglo Saxon, *gan*. As if she had never been. There was nowhere on this earth I could

ever again go to find her. She was ash in my home now, powdered and tamped into a hideous shoe-polish-brown box,
weighing little more than a feather, and slip-covered in a
purple-velvet pouch, reminiscent of Royal Crown liquor
pouches, something in which a member of the mortuary staff
had solicitously handed her to me. My father's body, cremated
by the same mortuary five years before, had not been pouched;
his squared remains, as brown as his surname, *dad-in-a-box*, had
been handed to me inside of a white shopping bag. Lord &
Taylor. As if he were a purchase, which in some sense and by
then, he was. I mentioned this to the mortuary staffer, confess-
ing too that I had stashed my boxed father behind my six published books, hidden him in my library these past five years. As
a result, I was given a velvet pouch for him, too. I left the mortuary, my mother tucked (my, what square, hard edges you
have!) into the crook of one arm, the royal purple pouch for
my father in my summer straw purse. Driving out of the parking lot while calling one of my daughters on the phone, I
would have been immediately killed had not my second daughter, in the car with me, shouted for me to stop before we were
slammed into by an oncoming, speeding four-wheeler. We
laughed—yes, like hyenas!—at the idea of being killed exiting
a mortuary, one dead mother in the car.

My parents, bagged in grape velvet, like tacky purple stuffed
animals, sit side by side (sit? repose? lounge? tumble-bumble?
decay? What does one say of dust and knobs and shards in a
box?) in an otherwise empty chest of drawers in the guest
room, guests now, waiting their flight to Honolulu, where, in
an outrigger canoe ceremony (as they had requested) my sister
and I will sift them like ingredients, blend them into the kel-
pish, blue-green broth of the Pacific.

I, on the other hand, am loath to let go. Can I not keep some little of their ashes, commingled? *("We are such stuff as dreams are made of . . .")* But in what? Where? And why? All at once, the logic of earthly interment is apparent, a specific place to visit, to show up at on holidays and bring flowers, to erect a granite stone or marble pillar or angel. A family gathering spot, a somber picnic ground. But my parents were not religious in any conventional sense; they were affluent gypsies, and in this age of global warming and impending environmental catastrophe, burial in the ground is passé, outdated, wasteful of precious space and vanishing hardwoods (for coffins). Cremation has environmental cachet, ash is green, even if it lends itself to moments of Beckett-like absurdity and comic pathos, like "Jack," my mother's teddy bear. For the five years she flailed miserably on after my father's death, "Jack" kept her company, a teddy bear in a blue print Hawaiian shirt, with a plastic Baggie holding a few thimblefuls of my father's ashes sealed up where the bear's imaginary heart would be. He was with her at the end, snuggled beside her in a hospital bed, his little eyes gleaming loyally, if blindly, his ash-heart thumping for her, his Hawaiian shirt faded, and at her demise, at her dissolution, at her burning, her auto-da-fe, "Jack" was there too, turning to flame in her enfolded, emaciated arms.

Father, Mother, Childe Forlorne

ROSSLYN CHAPEL

One night, in the drawing room at Hawthornden, I heard the story of Hardy, how his heart was cut out of his corpse, kept first in a biscuit tin, then interred at the cemetery where he had requested his body be buried (the rest of Mr. Hardy went to Westminster Abbey, sadly demonstrating the plight of being torn asunder, like a saint or martyr, by one's own fame). In the section of the church known as the Lady Chapel resides the earliest known stone-carved "danse macabre," sixteen human figures each dancing with a skeleton. Every inch of this chapel is obsessively carved with Christian symbols as well as gargoyles, Norse dragons, angels playing bagpipes, Lucifer tied and hanging upside down, and over one hundred heads of Green Men, male faces sprouting foliage, a Celtic symbol of fertility. Rosslyn Chapel is a book in stone, written in Celtic, Masonic, Templar, Pythagorean, Gnostic, alchemical, and biblical texts. The Stone of Destiny is rumored to be buried in the chapel, as is the Holy Grail and shards of the Black Rood, or True Cross, carried from the Holy Land by William "the Seemly" Sinclair. Christ's mummified head is said by some to be hidden inside the famous Apprentice Pillar; these tales abound and inspire theories, one wilder than the next. Stories of the Devil's Chord, of an Astral Doorway, of UFO sightings around Rosslyn, have given the tiny chapel a supernatural charisma attracting thousands of visitors. I am a visitor too, and Rosslyn Chapel, with its danse macabre, is more than a site of religious miracle and mystery. It is my second (silent) wailing room. Its graves, its symbols, speak of resurrection, of the infinite many gone into the dark.

HAWTHORNDEN CASTLE

Where better to grieve than in the same castle where a famous Scottish poet, Drummond of Hawthornden, born December 13, 1585, mourned as well? He grieved the loss of his parents, Sir

John Drummond and Susannah Fowler; he mourned poor Miss Cunningham of Barnes, his betrothed, who died on the eve of their wedding. He married, much later in life, a Miss Elizabeth Logan, because she bore a tender resemblance to Miss Cunningham, and of their nine children, six perished, giving him more occasion for grief. Drummond's fine sonnets, still subjects of scholarly research, all carry the strain, the gentle rumination upon death in them, an emphasis we might find morbid today, insulated as we are by the near-promise of a medically enabled old age. But Drummond lived in a time when death's gait evenly paced, if not outpaced, life's. What better spot to mourn than in the castle of a poet known for his many epitaphs and sonnets composed for departed friends, a poet who, thinking himself near death at age thirty-five, wrote to his good friend Sir William Alexander a sonnet ending with these lines:

> *To grave this short remembrance on my grave:*
> *Here Damon lies, whose songs did sometimes grace*
> *The murmuring Esk: may roses shade the place!*

His famous prose piece, "A Cypress Grove," a mystical meditation on death, was written in a cave inside a forest alive with roe deer, red fox, pheasant, rabbit, squirrel, and badger, near green meadows wandered over by horses, sheep, and cattle, in green, rain-swept air thick with stories of battles with Romans and Norsemen, of the Crusades, its monks and knights and ladies, of brutal warfare with the English for freedom, of Druidic wisdom, the teachings of the Celts still whispering if one stops to listen, in the ancient, black-limbed oaks, the gorse and Scottish broom, the flowering hawthorn, wild rose and foxglove, the springing leap of roe deer, or hoarse, raucous chorus of ravens, all of which accompany me on each daily walk, walks as healing as SHAKESPEARE, with its bed, its desk, its silence, its green view, the comforting sounds, beneath my feet, of food being prepared, nurturance delivered to the minds and souls of the resident writers, this writer, laboring, sorting her way to sanity, solitary, *danse seule*, in SHAKESPEARE.

ROSSLYN CHAPEL

A poem of stone . . . powdered with stars.

—THOMAS ROSS, 1914

I have walked fast this morning, the sky the bright enameled blue I remember from childhood. I left Hawthornden late, so I must walk fast, three kilometers through woodland glen and meadow, to be at the chapel for the Eucharist Communion at ten-thirty. I arrive barely in time, hot from an hour's walking, smelling of boiled wool from my green sweater, my hair turning to sheep's wool.

The service, preceded by organ music, is old-fashioned, sedate, as though we have all day, and the hymns we sing, found in our faded hymnals, are by George Herbert, Alfred Lord Tennyson, William Blake (*For Mercy has a human heart and Pity a human face*). In the organ loft above us, the morning's psalm is sung in plainchant by an unseen parishioner. Even in June, the stone chapel is bleakly cold, and the flames from white candles waver from unseen drafts. It is easy to float backward centuries and see the chapel broken into, seized as a stable for Cromwell's warhorses when he laid siege to nearby Rosslyn Castle, to smell the sweat, dung, and straw, to hear the rough shouts and curses of soldiers rather than the sweet singing of a dwindled, aging congregation of Scottish Episcopalians.

The grace of history, the dead, are those I feel most kin to now. The living seem removed, through no fault of theirs; they are meant to live and to savor all they can, and there will be that again for me as well, but for now I am more at home with the dead, with those who grieve, or with those who remember, with the Reverend, and the lay reader, as I cup my hands to receive the Eucharist, kneeling at the altar, below the statue of Mary, placed there in the age of Victoria. Layers comfort me. We walk upright awhile, then are divided, the lute from the player, the flesh returns to the sea or the earth or the air, the spirit becoming, perhaps, Light. A friend said of my mother, weeks before she died, she is scattering into Light. He was exactly right, and that is what we are all doing, though more slowly now than she—scattering into Light, in line to take our greater place, to be those distant stars, or a presence on the stair, unseen but felt, or that splashy violet bloom of azalea, or that midnight call of owl or nightingale, or that uneven fringe of cerise light on the horizon, or that deer, springing silent into the glen, or that pheasant, startled, flushed from its hedgerow or the black church cat, William, winding himself around the legs of the Reverend as he gives his Sunday announcements, his "adverts," for the church barbeque that afternoon, or for the archbishop of Brazil soon to visit, for this is the cat's home too, this chapel. We kneel above nine knights in the chapel vault, unopened for centuries . . . the story goes that when the vault was opened, and a small party went down to see, someone touched the first knight, laid out in his armor, a bell, a candle, and a book beside him, and the body, at the touch, inside its metal casing, fell to dust. The others were left undisturbed; the vault was sealed. I kneel this Sunday, June 15, Father's Day, my knees resting over the dust and bones of the St. Clair Knights Templar, five generations, my head bowed by the weight, growing lighter, of my own mortality, aging communicants on either side of me, devout, Scottish worshipers, growing lighter too as they keep their weekly covenant of flesh and blood, as the notes of "Ave Maria" soar like sweetest birdsong above our head, the sounds of Katherine Longville, of French Huguenot ancestry, mother of three, her boys home with their father, singing "Ave Maria" just as she had sung it the Sunday before for the wedding of a local couple, young Katherine Longville, who manages to keep up with her singing lessons every fortnight, for her boys, she says, are growing fast, and she too is only here a while. We are all engrailed.

In the woods where Drummond wrote, I write. Along mossy paths in the woodland glen where he walked, I walk. Where hearts were carved out of flesh, thus is my heart carved from my own chest, and carried, by me, to the chapel at Rosslyn, to be laid down, laid down too in the cemeteries I walk between, a permanent seeding of graves on either side, I, the living creature, sailing between so many dead with all the pride of uprightness, straight-up-ness, of breath, motion, thought, my gay distinction from poor-them, poor-dead, sorrily prone and purblind. Yet with my grandparents gone, aunts and uncles gone, parents gone, mother most recently, with all gone and but one sister living, my privilege narrows, my distinction dims, my allegiance shifting to those on either side of me, rather than with those walking all around me, strolling on a fair Saturday in June, families, visitors, the young, all of us on our way, pilgrims threading the path between two graveyards, to Rosslyn Chapel.

BETWEEN TWO GRAVES

Death is the sad estranger of acquaintances, the eternal divorcer of marriage, the ravisher of the children from their parents, the stealer of parents from their children, the interrer of fame, the sole cause of forgetfulness, by which the living talk of those gone away as of so many shadows, or fabulous Paladins.

—"A Cypress Grove,"
WILLIAM DRUMMOND, 1620

Written in Stone
"Lead, kindly light"
"At rest until He come"
"Sadly missed"

A Thimble of Dust
In Loving Memory of
Helen, aged 9 and ½
And
Alexander Simmons
Aged 8
Who were tragically drowned in
The South Esk
On 26th August 1932

✝

In memory of Jemima Arnott
Accidentally killed in an
Explosion at Roslin Gunpowder Mills
17th June 1925
Aged 20 years

✝

Guy Justly
The dearly loved child
Of Colonel Oliver and Mary Nicholls
At Rosebank, Rosslyn
26th February, 1850
Aged 7 months
"Of such is the kingdom of heaven"

Certain names catch at one. Christina Grieve. Tibbie Porteous. Fanny Law. Euphemia Todd. Proudfoot. Or an advertisement at the bottom of one monument: GIBB BRO'S. ROSLIN GRANITE WORKS, ABERDEEN. It isn't fair. We pause, our imaginations held, by the special tragedy of young deaths, or the mixed triumph of old deaths (the oldest a woman, age 102), or by the waste of the young in wars, or by parents left to grieve a child, or by the young husband left to grieve his wife, by the young killed in accidents, by disease, drowned. Less dramatic births and deaths, those whose dramas are recessed, we pass by. The sheer numbers of the dead render us frugal: we portion out sympathies.

✝

Here Lye
Anne Watson spouse of
John Sturrock merchant
In Edinburgh, Who died
The 17the of May 1782
Aged forty years
Underneath this stone Doth as . . .
Could . . . which . . .
Alive did vigor . . .
To . . . beauty as could . . .

What is it that draws us to linger over half-ruined inscriptions, puzzle out dates, to the romance of old cemeteries, stones sunk, overtipped, inscriptions blurred to unreadability, moss, scabs of lichen and rotting leaves overtaking the imperturbability of marble, the endurability of granite? One gravestone, fallen to the ground, is so covered over by an inch or more of grass and buttercup, a thick green hide, it could be mown. Near it, an angel of marble, once celestially white, soaring upward, now gray and black, tipping sideways and hidden beneath an overgrowth of hawthorn, a Cadbury biscuit wrapper obscenely prosaic by its base. All this is homily in stone, all this is what we are coming to ourselves, those of us who stroll with solemn pleasure among the dead, finding poetry in the biblical or sentimental or stark inscriptions on the stones, yet glad too to end our reverie, close the iron gate, and walk the graveled hill back up to the chapel or inn or tea shop, glad to turn our thoughts from a sweet melancholic ramble to our appetites, our calendars, our health, our families and friends, the petrol level in the car, the need for a drink or to take a child, or ourselves, to the bathroom. We need to pee, or to kiss and hold hands, or to help grandmother into the car, for we are, with thrilling vengeance, alive.

> *This passive place a summer's nimble mansion,*
> *Where bloom and bees*
> *Fulfilled their oriental circuit,*
> *Then ceased like these.*

—EMILY DICKINSON

Last Sunday, walking along the river path to Rosslyn, I came upon an injured magpie. It had tucked itself into some leaves by the side of the path, and as the sun broke over the soft green maple leaves, and with the rush of the river nearby, it seemed a not ungentle place to die. The earth is made of the dust of creatures lived before. We walk carelessly upon the dead, the world a rounded grave.

Mother, Father, Childe Forlorne

All this has laid a softness around my grieving.

In those last hours, my mother's laboring to die seemed like my own fight, as a younger woman, to give birth. The inescapability of it, the solitude, no matter who was there, the sense of magnitude. I wanted to know, to ask if it was like giving birth, this prising apart of the flesh and the soul, but something stopped me—reserve, fear, lack of temerity, respect for my mother's profound passage. When it was time for the hospice people to help, when I mentioned the seeming labor in this dying business, they said, oh yes, we think of ourselves as helping to birth people into the afterlife. Like midwives? Yes. Like that.

And I worried. For the eleven months she had lived after the stroke, my mother, paralyzed, smart as a whip, and fully conscious, could speak but one word. *Yes.* Even when she meant no. We communicated telepathically, or through touch, or my bad jokes, which made her laugh, or with her eyes and her yes and my prattling on. Was sitting with her, watching documentaries like *Winged Migration, The Wild Parrots of Telegraph Hill,* or *Ten Questions for the Dalai Lama* on my laptop, or my taking her out into the care center's garden in her wheelchair, enough? Was spooning bits of whipped cream with chocolate sauce into her mouth—the last thing she ever ate—enough? Was washing her face with a warm, then cool, washcloth, combing her sparse hair, putting aloe vera chapstick on her lips, massaging her temples and ear lobes, then rubbing lavender lotion on her face and hands, enough? Were these the proper rituals for death's hand-maiden? Love made me clumsy, tripping after the one who led the dance.

Hours before her heart stopped, my mother bolted half-up from her bed where she had been resting, struggling to breathe from the pneumonia, and grabbed hold of my sister's hand, staring at her with a look of terror my sister later refined, upon reflection, as a look that said, "Is this it, then? Is this death?" It was an intense, eyes-wide-open look, and the violent grip on my sister's hand, the strength of this frail, eighty-pound woman, a baby bird nested in white industrially washed linen, was so painful, so tight, my sister would have had to pry her fingers off if she had needed to. A death grip? I asked. We looked at one another, newly understanding the phrase.

We didn't want her to be afraid, so we asked the hospice nurse to give her a bit of morphine, a drop under her tongue, sublingua. She visibly relaxed, closed her eyes. Dozing, one might say, but for the struggle going on, the battle being lost. My sister tried to read a book she had brought; I tried to grade student essays. Who were we fooling?

When she opened her eyes twenty minutes later, we had music on, something she liked, instrumental, spiritual. I stood over her, smiling, and picked up her left hand, the paralyzed one, all bone now, and swung it gently back, forth, up, back, forth, up, as though we were waltzing. We're dancing, Mamma, I said. She smiled, then gave me a twinkling, openly flirtatious glance I remembered from childhood, the look she wore at parties, the look that had drawn so many young men to court her before I was ever born, and then, surprise upon surprise, my mother winked at me, a girl with all the world before her.

I leapt for the phone when it rang at 3 A.M. I woke my sister, who already knew. I had wanted to be there, to hold her in my arms, to murmur to her like a lover. *(I felt. I wanted. I!)* Her greatest fear, she once told me, was of dying alone. But she hadn't died alone, had she? We had all been there in the days preceding, and a nurse she'd liked, whose name I can't recall, was with her as she "passed" (the current euphemism). The hospice people say it is extremely common for people to "take their journey" (another expression) when everyone has gone home, has left the room. When we are with them, we hold on too hard, we won't let them go.

We drove the ten minutes to the care center, no traffic, the hour before dawn, took the elevator to the third floor, turned right past the dining hall, then left down the hall to her room. HELEN BROWN, said the sign by her door, a symbol beside it that meant "danger of falling." (They used to find her on the floor, having rolled somehow out of her bed; so they lowered her bed each night so that it was only an inch or so from the floor, and put gym mats down to cushion her fall.) The overhead fluorescent lights were on (ugh! turn them off!); flowers bloomed on the windowsill, stargazer lilies. The artificial Christmas tree from Walgreens which I had put up five months before and never taken down because I thought the colored lights and shiny ornaments added some cheer, and because I did not know what else to do with it, was there. The black and white photograph of her great-grandmother Zadrow, her grandmother, Fredericka, her mother, Rose Louise, and herself, little Helen Lorraine, five years old, hung above her bed.

She lay on her back in an overwashed gown of faded blue, her mouth gaping open. My sister said, "Can't we ask them to close her mouth?" We went to the nurse's station, asked, and were told they had tried, but that her jaw, loose now, as happens with death, kept falling open. We pulled the bed sheet up over the mouth that frightened us.

I asked for time alone with her. Corpse? *Mater Magnificat?* Oh, Mamma. I knelt by the bed, fell to my knees before the altar of my mother. I sensed her spirit, free, prised loose, and spoke aloud. I wept. I kissed her cheek, stroked her fine, soft hair. I went back to the nurse's station, asked for scissors, came back and snipped a lock of her hair, tinted light brown, her weekly hair appointment a last feminine pleasure.

> *When their bones are picked clean and the clean bones gone,*
> *They shall have stars at elbow and foot . . .*
> —"And Death Shall Have No Dominion,"
> DYLAN THOMAS

When I was fifteen, my mother, who knew I wrote poetry and burned Chinese incense in my room but did not know how many times I rode my bicycle to the cemetery behind our house, and wandered with solemn pleasure among the graves, gave me, for Christmas, a collection of poems by Dylan Thomas. I imagine her choosing this book for me, wanting to please me. She was not a literary person, she did not read poetry, yet she made the gesture within herself to understand my nature. She wrote, rather formally, in red ink, *"A Merry, Merry Christmas to our girl, with love from Mother and Dad."*

A female Anna's hummingbird appeared in my garden the day after her death. It hovered outside my study window, looking in at me for a long, suspended time. It came back the next day and the next, hovering before that same window as I sat at my desk. And one final time, as I sat in my garden, praying to her to show me a sign that she was free now and approved of how I was handling all the earthly details of life, for I was missing her terribly and falling under my burdens, the hummingbird appeared, this time hovering, hanging in the air, inches from my face. It stayed for a very long time. The next day, I hung a feeder in the tree outside my study window, but it had disappeared. There had been no hummingbirds in my garden before and none since.

According to Tibetan Buddhist teachings, the spirit has enough energy, during the first hours and days after death, to give signs to the living, but after that, the spirit moves on, signs fade, then are gone. *Gan.* My mother loved birds and fed them all, especially her elusive, iridescent hummingbirds.

The day before she died, I gave her two bouquets of stargazer lilies, pink-striped perfumed trumpets, the last blooms she would ever see. One month later, a clairvoyant came up to me and said, I see your mother has tiny little birds flying all around her—hummingbirds!—also, she says to thank you for the lilies you gave her, they have always been her favorites.

Mommy. Mamma. Gan.

✝

Journeying through the world
To and Fro, To and Fro,
Cultivating a Small Field
—From the gravestone of Joanna Dun, 1634,
Lasswade Cemetery,
Midlothian, Scotland

CHRISTOPHER SORRENTINO

DEATH IN THE AGE OF DIGITAL PROLIFERATION, AND OTHER CONSIDERATIONS

PUBLIC MOURNING: A KIND OF FAST

We are taught to respond with mannerly emotion to the inevitably dead—that is, to everyone else's dead, to the dead whom Ernest Hemingway attempted (in the most uncharacteristic of his short stories, "A Natural History of the Dead") to dignify by startling, or disgusting, us out of our misapprehensive complacency, the assimilation that permits us to see "them" (Katrina victims, World Trade Center first-responders, U.S. military casualties, etc.) not as graphically *destroyed* but heroically *fallen*. It is a seemly denial of the flesh, like a religious fast. It's hard to say whether Hemingway was more aware of the true conditions under which dead heroes meet their ends or of our own essential ghoulishness: These are the same dead we furtively revel in—the dead of the 3 A.M. websites, the secret autopsy reports and police photos, the dead reduced to recovered scraps of DNA, sumptuously interred femurs. These are the public deaths whose smell and feel we seek out privately, to plunge beyond the decorous piety of the news story, to move beyond the taunting simulacra of the movies into wide-open unknowns of anger, velocity, impact, decay. Public mourning says, *I am sad. Now show me the film.*

TRAINING WHEELS

With public mourning, the act to which we are called is the opposite of the grotesque social inappropriateness of true grief (see: keening, rending of flesh, hurling oneself into open coffins to embrace the dead, hurling oneself into open graves, the fulfilled suicide pact, discerning of supernal visitations and signs, etc.). When I was a kid I had a friend who thought that dealing with grief was a little like moving from the bunny hill to the black diamond on the ski slopes. You started gradually, with a nice, inconsequential death (we do not, as a society, really believe Donne's business about how together we comprise a continent unavoidably diminished by each individual demise), and then moved to the big ones, presumably at last to greet your own death with utter insouciance.

The idea of building up tolerance for grief, for death itself, has its weird appeal. What it overlooks is that there are the deaths that tip you over and those that are no trouble at all. There's a middle ground someplace, I know that: there are the deaths that arouse your hidden fears; there are the deaths that urge forth springlike effulgences of nostalgia; there are the deaths that elicit an unsettled emotional response strangely similar to what I've experienced when the Mets have lost in the playoffs. But—to paraphrase Philip Roth—there are some presences whose absence can undo even the strongest people.

I am a middle-class American, so I've managed to remain fairly sheltered from death (despite the invitation to psychological trauma issued jointly some years ago by Al-Qaeda and the New York City Department of Health and Mental Hygiene), and in fact the first death I remember that really startled me was the direct result of class inequality. It was a girl, Juanita, who was in my second-grade class at P.S. 41 and lived at the Broadway Central Hotel, a notorious welfare pit that eventually collapsed but not before claiming her life: She'd fallen down an elevator shaft when the doors had opened onto nothing. Lurking somewhere in there is a rueful joke about poverty; one with a punch line that has the landlord saying, "*Nu?* An elevator too you were expecting at these prices?" My handling of her death was consistent with the macabre norms of American boyhood. In a time before grief counseling was routinely made available to "survivors," my friends and I spent the day speculating luridly on the condition of her body. When I got home from school, I took one of the Magic Markers I was supposed to be drawing smiling suns and rigidly vertical stalks of grass with and drew instead an *X* over her image in the class picture, then crossed her out on the accompanying list of names, writing an explanation within parentheses—"dead."

Then came my grandfather. My mother has always possessed the gift of undaunted candor, a gift bestowed upon her that she, in turn, has liberally bestowed upon all. She always took it upon herself to disabuse me of my illusions—those I might have, for example, concerning any resemblance the movies might bear to real life. So when my grandfather died after losing what an obituary might have described as "a long battle with cancer," while I was away at summer camp, there wasn't any telephone call summoning me from the cacophony of the mess hall or the fellowship of the dingy bunk. There was a matter-of-fact letter, typewritten, composed in my mother's matter-of-fact style.

As if she had planned it thus, there also wasn't a moment when I walked down to the deserted lakeshore "to be alone"; no episode in which I stared at the millions of stars visible in the clear night sky upstate and wondered where in the universe my grandfather had gone. As it happened, when the letter arrived, I was laid up in the camp infirmary, aflame with the impetigo that my having been left to my own hygienic devices for over a month had incubated. Every morning a large middle-aged nurse would supervise me as I stripped naked, stepped into a scalding bath, and then scrubbed the crusty scabs off each of the festering pustules using a brush saturated with pHisoHex. It was painful on several levels. The nurse was not attractive. No one visited me. Quarantined without any other reading material, I read the same *MAD* magazine paperback reprint (*Good 'n' Mad*) over and over. And of course my mother's letter. In these circumstances, I attempted to experience grief for the first time:

I'm afraid I have some bad news for you, which I hate to have to tell you. Grandpa died last Saturday, and was buried yesterday, Tuesday. It was a very peaceful and a painless death. He really just slipped away, first into a coma, and then very quietly into death. I wish I could have given you the news face to face. If you want to we'll talk about it when you come home. Of course we were all expecting it, and the whole family has reacted very calmly. Grandma will be leaving on Saturday for a trip to Puerto Rico where she can relax and visit with the family.

By my reckoning, Grandpa had been dying practically forever (a variation, I guess, on that idea of building-up-to-it), and the interdiction that took hold, embodied right there in the letter, was that we were all to be relieved that he'd died; to be reassured that it was easier for him to be dead than it was for him to go on living. This myth of the blessed death raises questions, the biggest being: who and what, exactly, are relieved? Few would argue that leukemia and multiple myeloma are easy, but there is a clear distinction between relief and non-being (we are suspicious of precise meanings precisely because of such distinctions). The daily responsibility for dealing with my grandfather's decline was one that my grandmother accepted stoutly (although she enjoyed reminding people of it), and so fully that, having retired in her early sixties after working for decades as a Spanish-language interpreter for the state of New York, she had begun a second career working as a nurse's aide at Montefiore Hospital, encouraged to apply for the job by the staffers to whom her daily visits had made her a familiar presence. But while my grandfather's illness ended with his death, my grandmother's particular hardship—the affliction of the caretaker—ended in full recovery. She "got better." Her duties toward the dead man had been as completely discharged as his duties toward life. She not only went home to San Juan to "relax and visit with the family," but soon was treating her Co-op City apartment (smaller than the place she'd moved out of, near Bronx Park, when it had become apparent that my grandfather wouldn't be coming home again) like a way station where she dropped her bags and rested between frequent trips to Europe, South America, California, Las Vegas, and pretty much anyplace where some friend or relative would have her, indulging well into her eighties a wanderlust that apparently had built up, unsatisfied, during the years of her marriage.

I believe that some aspect of the relief the new widow felt

(along with other conflicts trapped in the opaque amber of the past), or its expression, offended my mother deeply. My mother is like certain cats I have known who ally themselves with and bestow most of their affection on one particular human, tolerate some others, and have little use for the rest. For much of my mother's early life, that human, I think, was my grandfather. She believed that my grandfather was ushered to his grave impatiently, almost gleefully, by my grandmother. As a consequence of this offense, and other, older ones, my grandmother became a criminal in our household; she was purged gradually from our emotional lives, and it occurred to me that death could begin an unraveling; that people themselves, their presence, held things together in ways that the memory of them never could.

Let me here append the first paragraph of this essay by suggesting that while another of the emotional purposes of organized mourning is to provide a comforting, if false, sense of death's uniting us, the inherent function of death is to separate us, first from the deceased and then, in a process of extension, from others.

MEMPHIS, SUMMER 2007

A life builds momentum (we hope); we hope that as a product of that momentum the living agency of the people we love persists in the form of their memory: we hope that their influence, the power of their "aura," buoys them, keeps them among the living, an illusion most convincing, I think, with the dead we love with narcissistic force. Last summer we drove into Memphis precisely on the August weekend when the thirtieth anniversary of Elvis Presley's death would be commemorated municipally. It was not a somber occasion, although it wasn't by any means clownish. The city fathers simply recognized that Elvis was and remains the star attraction of a very interesting town. It would have taken a certain mean-spiritedness to point out that in marking Elvis's life with a festive commemoration coinciding with the anniversary of his death, it seemed unavoidably to be celebrating the death itself. Again, the thing wasn't handled for comic effect; no souvenir miniature toilets mounted on pedestals thick with deep shag carpet denoting the place of the King's last act of volition—the attempt to void his narcotics-paralyzed bowels—were on sale. The customary level of vulgarity, and no more, was evident: a sort of polymerized adoration falling somewhere between that accorded JFK and that accorded Padre Pio. There was also the complete elision of the terminal fact itself. An act of self-preservation, surely: "love with narcissistic force" is the phrase I used: because if Elvis lives on, then the corollary to such a formulation must be that when Elvis dies "a piece of Memphis dies too. . . ." It was, in fact, shortly after Elvis's death that I first heard the now familiar phrase about the dead—the recorded, published, filmed dead—"living on." "The King may be gone," the announcer's voice said, "but the legend *lives on!*"

DEATH IN THE AGE OF DIGITAL
PROLIFERATION

I know I'm supposed to like the idea of a person's living on through some kind of legacy. Nowadays, certainly, with camcorders and HTML-enabled word-processing software, with Internet access, with free webpages and blogs, one has tools at hand to extend one's presence, one's utterances and likeness the length and breadth of the world, to be as omnipresent and plentiful as the heavenly stars and grains of sand to which God compared Abraham's posterity—to become, in effect, one's own posterity. The present ability to extend oneself beyond physical limitations as a result of the simplest act of will beggars the imagination; if every citizen of the world had been issued an airplane and a telephone early in the twentieth century, it would not have had the same impact. To be everywhere, forever! It's a marvelous thing, especially since nothing in particular needs to be achieved in life in order for this eternally globally instantaneously transmitted monument to have a reason to exist. It exists as a universal extension of the brain; as a poignant illustration of the "fixed fantasies" that we carry with us (as the web presences, publicized by newspapers and other "gatekeeper" media, of various recently dead mass murderers have demonstrated).

If we accept, for the sake of argument, that this is a form of "living" (NB: I don't accept it otherwise), then we need also to acknowledge that such perfected fantasy adumbrations of ourselves as websites, Facebook pages, and blogs also have as their corollary, trailing behind them, the inadvertent revenants of our less ideal lives. The best of several examples I saved to draw on for this essay is taken from a website called AOL Stalker, which purports to preserve, albeit under coded user IDs, the data concerning individuals' web searches that AOL injudiciously, and somewhat scandalously, released a few years ago. What story, what remainder of a life, are we to infer from the quests of user #672378, lingering there?

curb morning sickness	2006-03-01 18:54:10
get fit while pregnant	2006-03-09 18:49:37

he doesn't want the baby	2006-03-11 03:52:01
you're pregnant he doesn't want the baby	2006-03-11 03:52:58
online degrees theology	2006-03-11 04:05:24
online christian colleges	2006-03-11 04:13:33
barefoot contessa	2006-03-11 11:04:36
nightstand use	2006-03-11 22:09:02
why use a nightstand	2006-03-11 22:09:50
foods to eat when pregnant	2006-03-12 09:38:02
baby names	2006-03-14 19:11:10
baby names and meanings	2006-03-14 19:11:28
la tee da's charlotte nc	2006-03-18 15:57:48
physician search	2006-03-23 10:20:04
taste of charlotte	2006-03-27 15:56:49
best pampering trips	2006-03-27 16:33:26
best spa vacation deals	2006-03-27 20:04:09
maternity clothes	2006-03-28 09:28:25
outlets gaffney sc	2006-03-28 10:44:40
pottery barn furniture outlet	2006-03-28 10:49:09
furniture outlets nc	2006-03-28 11:14:29
pregnancy workout videos	2006-03-29 10:01:39
buns of steel video	2006-03-29 10:12:38
what is yoga	2006-03-29 12:17:31
what is theistic	2006-03-29 12:18:19
what is theism	2006-03-29 12:18:30
hindu religion	2006-03-29 12:18:56
yoga and hindu	2006-03-29 12:32:05
is yoga aligned with christianity	2006-03-29 12:33:18
yoga and christianity	2006-03-29 12:33:42
whitney houston	2006-03-31 11:29:33
www.coffeecup.com	2006-03-31 11:39:45
the coffee cup charlotte nc	2006-03-31 11:40:09

ashley stewart	2006-04-01 13:19:07
lane bryant	2006-04-01 13:22:40
www.patients.digichart.com	2006-04-05 20:04:37
federal government jobs	2006-04-06 18:16:16
jewelry television	2006-04-06 19:06:03
abortion clinics charlotte nc	2006-04-17 11:00:02
greater carolinas womens center	2006-04-17 11:40:22
can christians be forgiven for abortion	2006-04-17 21:14:19
roe vs. wade	2006-04-17 22:22:07
www.livethroughmusic.com	2006-04-17 23:17:41
effects of abortion on fibroids	2006-04-18 06:50:34
effects of fibroids on abortion	2006-04-18 06:55:57
abortion fibroids	2006-04-18 06:59:32
abortion clinic charlotte	2006-04-18 15:14:03
symptoms of miscarriage	2006-04-18 16:14:07
mecklenburg aquatics center	2006-04-18 19:39:00
water aerobics charlotte nc	2006-04-18 19:41:27
abortion clinic charlotte nc	2006-04-18 21:45:49
50th birthday gift	2006-04-20 07:51:19
total woman vitamins	2006-04-20 16:38:16
esteem vitamins	2006-04-20 16:42:42
engagement gifts	2006-04-20 16:57:04
zales outlet	2006-04-20 17:41:03
50th birthday gift ideas	2006-04-20 17:50:16
mom's turning 50	2006-04-20 17:51:13
high risk abortions	2006-04-20 17:53:49
abortion fibroid	2006-04-20 17:55:18
benefits of water aerobics	2006-04-20 23:25:50
new homes charlotte nc	2006-04-24 17:15:05
ethan allen	2006-04-25 15:55:48
wedding gown styles	2006-04-26 19:37:34

hewlitt packard computers	2006-05-05 13:15:15
ibm computers	2006-05-05 13:18:11
dell	2006-05-05 15:28:08
www.gateway	2006-05-05 19:12:13
notebook computer product reviews	2006-05-06 16:19:51
www.wedddingchannel.org	2006-05-06 21:22:18
define—oscillating	2006-05-07 11:21:35
st lawrence homes	2006-05-07 12:21:23
eastwood homes	2006-05-07 12:31:55
ryland homes	2006-05-07 12:41:41
www.substanceabusepreventionservices.org	2006-05-14 13:21:50
virginia credit union	2006-05-14 23:02:46
hgtv	2006-05-16 18:43:34
test taking tips	2006-05-18 14:49:58
northern star credit union	2006-05-19 18:23:08
hotel deals	2006-05-19 21:11:21
courtyard new carrollton	2006-05-19 23:27:55
dead sea scrolls	2006-05-19 23:35:13
dead sea scrolls discovery place	2006-05-19 23:35:44
blueletterbible.org	2006-05-21 07:24:00
recover after miscarriage	2006-05-22 18:17:53
travel deals	2006-05-24 16:27:52
combat uterine fibroids	2006-05-24 16:28:31
degenerative vertebrate	2006-05-25 20:58:19
degenerative disc	2006-05-25 20:59:16
demetrios bridesmaid dresses	2006-05-26 19:32:52
marry your live-in	2006-05-27 07:25:45
juice fasting	2006-05-31 11:54:14
www.healthyliving.com	2006-05-31 12:48:29
community pathways	2006-05-31 13:11:09
carolinas healthcare system	2006-05-31 13:12:48

family specialist   2006-05-31 13:17:29
what is the average merit raise   2006-05-31 13:31:41

The story here is truer than ego would ever permit; as unintended for public scrutiny as the telling gesture of a stranger on the street who believes she is unobserved—is it only the novelist who doesn't require the name to envision the whole person? American dreams and worries are adrift, forever current, within the massive servers that conserve them—672378's dreams of a baby, of a happy father for it, of a wedding; dreams of new furniture, a new home, of a getaway vacation, of a better job, of healthier ways of living; worries about sin, about the emotional and physical impact of medical ordeals; and those strange wild cards (nightstand use?); all will outlast the dark nights and bright days that gave rise to them. And as one reads this plain document, a simple enumeration of the complicated things on one woman's mind, it's difficult not to read *into* it—did 672378 look up miscarriage symptoms on May 14 so that she could smoothly lie about having "lost" the baby after having an abortion? Did she resolve to have the child with or without "him" only to suffer a miscarriage around May 21? Did she lose the baby because of some substance abuse problem she belatedly sought help with? Did "he" have the substance abuse problem? But as long as it endures, and as true, as minutely real, as it is, this is no second and more durable life, it is only another document positing with each affirmative the expansiveness of the unknown awaiting our interpretation, and interpretation is no more than the empty hole we fill with our own reckoning. Elvis does not "live on"; death is that moment when any possibility of learning the unknown is lost, when the inadequate sum of what is known becomes the totality of what there is to know.

Narratologically, this isn't much help. What we like and respond to, in forming the narratives that give our lives and those around us coherent meaning, is something far more than the unadorned accounting of 672378's lonely keystrokes. Think of De Palma's *Black Dahlia,* in which Aaron Eckhart pretending to be a detective watches Mia Kirshner pretending to be the murdered Elizabeth Short pretending to be someone else in one of the silent stag movies she made; Eckhart's rapt face is a testament to the phony power of "living on."

MY FATHER

If I seem to be cynical about a perfectly inoffensive way of ordering reality, it may be because of my father. I tried all this business with him (let me say here that the building-up-to-it method I discuss above proved to be of absolutely no help in dealing with his illness and death; the absence of his particular presence ruined who I'd been and made a different man of me) and it made no sense. My father was a wonderful writer (*pace* the blogger—another potential immortal, of course—who wrote that 2006 was turning out to be a great year for literature because Pynchon had published another book and Sorrentino had died), and as such his books leave me with something of considerable substance, but it was as a father that I loved him. Besides, the books make up an artistic legacy, and a public one; there are scores of "sons" out there who can take from those books precisely what I can, and who have no interest in trying to extract from them what I can't, his essence.

That's thorny, isn't it? Another thing we want to believe is that the artist invests himself in his work. Wit, intelligence, facility, profundity, skill, style—all are present, each individually amounts to more than the whole of 672378's found drama, but neither are they life.

I made a Super 8 film of my father once; like nearly everything else from my childhood, it's long gone. It was an actual filmmaking project, titled *Pop on Memorial Day,* which suggests that a suitable subtitle might have indicated that I was home from school, bored, and probably had received the camera about ten days earlier for my birthday. Certainly, I wasn't thinking of posterity; I was thinking about getting the developed reel back from the lab and running it through my little Bell & Howell projector. Does he live on in this film in a way that he does not through his books? Certainly, if it were to be restored to me, the film would depict many of the lost corners of my life, because for my parents (unlike for me) only a handful of material things ever accrued sufficient sentimental value to require their preservation, but the film would only confirm the things, in altogether inadequate shadowed blurs, that no document is necessary for me to remember, and the memory of my parents' tables and chairs, appliances and decorations, the combination of the timeless comforts of high bohemia and the dated 1970s particulars, is more than enough.

The memory of my father is not enough. When I think abstractly of "my father," the image my mind summons forth is of him at about this time—1973, when he was a year younger than I am now—and of his ultrapredictable habits and mannerisms I would likewise never need a film to remind me of. The only time my father ever surprised me was when he got sick and died.

My father would have ridiculed the suggestion that he'd devoted his life to leaving a record of himself, or of his thoughts, and he would have been especially scornful of the idea that a record of any kind could substitute for, let alone possess, life. He wanted to make things that were beautiful yet, as he put it once, "do not live." He made that clear to me so that I'd always know it. What I always knew I should have known better; I look at the shelves and shelves of books—about twenty-five hundred, I figured during a recent move—everything lying in wait within the dark pages between the two covers, every conceivable situation, and the inconceivable ones, helping not a bit.

THE SIEGE

HOW ARE YOU?

This query has always been baffling to me. For I have no idea how I *am*, usually.

Far more logical to reply *How do I appear to you? That's how I am.*

For truly, my "self" is a swirl of atoms not unlike the more disintegrated paintings of John Turner—almost, if you peer closely, you can see *something* amid the atoms, perhaps on the brink of coalescing into a *figure*—but maybe not.

Even when Ray was alive, and I was Ray Smith's wife and not yet Ray Smith's widow, I found it difficult to respond to this totally innocent, totally conventional social query.

"How am I? I'm fine! And how are you?"

From time to time, in a social situation, an individual will acknowledge that things aren't so good, maybe he/she isn't so fine, which will derail the conversation in a more personal, pointed direction. But this is rare, and must be handled with extreme delicacy. For it's in violation of social decorum and people will be sympathetic initially—but finally, maybe not.

Now, when people see me, when they ask, often with ten-der solicitude, *How are you, Joyce?*—I assume that they mean *How are you managing, after Ray's death?* Usually I tell them that I am doing very well. For I am, I think—doing very well.

Interminable days have passed, and interminable nights—and *I am still here.* This is amazing to me.

More and more it seems to me, I may have made a wrong decision at the time of Ray's death. Picking up the phone, call-ing my friends—making of my plight their concern. Making them feel that they are responsible for me.

A nobler gesture would have been to erase myself. For there is something terribly wrong in remaining here—in our house, in our old life—talking and laughing with friends—when Ray is gone.

I feel that others might think this way about me too. For there *is* something ignoble, selfish, in continuing to live as if nothing has been altered.

But I am not strong enough, I think.

And then—so I tell myself!—I had—I have—many respon-sibilities to which Ray would have entrusted me. And in the terms of Ray's will, he has entrusted me.

Though Ray has left me, it is not so easy for me to leave *him.*

The thing with the beady dead gemlike eyes—that thing, which now more clearly resembles an ugly lizard of some kind, or a Gila monster, than a sea-creature—this thing is more fre-quent now in the corner of my eye, when I am alone.

Erase yourself—of course!

What a hypocrite you are, to pretend not to know this.

So, it's good not to be alone! Except, when I am not-alone, I am in the company of other people, and aware of the fact that the one person I wish might be there is not there.

Thinking always of yourself. Only of yourself. Hypocrite!

This is true. I am obsessed with my "self" now—whatever it is, it seems to be about to break and be scattered by the wind, like milkweed pollen. Though the "self" has no core yet it is a nexus of random sounds, voices—some of them tender, and some of them jeering, accusatory—

Love to my honey and my kitties.

Hypocrite!

Really, I have no idea how I *am.* I have become a sort of wraith, or zombie—I know that I am *here* but have a very vague idea of what *here* is.

I have been observed laughing, with friends. My laughter is not forced but seems natural, spontaneous.

I have been observed staring into space, in the company of friends. Though I am aware of being observed—I try to shake myself, into wakefulness—sometimes it isn't so easy, to haul myself back.

Talk at Princeton gatherings is of politics, mainly. America has become a rabidly politicized nation since the election of George W. Bush—since 9/11, ever more a virulently divided nation—it is quite natural that the personal life is submerged in the public life, but how lonely, how empty, how spiritually depleted it seems, to one on the outside.

And so, often I leave for home early. Where Ray and I often stayed late—and were among the last to leave a party—I am now the first person to leave.

When I am departed, my friends talk about me, I suppose.

I hope that they are saying *Joyce is doing very well isn't she!*

I hope that they are saying *There's no need to worry about Joyce.*

I can't bear it, if they are saying *How tired Joyce looks!*

If they are saying *How thin Joyce looks!*

Poor Joyce!

Often when I am driving our car, I begin to cry for no clear reason. Often it's night, I am dreading my return to the (empty, deserted) house in which, on the dining room table, "sympathy baskets" and "floral displays" are still crammed together, and wilted petals are strewn underfoot like tiny bruised faces. Only a light or two will be burning—no longer is the house lit up as if for a festive occasion—the first instant, of unlocking the door—(unless it's unlocked, I'd forgotten to lock it)—is the hardest, a horrible moment—then, if I can manage, I will slip into the bedroom without having to pass through most of the house—though I can't avoid passing by Ray's (darkened, deserted) study where, on his telephone, a red light will be blinking—new messages! unanswered messages!—these responsibilities clawing at me, I am too exhausted to contemplate.

But in the car—there's a kind of free-fall no-man's-land inside a car—in which one is neither *here* nor *there* but *in transit*.

If I am in tears while driving, by the time I reach my destination, I am no longer crying—I am *fine*.

A widow's emotions—I think this must be generally true—resemble the "lake effect" of the Great Lakes. One moment, a clear sky and sunshine; minutes later, enormous dark thunder-heads moving like battalions across the sky; soon after, a lightning storm, churning waves, danger. . . . You learn that you can't predict the weather from visible evidence. You learn to be cautious. The "lake effect" is ordinary time, speeded up.

But I have become so—*sad*. I have become one of those blighted / wounded / limping / sinister malcontents in Elizabethan-Jacobean drama—an observer who glances about seeing, not happily smiling individuals, not friends whom I love, but individuals destined for terrible, tragic ends—the women to lose their husbands sooner than they would expect; the men to become ill, to age, to vanish within a few years. I feel a kind of sick terror for my friends, who have been so kind to me—what, one day, will happen to *them*?

Of all malcontents, Hamlet is the most eloquent.

> How weary, stale, flat and unprofitable
> Seem to me the uses of this world . . .

This is the very voice of paralysis, depression—yet it seems to me in my zombie-state an utterly astute reading of the human condition.

Still, one must not say so. One must *try*.

Asked how she is, it is a good idea for the widow to say, brightly, like everyone else, "How am I?—fine."

Back home, I am likely to replay Ray's final message—the one he'd made from his hospital bed just a few hours before he died.

Though sometimes, I call our home number from my cell phone, to hear Ray's recorded voice that is so comforting and which, when they call this number, our friends will hear for a very long time.

> *Joyce and I are not here right now to take your call.*
> *Please leave a detailed message and we will return your call as*
> soon as we can.

BELLS FOR
JOHN WHITESIDE'S DAUGHTER

In Detroit, in the mid-1960s, when Ray taught English at Wayne State University, one of his courses was "Introduction to Literature," and among the poems he assigned his students was the elegy "Bells for John Whiteside's Daughter," by John Crowe Ransom.

This beautiful short poem Ray read to me with such feeling, in his deep, subtly modulated voice. I am moved to tears recalling it.

Reading the poem, which I haven't looked at in years, I realize that I've memorized it, and I've memorized it in my husband's voice.

> *There was such speed in her little body*
> *And such lightness in her footfall . . .*

Was this Ray's favorite poem? When I'd first met him in Madison, Wisconsin, Ray could recite a number of classic poems—sonnets by Shakespeare, John Donne, and Milton ("When I Consider How My Light Is Spent"); and he was much admiring of Whitman, Hopkins, Frost, and William Carlos Williams, as well as poetry by certain of our contemporaries, which he published in *Ontario Review*—but no poem moved him as deeply as "Bells for John Whiteside's Daughter." It is his reading aloud of this poem that is imprinted in my memory—my handsome young husband, his voice quavering with emotion, in our house on Sherbourne Road in the small room at the front of the house, a kind of sunroom, where we sat most evenings to read, or prepare our classes for the next day.

How I wish that I could remember what we'd said to each other then! In that little room, one of the few comfortable rooms in that not very comfortable house, where for so many nights after dinner we sat at opposite ends of a sofa.

What could have so absorbed us, in those days? I know that we talked a good deal about our teaching, our classes and colleagues—Ray at Wayne State, me at the University of Detroit—but all this is vanished now. What was I thinking, what was I writing, what had seemed to me of supreme significance at that time? If Ray was writing, what was he writing? And did he show it to me?—I think that he must have, but I can't remember with certainty.

Of all those years, how many thousands of exchanges of words, I can remember so very few—this is heartrending to me.

This is terrifying to me—so much that is human is lost. . . .

Except, there is "Bells for John Whiteside's Daughter."

> *But now go the bells, and we are ready . . .*

Now Ransom has been dropped from the American poetry canon. No one younger than sixty, probably, has even heard of this poem. Much-admired in his time, and a figure of considerable influence, Ransom is a casualty of the academic-literary culture wars of the late twentieth century—a Caucasian male poet like Delmore Schwartz, Howard Nemerov, James Dickey, James Wright.

All of them, casualties of time.

THE NEST

Nothing is so wonderful in my posthumous life as retiring to my nest!

Even to die here—*especially* to die here—will be wonderful, I think.

This "nest"—in our bed—on my side of the bed—is a swirl of pillows, bedclothes, a rainbow-hued quilt crocheted by my mother—books, bound galleys, copyedited manuscripts and page proofs, drafts of things I am working on—whatever I am working on, or trying to work on, each night. And now, in the nest, I am reading—rereading—all that I can find of Ray's published work.

When we were alive—when Ray was alive—I did not read in bed, ever. I did not have a "nest" in bed. I would have considered working in bed, especially, clumsy and messy and not very efficient—excusable if one were ill, or an invalid. Our evenings at home were spent in the living room, on our sofa, where at opposite ends of the sofa we read—or Ray copyedited manuscripts, or read page proofs—or I took notes on whatever it was I was writing at the time, or trying to write—the effort of "Joyce Carol Oates" to compose something of more than fleeting value out of our (unknown to us at the time) rapidly fleeting lives.

Now, I have to wonder if I'd spent too much time in that other world—the world of my/the imagination—and not enough time with my husband.

This nest, that draws me to it like water swirling down a drain, is my respite from the day, and from thoughts like this; my reward for having gotten through the day. It is a place where I am not "Joyce Carol Oates"—still less "Joyce Carol Smith"—whose primary worth has been to sign legal documents multiple times, a smile clamped in her face like a steel trap. In the nest, there is anonymity. There is peace, solitude, ease. There is not the likelihood of being asked *How are you, Joyce?*—still less the likelihood of being asked, as I am beginning to be asked *Will you keep your house, or stay in it?*—a question that makes me quiver with rage and indignation though it is a perfectly reasonable question to put to a widow; as one might reasonably ask of a terminally ill cancer patient *Is your will in order? Have you made peace with your Maker?*

In the vicinity of the nest no one speaks at all. In the vicinity of the nest, except for, sometimes, the TV—usually turned to one or the other of the classical music channels on cable TV—there is a reliable silence. The nest is a warm-lighted space amid darkness, for the rest of the house is darkened at night. In a belated effort to save on fuel—for I have been careless about leaving the furnace on too high, without Ray to monitor the thermostat—as I've been careless about leaving doors unlocked, even at times ajar—and worse—I make it a point now to turn down the furnace at night—I know that Ray would approve of this—and so much of the house is chilly, and forbidding.

I don't undress, entirely. Partly because I am so very cold—sometimes my teeth chatter convulsively—unless I am feeling feverish and my skin is sweaty-clammy—but mostly because I want to be prepared for leaving the bed quickly—running from the house if summoned. Never will I forget—I hear the voice often—as I see the lizard-creature with the beady dead gemlike eyes—*Mrs. Smith? You'd better come to the hospital as soon as you can—your husband is still alive.* Especially, I wear warm socks.

If you are likely to be summoned unexpectedly from bed, it is a very good idea not to go to bed barefoot.

Precious minutes are wasted pulling on socks! In a time of desperation, nothing is more awkward.

And so I have become, even in the nest-sanctuary, *incapable of removing my clothes* at night, and wearing what is called *night-wear* as I'd used to wear, in my former life.

In fact, it has come to seem to me utterly brazen, reckless, and plain ignorant, that one would even consider *undressing*, and making oneself needlessly *vulnerable*, like a turtle slipping out of its shell.

Is he still alive? Is my husband still alive?
Yes. Your husband is still alive.

Though the nest is very comforting, and very welcoming—though *the nest* has become the (emotional, intellectual, spiritual) core of the widow's life—yet it should be acknowledged that the nest is not an antidote for insomnia.

When I can't sleep—which would be every night unless I take a sleeping pill—or a capsule of something called Lorazepam ("for anxiety") that our family doctor has prescribed for me—the nest is my place of great solace and comfort, and though I am awake, I am not the desperate person I am during the day. Here, to the extent to which I can concentrate, I am able to mimic my old self to a degree, by taking a sort of pleasure—"pleasure" might be an exaggeration, but let it stand—in going through page proofs for an upcoming review, or working on a draft of a short story abandoned at the start of Ray's hospitalization; there are myriad scattered notes for a novel, which I will not be able to write, but there is a completed novel which I'd intended to revise, and may soon begin revising; this novel, about loss, grief, and mourning, in a mythical upstate New York river city called Sparta, will come to be primary in my life, if not indeed a life-line; but at the present time, I am not able to concentrate on even rereading it, let alone undertaking a revision.

How frail a vessel, prose fiction! How fleeting and insubstantial, the "life of the mind"! I must fight against the terrible lethargy, despair and self-contempt so many of us felt after the catastrophe of 9/11 when the very act of writing seemed of so little consequence as to be a kind of joke.

Yet, working on short things—reviews, essays, stories—is a solace of a kind. Almost, immersed in work, I can forget the circumstances of my life—almost!—and if I become restless in bed, I leave the nest to prowl about in Ray's study, which is the next room; or, I drift into my study, which is on the other side of Ray's, to answer e-mail, which has already come to mean a great deal to me, far more than it had ever meant when Ray was alive; but always my late-night excursions are predicated by the fact that I will return to the nest in a few minutes.

The possibility of remaining awake through the night, outside the nest, is frankly terrifying.

And if I am very lucky our tiger cat Reynard will appear suddenly in the bedroom—with a leap, onto our bed—he will curl up to sleep with me, not exactly beside me but at the foot of the bed, on Ray's side, where as if inadvertently—in the feline imagination, such nuances are not accidental—he may press against my leg; but if I speak to him cajolingly—*Nice Reynard! Nice kitty!*—or reach down to stroke his somewhat coarse fur, he may take offense at such a liberty, leap down from the bed, and hurry away into another part of the darkened house.

I can't bring myself to recall the summer day ten or eleven years ago when Ray brought Reynard home from a local animal shelter, to surprise me. We'd lost a much-loved older cat—I hadn't thought that I was ready for another so soon—but when Ray brought the tiny tiger kitten home, mewing piteously for his mother, or for food and affection, my heart was completely won.

And how I loved Ray, for these impulsive, seemingly imprudent unilateral gestures that turned out so well.

The other, younger cat, Cherie, though the friendlier of the two, and the less anxious, has not entered this bedroom since Ray's departure and will not enter it no matter how I cajole her. Cherie will not sleep with me, or near me, in this nocturnal nest-life, nor will she enter Ray's study when I am in it, though she might sleep in his desk chair; she refuses to enter my study, where I sit working, or trying to work, at my desk. Only if I sit on the living room sofa—which I must now force myself to do—as I'd done when Ray and I read together in the evening, will Cherie hurry eagerly to me and leap into my lap and remain for a few minutes—until she sees that the other individual who shared this sofa with us isn't here, isn't coming, and so she departs also without a backward glance.

The cats blame me, I know. Animal reproach is not less palpable for being voiceless.

The nest is my solace for such cruel—such ridiculous—cat-rejections that, in the radically diminished household in which I now find myself, a hapless cartoon character marooned on a shrinking island, actually loom large, and have the power to *wound*.

Absurd, to be hurt by an animal's behavior. Yet more

absurd, to be so reduced in scale, to care about an animal's behavior.

For this is the fact of the widow's posthumous life—all things are equally profound as all things are equally trivial, futile, pointless.

As all acts—actions—"activities"—are, to the widow, alternatives to suicide of more or less equal significance.

Except—the widow must not say such things. Better to be reticent in grief, mute and stoic. Better to hide away in her nest than to venture into the bright peopled world outside her door.

During the week of the hospital vigil, often late at night huddled in the nest, I would stare at the television screen entranced—it seemed too much effort for me to concentrate on reading, or on my own work—restlessly I would scroll through the channels—for insomnia makes of us explorers of the most bizarre landscapes: I was fascinated and appalled in equal measure by a rerun of the *X-Files*—a popular television series Ray and I had never seen during its run—in which the intrepid FBI agents pursue a man whose kiss turns women into rotting phosphorescent corpses—the female victims are so physically repulsive, even the FBI agents are stunned, revolted—here is an allegory of sexual contamination worthy of Nathanial Hawthorne, though somewhat crudely portrayed, and self-consciously sensational. Watching late-night TV, I came quickly to discover, is like trolling through the uncharted deeps of the ocean—a roiling Sargasso Sea of high-decibel melodrama, gunfire, car chases, helicopter pursuits, CNN and Fox News repeats—the collective underside of our culture—the banality of our fetishes. What a lovely silence, switching off the TV to hear wind, rain pelting against a window.

And there was a time, later, shortly after Ray died, when

weirdly at 4 A.M. there appeared on the TV screen a replay of the historic *What's My Line?*—the animated ghost-figures of Steve Allen, Dorothy Kilgallen, Arlene Francis, Bennett Cerf, and John Daly of a long-ago decade preceding color TV— suddenly so vivid, so real, familiar to me as long-lost relatives. This low-tech show, allegedly the most popular game show in the history of network television, on the air from 1950 to 1967, was one I'd watched for years with my younger brother Fred and my mother, on our small black and white television set, upstairs in our half of the old farmhouse in which we'd lived with my mother's Hungarian step-parents in rural Millersport, New York. How impressed we'd been by the witty repartee of the panelists and their coolly affable moderator John Daly! Yet I don't recall a word we'd said to one another.

Why is so much lost? So much of our spoken language? It's said that distant memories are stored in the brain but so little is accessible to consciousness, of what value is this storage? In memoirs, dialogue is reported with exacting precision decades later but I think, to be truthful, we should acknowledge that we forget conversations almost immediately; our aural memories are weak, unreliable. I have witnessed individuals repeating—inaccurately—conversations they'd heard only a few minutes before—yet more often the tone, the emphasis, the *meaning* of spoken language is lost.

My loss is compounded by the somewhat unusual fact that Ray and I had no correspondence—not ever. Not once had we written to each other, for always we'd been together, virtually every night since our first meeting.

We had had no "courtship"—no interlude of being apart, that would have warranted letter-writing. From the first evening we'd met—Sunday, October 23, 1960—at a graduate-student gathering in the massive student union at the University of Wisconsin, overlooking Lake Mendota—we'd seen each other every day.

We were engaged on November 23 of that year and, to maintain some small constancy, we were married on January 23, 1961.

It wasn't until years later that as "JCO" I began to be invited to visit colleges and universities, usually just overnight. At first Ray came with me, but then, as the invitations increased, I began more often to travel alone, and so we were apart more frequently in recent years.

And so I'd gone to UC Riverside. On the eve of Ray's illness.

Of course, I think that possibly he might not have become ill, if I'd stayed home. However he'd caught a cold, whatever he'd done that he might not have done if I'd been home, I don't know. *You are being ridiculous. This is reasoning too finely!* It is difficult not to feel sick with guilt, that a husband has died, and you would seem to have been helpless to prevent it.

And then, Ray hadn't wanted to go to the ER. You'd insisted. Maybe he would have done better at home, untreated.

Always when I was away, I called Ray in the late evening. After my reading, after a dinner in my "honor"—my hosts are invariably very nice, very interesting and engaging individuals—most of them academics, like us—and so I would tell Ray about my reading, about the dinner; and Ray would tell me what was far more interesting to me, about what he'd done that day—what had happened in our life, while I was away.

All this, you have lost. The happiness of domestic life, without which the small—even the colossal—triumphs of a "career" are shallow, mocking.

But this is wrong! In the nest, huddled beneath my mother's quilt, listening to a Chopin prelude on the classical TV channel, I am supposed to be shielded from such thoughts.

It is the night of February 26—or, rather, the early morning of February 27—2:40 A.M.—a full week after Ray's death. Earlier this evening I had dinner with friends—it isn't possible for me to "have dinner" alone in this house, or anywhere—but with friends, a meal is not only possible but wonderful—except that Ray is missing. . . . In the nest, I have spread out some of Ray's published work, and have been reading an essay on Coleridge's famous poem "Christabel"—an "enigmatic fragment," Ray calls it—titled "Christabel and Geraldine: The Marriage of Life and Death," which appeared in the *Bucknell Review* in 1968. Astonishing to discover so much in Ray's essay that relates to our shared interests—in the English and Scottish popular ballads, for instance—and there is the striking stanza from a poem of Richard Crashaw that Ray quotes:

> *She never undertook to know,*
> *What death with love should have to doe*
> *Nor has shee ere yet understood*
> *Why to show love shee should shed blood.*

How powerful these lines are, how vividly they come back to me, like a half-recalled dream! The Crashaw poem had made such an impression on me, I'd appropriated the second line for the title of a short story—"What Death with Love Should Have to Do"—a mordant love story of sorts, of 1966.

(I should reread this old story of mine, that was reprinted in my second collection of short stories, *Upon the Sweeping Flood.* I know, I should reread it to recapture that time, those emotions. But I can't. In the nest I feel enervated, paralyzed. I just can't.)

As I read Ray's critical essays of this long-ago time, I realize how close we'd been. . . . We had shared every detail of our teaching jobs—our classes, our colleagues, the high points and low points and surprises of our lives—we'd discussed the Coleridge poem together and I'd read drafts of Ray's essay—our lives were entwined like the conflicting emotions of love/hate—beauty/a snaky sort of ugliness—in the haunting Coleridge poem.

In the nest, reading—(re)reading—this material, I am beginning to shiver violently, though I don't think—I am sure—that I'm unhappy. I can't seem to stop trembling. I must go into my bathroom to run hot water on my hands, which have grown icy. How strange this is! I've been thoroughly engrossed in my husband's literary criticism—I'd totally forgotten that he had once reviewed for the journal *Literature and Psychology*, and that he'd ranged far afield to publish a brief piece on Dostoyevsky's *Crime and Punishment*—a novel we'd both taught in the 1970s—yet now this fit of shivering has come over me, even my teeth are chattering.

On my bedside table is Ray's novel manuscript, on which he'd worked for years in the 1960s, but which he'd never completed. I can't recall if I have seen the most recent draft, or if for some reason Ray hadn't shown it to me; I think that he'd intended to revise it, but set it aside. I am eager to read the manuscript I found in his closet, which has been untouched for years, but I am beginning to feel anxiety, too. I wonder if Ray would want me to be reading this manuscript, still far from completion; I don't think that, since moving to Princeton in 1978, he'd so much as glanced at it, and had long since ceased alluding to it. I look at the first page—the title is "Black Mass"—the manuscript looks old, worn—very like a manuscript that has been hidden away at the back of a closet, forgotten for decades—and I feel very sad suddenly.

This is a mistake.

You don't want to read it.

What you don't know about your husband has been hidden from you for a purpose.

And in any case, your husband is gone, and is not coming back.

You can resolve to be "brave"—"resourceful"—you can cheer yourself up by (re)reading his writing, or trying to—but he is not coming back, he is gone and he is not coming back.

He is gone. He is gone.

He is not coming back.

GHOST ROOMS

The vigil continues. Though there is no hope, the outcome is known.

In the nest, I had hoped for some protection. But the nest has failed me, in the matter of Ray's novel which I have put away, for the time being.

Thinking *If he'd wanted you to read it, he would have given it to you. You know this.*

During the hospital vigil the rooms of the house were well lighted in anticipation of a homecoming. Outdoor lights were left on through the day. Now most of the rooms of the house are never lighted. Most of the rooms are off-limits to me, I dare not enter them, nor even glance into them.

The outdoor lights I never use for fear that soon they will burn out and I will have no idea how to replace them.

Now the flurry of death-duties has abated, the siege is taking other forms. As virulent bacteria will mutate, to ensure their virulent survival.

One by one regions of the house are becoming ghostly, unoccupied. The living room that was once so welcoming—the sofa, the white piano, the dark rose Chinese rug Ray and I selected for the space, when we'd first moved to Princeton. On the marble-topped coffee table we'd bought together in a furniture store in Detroit, in 1965, are Ray's books which I'd brought home from the hospital, at his end of the sofa—*Infidel, The Great Unraveling, Your Government Failed You.* Back issues of the *New York Review of Books* and the *New Yorker.*

I have taken away the stacks of *Ontario Review* submissions, however. A scattering of pens and paper clips Ray had accumulated.

But the living room is a ghost-room, and the small solarium that opens off the living room where every day Ray and I had lunch—except when we sat outside on our terrace, in warm weather. This glass-walled room with a glass-topped round table and wicker chairs and a red-brick floor that seems, bizarrely, even in winter to attract spiders and, in abundance, the insect-prey of spiders, is an unlikely ghost-room since it is flooded with light on even overcast days—yet so it has become.

I will not enter the solarium for months, not even to sweep away the cobwebs.

I will avoid looking into the solarium. There is too much heartbreak in even a glimpse of the glass-topped table with the pale beige cloth place mats.

The farther wing of the house that we'd designed with such enthusiasm for my parents to stay in has become a ghost-region—of course. This is a part of the house I can shut off

from the rest—I have turned down the heat—there is no reason for me to step inside this space for days, weeks at a time. It
was in a room here, at the long white Parsons table, that Ray
ate, or tried to eat, his final breakfast at home. Read, or tried
to read, the *New York Times* for the final time at home.

Often Ray worked at this table. It was—it is—an ideal place
to spread out photographs, galleys, page proofs. Passing along
the gallery on the far side of the courtyard, I would look over
and see my husband there—he would glance up at me—we
would smile, wave.

We occupied the house often for hours at a time without
speaking to each other, or needing to speak.

Now, I dare not look across the courtyard at the plate-glass
window that runs the length of the room. I think that I am
terrified to see no one there. Yet more terrified, to risk seeing
a reflection in the glass—for in our house there are myriad
reflections of reflections in glass—a kind of vertigo springs
from such reflections, like the sharp flash of light that precedes
migraine.

Mirrors too have become off-limits, taboo. As if toxic
fumes inhabit these ghost-mirrors, you dare not draw too close.

Of course, you dare not glance heedlessly into any mirror!

Except that I must pass through it on my way to the
kitchen—a part of the house hardly to be avoided though it has
become a very lonely region of the house, for so often Ray and
I were in this room together—the dining room would be a
ghost-room, too.

On the long, gleaming mahogany table are piles of mail as
well as remnants of the floral displays, potted flowers, "gift
baskets" that were delivered in such profusion soon after Ray's
death. The miniature rose for which I'd had some hope had

prevailed for a few days but finally withered, and died—most of the fresh-cut flowers have died, and have been thrown away in the trash. Other plants, in pots, are scattered about the room. At the far end of the room is a hefty plant in a stoneware pot, so heavy my fingernails were torn trying to move it.

Empty now of flowers is a squat pearl-colored ceramic vase on a side table wound about with a white satin ribbon stamped COMFORT   COMFORT   COMFORT   COMFORT at which I find myself staring as if hoping to be hypnotized.

Sometime soon I will thank people. This is my resolve.

Except that I've lost many of the cards that came with the sympathy gifts. In my frantic need to get rid of trash.

Each day, the mailbox is filled with sympathy cards and letters as well as with the usual junk mail and unwanted packages. Some of these cards and letters I can read, depending upon my emotional state, but many I am not (yet) able to read, and have put away into a large green bag kept in my study.

Yes I am grateful for these cards and letters! I know that Ray would be deeply moved as well.

Better to be alive and nobody gives a damn about you than to be dead and "missed."

(Is this what Ray would say? Almost, I can hear his droll voice in its eighteenth-century satiric mode.)

Is a widow expected not only to write thank-you notes for presents, but for sympathy cards and letters as well? I think that this is so—it's a very cruel custom.

Yet I hope to be a conscientious widow. I hope to be a good widow. A Princeton acquaintance who'd lost her husband last year told me how painstaking she was to reply even to sympathy cards, how much pleasure she took in writing letters to the many people who'd written to her. *It was something for me to do. I was grateful.*

Unlike my Princeton acquaintance I am not lacking for things to do and though I am grateful for the kind attention I think that I will continue to put away the cards and letters in the green bag with the resolve that I will read them when I feel a little stronger.

This may not be for a while. Months, years.

Eventually, I move the green bag into Ray's study. The corner of my room in which it was placed had become a corner into which I dared not look.

Other ghost-rooms: the small guest room adjoining Ray's study in which he kept, in a closet, some of his clothes; and Ray's bathroom in the hall.

When I'd returned from the hospital that night, with Ray's toiletries, I'd replaced them in his medicine cabinet and on his sink counter. As I'd replaced his clothes in his closet and put into the laundry his (very mildly) soiled things, and when I did the laundry, I put into his bureau his socks, underwear, shirt.

All of his clothes are in place. Not an article of clothing has been discarded. As all of his mail, papers, financial statements, etc., are arranged on his desks and on the floor of his study.

His clothes are very nice clothes, I think. A camel's hair sport coat, still in its dry cleaner bag. A coat of soft dark-gray wool. Dress shirts, newly laundered and not yet worn. A blue-striped shirt which is a favorite of mine. Neckties—so many!—dating back to a long-ago era when men wore inch-wide ties—was this the 1970s?—my favorite is a silk tie imprinted with scenes from the Unicorn Tapestry which we'd bought at the Cloisters one giddy spring day when we'd slipped away from the interminable ceremony at the American Academy of Arts and Letters in upper Manhattan.

Sure was glad to get out of there alive!—this phrase from a song of Bob Dylan—"Day of the Locust" (coincidentally, set at Princeton)—often passed between us.

And also *One would not have wished it longer*—as Samuel Johnson said of Milton's *Paradise Lost*.

Earlier today I was drawn to look into the manuscript of "Black Mass"—Ray's unfinished novel. My heart beat so strangely, I could not continue.

There is some secret in Ray's life, I think. Or perhaps "secret" is too strong a term. Things of which he didn't care to speak, and after the early months in which we'd talked of our family backgrounds—as I suppose everyone does, when new to each other—these things passed into a kind of taboo territory about which I could not make inquiries.

Quietly, the other evening at her house my poet-friend Alicia Ostriker said to me *I can't imagine what it's like to be you* and I said *I can't, either.*

Friends have been wonderful inviting me to their homes. I think that they are trying to watch over me—I think they must talk about me—I am deeply moved, but also anxious—I can't fail them—I am most fascinated by the absence of ghost-rooms in their houses—the unwitting ease with which they speak, smile, laugh, move from room to room as if nothing is threatening to them—they will live forever; there is no *Why?* in their lives.

Sometimes if I fall asleep toward dawn it is very hard for me to wake up in the morning and very hard for me to leave the nest and the thought comes to me *Why?*

I am utterly mystified *why* there is life and not rather the cessation of life. The earliest effort of *life*—single-celled organisms in a sort of seething chemical soup—millions of years before Man—to prevail, not only to prevail but to persevere, not only to persevere but to triumph by way of reproduction—*Why?*

Once in a while when I am feeling a need for exercise, excitement, I run the vacuum cleaner through the rooms. I am always happy vacuuming—the thrumming noise drowns out the noises inside my head and, underfoot, a sudden smoothness in the texture of a carpet has the visceral feel of a spiritual calm, almost a blessing.

Well—not quite a *blessing*.

Ghost-rooms! But there are ghost-acts as well.

For instance, I can't any longer "prepare" meals in the kitchen. I am not able to eat anything that isn't flung together on the counter, spoonfuls of yogurt into a bowl, some cut-up (rotted?) fruit, a handful of (stale) cereal; maybe in the evening, a can of Campbell's soup (chicken with wild rice) and those Swedish rye-crisp crackers of which Ray was so fond.

The prospect of sitting at the dining-room table for any meal is repellent. All my "meals" are at my desk while I do e-mail or work or in the bedroom where I might watch TV, read, or try to work.

When you live alone, eating a meal carries with it an element of scorn, mockery. For a meal is a social ritual or it is not a meal, it is just a plate heaped with food.

When I traveled and Ray was home alone, he took advantage of my absence by bringing home a pizza. When I called home I would ask how he'd liked the pizza and he would say *It was all right* in the way of a shoulder shrug and so I would ask what had been wrong with it and Ray would say *It was too big for just one person* and I would say *Well, you didn't have to eat all of it—did you?* And Ray would say *I guess I did. I ate it all.*

Better even than meals hastily dumped into bowls are bottles of Odwalla fruit-blend drinks. These were left for me in the courtyard a day or two after Ray died, a dozen or more in a plastic shopping bag, from a woman friend who is also a novelist. *You have to eat, Joyce* she'd said *and you won't want to eat. So drink this.*

Bottles ideal for gripping while one is driving. The ordeal of eating alone is mitigated by subordinating eating to another activity, like driving a car.

Long I'd noticed that friends/acquaintances of mine who live alone often seem to be eating when we speak on the phone. I'd assumed that this must be incidental, or that the individual had a nervous habit of eating continuously, hence could not stop just because I'd called; but now I think that the opposite is the case—eating alone is so terrible, one must subordinate it to something else, like talking on the phone.

If I am heedless, walking quickly through the house to the kitchen, or from the kitchen, my eyes might swerve into one of the ghost-rooms—the living room, for instance—where at Ray's end of the sofa a shadowy figure might be imagined, or the outline of a figure—what is called an "optical illusion"—which is to say the *idea*—the *memory*—of a figure.

Oh, God! My heart stops.

Quickly I turn away. Run away into a safe part of the house.

"Safe" parts are the bedroom, which I can't avoid, and my study, in which I was usually alone in any case.

Thinking *But I can't live like this. I can't live.*

ROBIN HEMLEY

FIELD NOTES FOR
THE GRAVEYARD ENTHUSIAST

In creating a taxonomy of graveyards, let's start with the obvious: Graveyards in Which We Are Not Buried along with Graveyards in Which We Are Buried. At first glance, both of these classifications would seem simple enough. The first consists of all Graveyards Known and Unknown, and the second contains no graveyards, Known or Unknown. Given a few years, our relationship to these categories might well change, and the first category will contain all but one graveyard, and the second will contain that same graveyard, while excluding all the rest. If, however, you choose cremation, the categories will remain unaltered from your first encounter with them. However, as a Jew, more superstitious than observant, cremation is not an option for me—I can't, in any case, separate this option from the fate of so many of my coreligionists at the hands of the Nazis. As I age, the consideration of where to be buried occupies more and more of my time, in direct contrast to the fading of my preoccupation with where to live. My father and sister are buried in a rural cemetery in Athens, Ohio, while my mother and grandmother and several other relatives are buried in a vast necropolis in Queens, New York. Considering this split in my family, which bears absolutely no relation to their closeness in life (my father and sister were often at odds while my mother was extraordinarily devoted to them both), I feel an almost giddy amount of latitude in my eventual choice—happily, I have always loved graveyards, but my enthusiasm for so many graveyards makes me unable to settle on one, to settle down, as it were. As I am a restless spirit in life, unable to choose a more or less permanent place to live, never having lived in one place for more than eight years in my half a century on earth, I imagine I will make an equally restive spirit. If I had the means, I might simply have a codicil in my will drawn up, obligating my heirs to disinter me every few years and move my remains to some new pleasant and/or unusual location. As this eccentric request is unlikely to be followed, even if I somehow accrue the riches necessary to make the request financially possible, I suppose I must choose one. I'll leave that decision for another day, and instead will spend these several hours of my existence contemplating some of the varieties of graveyards and will try to convey some measure of my enthusiasm for them.

As a child, I used to hold my breath when passing a graveyard, but now I breathe deeply—in any event, there will be plenty of time for holding my breath. If you are a breath-holder, imagining holding your breath does some good, then you might want to forgo this small tour of Graveyards I Have Known and Loved, and instead eat some ice cream or have a tumble in bed, both activities I would take to the grave if I could.

Perhaps the two largest categories of graveyards are Graveyards Known and Graveyards Unknown. A subset of the latter is Graveyards Forgotten, and a subset of the former is Graveyards of Historic Note. A subset of either category is Unintended Graveyards or Cemeteries of Happenstance. These would include mass graves, or as-yet-undiscovered graveyards. Of the latter, we might surmise that graves are all around us, from the unmarked graves of vanquished if not forgotten peoples to some spot in the woods where a lone traveler froze in the snow, starved, or sat down, feeling ill, by a tree and never stood again. Under the streets of London, for instance, lie at least 37,000 bodies, according to the London *Times*. Is it proper to call the city of London a graveyard? Perhaps in the strict sense, no, but conceptually, let's consider the graveyard's boundaries as limitless as the earth's, at least potentially so. In this way, we begin to demystify the graveyard (and possibly death) while conversely making into sacred if not consecrated space every inch on which we tread.

Walking through a graveyard is how most of us, at least those not in the medical profession or undertakers, come into our closest contact with death while remaining alive. An appreciation of this vast category of Unknown Graveyards is the cornerstone for a kind of mindfulness that those who don't hold their breath have when walking through a Known Graveyard—we might, as the Japanese do, hold a picnic by the grave of a relative, share beer and rice crackers, enjoy our outing while at the same time including our loved ones. Whether or not I might enjoy Spirit Beer and crackers, I like the thought of at least being included. When Janis Joplin treated her friends to a round of drinks in the Afterlife, she had the right idea, but perhaps she shouldn't have stopped there. Perhaps she might have requested to be entombed beneath her favorite bar, not that she might continue to let the good times roll, but so the combination of spirits and Spirit might give patrons a buzz that was simultaneously intoxicating and sobering. It's this paradoxical and powerful combination of inebriation and sobriety that is one of my aims as a devotee of the Unknown Graveyard.

The antithesis of the Unknown Graveyard is the Graveyard of Historic Note. Of these, the largest subset by far is the Military Graveyard. I'm stopped (dead, I'd like to say) in my tracks, left speechless at most such graveyards. Most recently, I visited the town of Aquileia in northeastern Italy, a town within a region that has changed hands and nationalities innumerable times, once the second biggest town in the Roman Empire. My companion wanted to visit the ancient mosaics that line the subfloor of the basilica that was later built on top of the Roman temple. I'm not the biggest fan of either mosaics or basilicas—perhaps having seen so many splendid cathedrals over the years that they have blurred, and mosaics, well, after exclaiming how meticulous the craftsmanship is, I quickly become bored by shallow Roman faces staring up at me, or birds or lions. No matter how beautiful the image, virtually none of them will stay with me longer than five minutes after viewing, unless I take a photo. I've ceased carrying a camera while traveling because I never look at trip photos and no one else is interested.

Attached to this church was a graveyard, and for me the graveyard was a hundred times more fascinating than the Roman mosaics. This was a cemetery of the fallen—*Cimitero dei Caduti*—of World War I. In this shaded courtyard lay perhaps a hundred soldiers whose deaths were as strikingly meaningless as any I've ever heard of. This was a Hapsburg cemetery—the men buried here died fighting to prop up the Austro-Hungarian Empire that collapsed as a result of this war. The cemetery is replete with iron crosses and encased photographs of young and middle-aged mustachioed men with stiff hats and stiff expressions that have somehow withstood the elements, dating to World War I.

MARIO BRVA, reads one inscription. MORTO PER LA PATRIA. But what country did he die for? As his name and the names of others suggest, part of his name was Italian and part Slovenian. In this region of the Istrian Peninsula, Hapsburg census-takers were often confounded by the question of ethnicity. A village might self-identify one year as Italian and ten years later as Slovenian, depending on what the parish priest told them to say they were. Almost a hundred years after these men died in a war fighting for a monarchy that no longer existed, I was left feeling more bereaved than if I had been standing in front of the thousands of white crosses at Normandy. At Normandy at least, I could make sense of why the men had died in such vast numbers, but not in Aquileia. Not too long after these men died, the Italians switched sides and fought against the monarchy for which these men had given their lives.

To offset these ironies, I suppose, the people who had designed this graveyard aimed for greater glory by commissioning a statue of Christ supporting two fallen soldiers. The statue, a massive chunk of marbled sentiment, depicts Christ on the cross, or mostly on the cross. He has freed his right hand from its nail and reaches down to touch the brow of a dying soldier, the soldier's face lifted like a beseeching child to the Savior's face, a model of compassion and pity. Below the dying man lies another soldier, already dead, but the dying man has a hold on his dead comrade, lifting him up too, to heaven. All three men are bare-chested, though Christ at least doesn't wear a cartridge belt like the other two. The statue, of course, is largely ignored by the few other tourists in this courtyard. On the day I visited, I alone succumbed to the great sentimentality of this statue, feeling pity for everyone involved, including the donors and the sculptor.

Often, though not always, the Military Graveyard, the Historic Graveyard, as well as what we might term the Cemetery of Happenstance are linked, but not always (as in the case of London—a Cemetery of Happenstance, but neither military, nor particularly historic, as a graveyard). A famous example of the Military/Historic/Happenstance Graveyard is the Little Bighorn Battlefield, which was never intended (by Custer at least) as a graveyard. The soldiers in Custer's detail were buried in the spots at which they fell—220 bodies were later reinterred in a single spot on Last Stand Hill, except for Custer's body, which was transferred to a grave at West Point, and a number of the officers under his command, which were shipped back to eastern cemeteries. But the markers remain in the spots where the soldiers fell, and in recent years new markers have been added in locations where Cheyenne and Sioux warriors reportedly perished. And so, the remarkable feature of this graveyard is that unlike any other Known Graveyards (at least by me), one can mark the progress of a battle by the location of the points of death. There's something immediate and visceral about seeing a battle marked in such a way. Instead of the ordered and stately crosses of Normandy and Arlington, perhaps it would be wiser in the long run to bury all casualties in all wars on the spots where they died. Imagine coming upon such reminders at random in some European village or city— we should see death inflicted by war, in any event, as surprising, random, chaotic, not ordered and stately.

In some cases, an Unknown/Happenstance/Military Graveyard (belonging, as in the cases of all Military Graveyards Known and Unknown, to the larger category: Graveyards in

ROBIN HEMLEY   201

Which I Am Not Buried) will shift categories to Known/Hap-
penstance/Military/Historic Graveyard. One such instance on
which I'd like to touch briefly is the Japanese Military Graveyard on the island of Corregidor in the Philippines. On this
island, General Douglas MacArthur's American and Filipino
forces held at bay the Japanese Imperial Forces from December
1941 until May of 1942, far longer than the superior Japanese
forces anticipated. When MacArthur and President Quezon of
the Philippines were smuggled off the island before the island
fell to the Japanese, the general made his famous "I shall return"
declaration. Like MacArthur, I have had a repeated urge to
return to Corregidor too, though for different reasons. If one
believes in ghosts, then this island is surely haunted. The entire
island is in essence a graveyard. Not an inch was spared by Japanese guns in taking it at the beginning of the war, nor an inch
spared by American guns reclaiming it. Ruined bunkers, hulks
of gigantic guns, barracks with trees and metal cables and
twisted vines grown together, even the ruins of a movie theater, dot the island. Here is where the memorial to the War in
the Pacific was placed, but this memorial has about as much
relevance to war as a bombardier's eye to his target. The real
memorials are the ruins and the graves—here the Japanese
graveyard holds the most promise for the graveyard enthusiast
because it is the rarest of military graveyards. For many years,
its location was unknown, but was rediscovered forty years
after the war. Very well tended now, the memorial has a spectacular view and a large statue of the Goddess of Mercy, upon
whose foot my Filipino guide, a man old enough to have been
a child during the war, made a point of taking a piss on when
we stopped at this site.

Graves We Might Piss On could take up pages of notes, per-

haps starting with Hitler's unmarked grave in a parking lot of
the former East Berlin and no doubt including the well-marked
grave of Custer at West Point. But let's not go there, to coin a
phrase, or else we might veer off onto a bitter tangent that strays
too far from our aim, which is, after all, to familiarize ourselves
with our eventual homes rather than alienate ourselves further.

Instead, we might consider Historic Graveyards That Are
Not Military Cemeteries. These include your standards, Père
Lachaise and the Panthéon in Paris, the catacombs of Rome, as
well as La Recoleta in Buenos Aires. We might also include
most such cemeteries in a subcategory of Historic Graveyards:
Known Graveyards in Which Famous People Are Buried. We
must acknowledge at the same time that not all Famous People
Are Buried in Historic Graveyards, nor are all graveyards necessarily considered Historic if, say, one famous person is buried
there, or if that person's star fades over time, and not all the
graves of famous people are Known. But of Known Graveyards
in Which Famous People Are Buried, few hold my attention or
interest for long. I have little interest in visiting Molière or Jim
Morrison at Père Lachaise, nor Victor Hugo and Marie Curie
at the Panthéon. At La Recoleta, I was more interested in the
graveyard's cats than in the tomb of Evita. And I would surely
skip the Catacombs of Callixtus, in which assorted popes and
martyrs are entombed, in favor of the anonymous stacks of
skulls in the Capuchin Crypt, or in favor of the so-called Bone
Church of Kutná Hora in the Czech Republic, in which the
bleached skulls and bones of 40,000 victims of the fifteenth-
century Hussite Wars and the Black Plague were arranged in
the church in 1878 into chandeliers, crowns, chalices, and bells
made of bones and skulls. While studying a blackbird made of
bones pecking out the eye of a Turk (the Schwarzenberg family

coat of arms, the family that commissioned this ossuary), I marvel at the thought that the skull of the Turk was never a Turk at all in real life, but some poor local peasant struck down by illness, that in death he or she has achieved a kind of anonymous fame. The fact of the skull reminds me of the fact that he was a person once with a life, a history, passions and unhappiness, but someone whose sense of personhood has been bleached as thoroughly as his bones.

For this reason and others, the Famous hold much less interest to me in death than the Anonymous dead. While viewing the crypt of Shakespeare at Westminster, for instance, my thoughts of death are subsumed by thoughts of fame. The anonymous dead are my brethren, and to the skulls of Kutná Hora, I can imagine adding my own to the fragile pile, from which nothing tumbles. At Pompeii, I can gaze for an hour— as at a painting by a master—at the anonymous pyroclastic cast of a slave forever trying to shield his face from the mountain that has buried him.

Perhaps the largest category of graveyard, in any case, is Graveyards in Which the Anonymous Lie, a grouping that contains nearly every graveyard Known and Unknown. My favorite of these—and I use the word "favorite" advisedly—is Auschwitz. People are buried in the form of ash at various points in the death camp, but these are not the most affecting grave sites—still, the various urns made out of ash are perhaps the closest we Jews have to reliquaries. Each room at Auschwitz is a tomb of sorts, each containing, if not actual DNA of the departed, then something of their history and humanity. We follow our guide to the room of women's shoes, to the room of prayer shawls, to the room of artificial limbs and crutches, to the room of eyeglasses, to the room of pots and pans, to the room of suitcases and baskets, to the display of broken dolls. The suitcases are grave markers as are all the other markers. On many of the suitcases are stamped the names and sometimes the date of birth and the city from which the owners came.

Klement Hedwig
8 10 1898

Jnes Meyer
Koln

Neumann Friedrich
1890

My own aunt Rose, an aunt by marriage, was one of the 430,000 Hungarian Jews brought here toward the end of the war. Most of her family was killed, except for her and a son. She told me about Auschwitz when I was a boy, how the Nazis shaved her hair and pulled out her fingernails, how she didn't know her son was alive until ten years after the war. My father's family were all Hungarian Jews. Those who didn't emigrate surely perished here or in nearby Birkenau.

This is the closest I can come to visiting their graves. At Auschwitz there is a room of hair, two tons of it. Every prisoner was shaved and the hair that was of any length was sold for half a mark per kilo. The two tons of hair behind the window in the room of hair at Auschwitz represents 40,000 people, only a fraction of the seven tons of hair the Soviets found here, which itself was only a fraction of the hair that was shorn from the prisoners about to meet their deaths. The hair has all turned grey over time because of the light, but once it contained all the colors that hair can be, and here, as close as anywhere you can stand, you stare at stacks of bodies disguised as filaments.

Perhaps I should include Auschwitz in the category, Grave-yards in Which I Am Buried, a category I previously thought uninhabited. At first glance, this might seem merely a senti-mental gesture, or grandly symbolic, but I would argue that all graves are sentimental gestures, all of them grandly symbolic. That makes them no less necessary, but does one really take up residence in the ground? As with an honorary degree, an hon-orary burial has little in the way of actual benefit, and so I must include myself in Auschwitz in the honorary sense—my con-nection to the place, in any case, is not arbitrary.

But here I'd like to add a tiny category of graveyard that the enthusiast should not miss or fail to notice: the Graveyard Guarded by Avatars. Before now, I have tried to keep my feet on the ground, as it were, considering that my subject itself is so earthbound. Yet graveyards exist as habitat for living things as well as dead, and while the animals that inhabit these spaces might do so solely out of a need for unoccupied space, certain species take on the form almost of sentinels at the graveyards they occupy. The cats of La Recoleta in Buenos Aires, for instance, seem like perfect companions for the wealthy inhabit-ants of the grand mausoleums that crowd the streets of the cem-etery. From around corners, they peer at you, as if to question your intentions and to report your business.

The day after Auschwitz, I visited the main Jewish ceme-tery in Krakow. This cemetery belongs to the subset of His-toric Graveyard that might be termed Graveyards of Lost Civilizations. The "New Jewish Cemetery" ("new" only in the sense that it is distinguishable from the nearby Medieval Jewish cemetery) holds many more dead Jews than the city of

Krakow holds live ones. While the Jewish population of Krakow numbered a quarter of the city's inhabitants, or about
60,000, at the outbreak of World War II, only about 150 self-
identified Jews remain in the city. The day I found the cemetery, I was the only live Jew (or live human of any kind) inside
the graveyard. It was me and a minyan of pigeons, milling
around as I walked among the ancient trees and ancient gravestones, many graves well tended still, and stretching the length
and width of a sports arena to its far walls. As I always do in
graveyards, I read the gravestones and tried to imagine what
the lives of these people might have been. I came across relatively new gravestones as well as older:

MAURYEY WIENER
ADWOKAT
1906–1990

HELENA GOLDMAN
1909–1983

HELENA KRISCHER
1902, Krakov–
Bergen Belsen, 1945

A number of the graves had stones on them, a sign of
remembrance that's part of Jewish tradition. I gathered up a
dozen stones and then another dozen and placed them on the
graves with the most faded inscriptions, many completely illeg-
ible. I placed stone on stone—a stone finally is the only pay-
ment the dead expect, the only language worth sharing. For
the graveyard enthusiast, it's best to always have a pocketful.

Jews say Kaddish for the dead and remember the day of

death, the Yahrzeit. Remembering feels good, but forgetting is inevitable. In the graveyard, we all lie down together, the Remembered, and the Merely Dead. It's not with acrimony that I say the Remembered will also eventually be merely dead, but to point out that the solace of anonymity is that it is what bonds us finally with every other human. My gravestone will be blank. In that way, I will have beat Time to the punch. This wish at least I expect my heirs to carry out.

PETER STRAUB

INSIDE STORY

I used to think that it was misleading to say, *In life we are in the midst of death*. According to me, the proper way to say this was, *In death we are in the midst of life*. The first made no sense to me at all, but the second seemed self-evident. I had no idea why this should be true, neither had I any real understanding of what these sentiments actually meant: the inside-out version just struck me as accurate, and the straightforward one sounded like nonsense, apart of course from the recognition that people were dying all around us, everywhere, one at a time and all the time. But didn't that actually prove that the dead were in the midst of life? And in a sense, weren't the dead all around us, at least in memory? Six months after my mother died, I saw a white column of steam rise up from the corner of Central Park West and West 86th Street, and I thought, *Oh, there she is*. According to my version of the verbal formula, my mother's ghost had appeared on the busy corner to offer me reassurance, also to take in the unregarding life— taxis, buses, women pushing strollers—passing by. In other words, without ever having decided to frame matters in this way, I was looking at the formula from the point of view of the dead.

I was not, let me say, a creepy child. However, I did possess a

flair for the invention of macabre and frightening stories, and
many of the reminiscences of various first cousins of mine prepared for a recent family reunion include a sentence like "After
dinner, we walked up into the woods and Peter told us a scary
story." I do not actually remember ever doing this. What I do
remember are scenes of other children, sometimes my cousins
and brothers, sitting in loose circles around little fires or otherwise disposed over the ground, staring at me in expectation. The
only other aspects of these occasions I can remember are that I
never had anything prepared and that at least half of the time I
did my best to be amusing, to make them laugh. The entire process was not about fear and death.

Fear had always to be tamped down, turned away from; the
imminence of death had always to be denied. A constant presence, fear lurked behind every surface, no matter how harmless
or benign it appeared: it lay, waiting to be discovered, within
doorknobs, beneath wallpaper, in telephones and coffee cups, all
the objects that furnish a life. The intensity of this amazes me
still, as does the simple fact itself; so does the contemplation of
the effort required to even halfway deny or ignore this simple
fact. Looked at the right way, everything sizzled with terror's
unseen payload. Fear of this magnitude is unmanning, especially
to a young male moving into and through adolescence, and it
was both my duty and my job to thrust it from view, especially
the view of others. So that was how I lived, how I got by. Most
of the time, I seemed pretty normal, mostly, if "nervous."

At the end of a seventh-grade school day in Marcy School,
Marcy, Wisconsin, a tiny village just beginning to melt into

the suburbs of Milwaukee, a girl named Judy Johnson spoke my name from behind me in the aisle between our desks, and I jumped. This is what is called an Exaggerated Startle Response. Judy Johnson was smart and confident. "Wow, Peter," she said. "You looked like a scared rabbit." For a couple of seconds, I hated Judy. I was brimming with ambitions, and I did not want, ever, to resemble a frightened animal.

Not long ago, I came across a manila envelope stuffed with old reports from the grade schools I had attended. Sure of meeting astonished praise, I leafed through the reports from second and third grade. Instead of what I had anticipated— universal appreciation—I found one comment after another that said, "Peter is talking to himself a bit less this quarter," and "Peter did not talk to himself so much this year." This *year*? These comments from my old teachers brought back the atmosphere of a childhood very different from the one I thought I remembered. Instead of being bathed in admiring expectations of success, this child moved through an atmosphere simultaneously bright with terror and dark with anxiety. When rebuffed or misunderstood or lonely, he talked to himself. (Also, he stuttered terribly, except for when singing or talking to his favorite auditor.) The things he said were comments on whatever passed before his eyes, a ceaseless unfurling of language deployed in the need for distraction: real chatter, some of it observational, some of it cruel. He was only pretending to be a child, anyhow. Far too closely, death had approached him—no, it was worse than that, death had swarmed into him and briefly snatched him away. His childhood had been murdered the year before he finally reached second grade, in 1950, on Capitol Drive in wide-open western Milwaukee.

We are nearing the unspeakable that must be hidden behind

endless speech: a substance dark, rich, and lavalike; the memory of a fire, the memory of an explosion, the actual fire, the actual explosion; the experience of being tortured for what feels like time without end; torn apart, battered, smashed. I felt sorry for this child, but I'm glad I do not have to live with him. I'm happy he is not in my care. He is in my care. I do have to live with him. At least, I did until very recently.

That which is not understood compels us toward it, urging us in while refusing entry.

I once told an audience at one of the Mohonk Mystery Weekends that I had a seven-year-old twin, and he lived in eternity. "Every now and then," I said to these puzzled champions of the mystery novel, "he grabs the pen." He was always in a rage, I said, at having been stripped of the illusion of protection, at having been broken in so many places, then at having gone on unconsoled.

Fear is shameful. Fear of what cannot be admitted—the intensity of death—is beyond shame. Rigid defenses must be built against it, a suit of armor must be made by hand and worn so continuously that you no longer notice that, like the Tin Man, you are entirely encased in metal. Inauthenticity spreads like a stain.

After trauma, what you know most deeply is what you do not want to know, so you do not know it, imperfectly.

Knowledge crawls through the unprotected places.

Twenty-five years ago, I used to walk my daughter to preschool classes at the Walden School, on West 89th Street. One day, just after coming out of the building, I had an experience unlike anything else that had ever happened to me. Although this experience was both disturbing and frustrating, it began with a kind of beguilement.

It was as if something strange, curious, and compelling had just come into view within a far corner of my mind's eye: this bizarre *thing* gleamed and sparkled with the power of the unknown and unforeseen. *What's that?* I wondered, and turned mentally to get more of it in view. At that moment, just before I could get my first real look at the glittering, compelling curiosity, a dark, heavy curtain, a curtain made of lead, slammed down and struck the ground with an enormous internal crash that was of course completely inaudible on West 89th Street, but would have terrified the half-dozen sparrows and pigeons fussing over some morsel in the gutter. Had the crash been audible, the birds would have rocketed off to the tops of buildings.

I stood there, open-mouthed and more than startled, shocked by what had just happened. There existed in my mind a massive and, I had to assume, terrifying memory area I was not allowed to visit. I was not even supposed to be aware of its existence. The brute force of the sacred seemed to underlie this prohibition. I thought this unilateral mental denial could refer to one thing only, that which was the source of the nearly lifelong suppressed terror which in those days I had, on the famous, often-derided analytic couch, just begun to reckon with and map.

Now. Nineteen-fifty, maybe it was September, maybe October. My brother John and I bought ice-cream cones at a candy store on the far side of busy Capitol Drive, only a five-minute walk from our red-brick house on 100th Street, and ahead of John, I started to walk across the Drive.

In the middle of the far, westbound lanes, I turned my head to the right and saw, perhaps ten feet away and hung stationary in space and time, unmoving, the broad, rust-speckled grill of an old car. Even if I had time to escape my fate, that I was literally frozen with terror made escape impossible. The hideous grill advanced all at once across three feet of roadbed. It was a sudden transition, like a jump cut in a film. The grill became clearer, more focused. Within my body, fear shot up like mercury in a thermometer. I was not capable of thought. A bright, hideous clarity infested the ambient air. Then the grill jumped to within a foot from me, and it was too late for the driver to swerve, and everything disappeared, including me, at least for a time.

Afterward there came a long period of hospitalization, surgeries, surgeries to correct the errors of previous surgeries, pain unto weeping/screaming/sobbing, half-body plaster casts, the progression, over nearly a year, from bed to wheelchair to crutches, the grim effort to relearn how to walk, then how to walk without limping. I spent an amazing amount of time alone in my house, feeling completely abandoned. (It was during this period that I discovered how terror inhabited simple objects like doorknobs and coffee cups.) My parents' advice about this material was to forget about it, to put it safely behind me. I tried. Pulsing away deep in my mind was the image of having been smashed, broken, turned into a bloody rag. When you got to the center of my being, that's what you found: a bloody rag and a smear on a four-lane thoroughfare. The child I had been had died, and a twitchy, fearful, furious, embittered, larval-stage sociopath in a perpetual state of denial now bore his name.

Happily, I discovered that I had a great two-way appetite for narrative. I loved reading and writing both, and what I most loved reading and writing was fiction. (Also, thank God, I was an absolute swot.) Fiction, along with my capacity for work, rescued me. Instead of becoming a teenage housebreaker who pissed on the furniture and slaughtered the pets, I majored in English and cheerfully read, at an only slightly optimistic estimate, ten thousand novels. When I was twenty-six, I stopped pretending to be a Ph.D. student and wrote a novel, and that was that, especially when my work began to be read by carpenters and bartenders, high school students and retirees, jazz musicians, women lawyers and women in maternity wards. What would a former embittered larval-stage-sociopath-turned-novelist write but horror, a genre then enjoying a lengthy period of dizzying commercial success? Everything appeared to be worked out and resolved.

Except that it was not, not at all. The near-death trauma that I had wrapped in chains and dropped into the psychic sea began to bubble up, and I went off the rails. After a couple of years, I started seeing a therapist, and after the immediate problems began to move toward their best solutions, the therapist, who knew that she had a live one, suggested I enter into psychoanalysis with her, four days a week, supine on the couch, freely associating to the ceiling.

"I don't know how you could resist," she said, and I didn't.

Both gloriously neurotic and astonishingly ignorant about my own motives, I began the mapping process I mentioned before. Over the next four to five years, I opened and explored, often shaken and weeping, an internal seam of misery, sorrow, rage, and endless injury. This was amazing to me. All of that terrible deathly darkness inhabited me? It seemed that my sanity, or at least my psychic balance, depended on never losing consciousness of this reality. After psychoanalysis had revealed to me that my encounter on Capitol Drive with an automobile was, whether I liked it or not, the center of my experience and the source for all that followed, I wrote about it in two novels, *Mystery* and *The Throat*, trying to fit it into me, me into it, with as much truth as I could find, remember, or invent.

In fact, I had a milder version of PTSD, which explained all the fear that I had tried to ignore, or to wish out of existence. This understanding, which had led me to hundreds of the hard-won insights known as "breakthroughs," did not, however, explain whatever had been pulsing away on the other side of the leaden curtain that had crashed down onto West 89th Street.

To glimpse, however briefly and partially, what lay beyond that curtain, I had to release the last, most strenuously pro-tected secret I was keeping from myself. It had to swim up to the surface of my consciousness, this secret, and reveal itself at a moment when I felt relaxed, secure, unguarded, and recep-tive. These conditions meant that were this marvelous and confounding event ever to occur, it would have to take place in the consulting room, a space like an enchanted clearing in a jungle, a space where magical prohibitions profoundly ward off all harm.

One of the first questions that I asked my mother afterward in the hospital was if I could have the clothing I wore that day. I wanted to wear my own blood. When I was able to get on my feet again, I wanted to walk around in the costume of my worst, most decisive, most mysterious and appalling moment.

Horrified, my mother explained that after my clothes had been cut off my body, they had been burned. Of course, a strange notion about bloodstains and glamour had prompted my question, but it seems clear to me now that also at work was an impulse toward narrative: my secret, unseen goal was literally to insert myself into my own history, that I might court an area of my memory I was not consciously aware of having lost. I wanted to plug myself back into the fearful story to recover what had been lost. The wish to dress myself in that ruined clothing, it strikes me now, represented a childish, cartoonlike attempt at self-analysis.

If you think "the talking cure" is outmoded, misguided, or delusional, you will be unable to trust what I am to describe next.

I'm not sure I should trust it myself. I do, though, I trust it absolutely.

Perhaps this next part was merely a suffering dream, a vision created within a fractured skull by a concussed brain. By a large margin, I prefer the world in which what came to me in the familiar couch cannot be taken to be the truth. That human beings should experience anything at all after the moment of death strikes me as so impossible that its proposal as a serious possibility verges on the immoral. I want this life to be all we have, all we get—a brief passage from darkness through the light and back into darkness. *That*, according to me, is how you create a moral life, by learning how to do so in the absence of theological prompts and goads. Our life seems more beautiful if it is understood to begin and end, really *end*. Thus, we may choose salvation and experience resurrection, but only in the brief journey between leaving oblivion and entering it again.

Despite my preferences, what I glimpsed on the other

side of the lead curtain arrived with the taste, the in-fact-unmistakable clout of the authentic. Overwhelmingly, it felt like truth.

I lay supine on a couch in the familiar consulting room, with the beloved presence of Lila, my companion and confidant of decades, behind me. Out of my mouth came words directed at both the listening presence behind my head and myself, who spoke them. A lovely, mysterious image had just occurred to me: in the imaginative space, I saw a child, a boy, step forward out of a foreboding, dark sky, his right arm extended, offering the open palm of his right hand. On his palm was written a great, explanatory word, a *necessary* word, in some sculpted, ornate language I did not know and had never seen before.

Oh, there he is, I said to myself, and out loud, said, "A child . . ."

The world as I knew it was no more, had been left behind.

As had I, for I had escaped myself, exited my body. What remained was a speck of being hurtling through a void toward an unknowable but powerfully magnetic destination. (Remote and untouchable, other being-specks were also shooting through the void.) I was no longer a self, for all of what I understood as selfhood lay behind me. I was what remained after the body, and the personality, and the mind with all its memories had been husked off and stripped away.

A powerful, labyrinthine emotion filled the traveling speck that was the essential portion of what had been my being, an unbearable mixture of ecstasy and terror. In the grip of this dread yet exalted emotion, ecstasy *was* terror, because it spoke of an immanent, absolute transformation that involved the utter loss of everything earthly. Within the promise of an upward escape from the mundane, ecstasy always contains this suggestion of a darkness. The ecstasy/terror of this moment, however, flooded into me and was instantly beyond my capacity for coping with it, even to contain it, and in my terror I refused to go further.

Throughout this experience, I knew that I was myself, Peter, stretched out across the couch in that protected and meaning-soaked space. I knew this was a sliver of memory miraculously returned, and I lingered a moment longer within the visionary territory, transfixed with a terrifying conviction. What had once been promised would this time reach its conclusion, and I would not only die on the spot but on the instant disappear from the couch. I would be *gone*. The compounding ecstasy was on the verge of bursting into flame, and with every intentional muscle I possessed, I pulled myself out of the experience and returned to this world, panting, trembling.

I thought—no, I was certain—that Lila had witnessed everything that had just happened. She lived through it with me and was as astonished, moved, frightened as myself. She had the sense not to say a word. Although that may seem unsurprising, she is not an analyst who has taken a vow of silence. However, she let me retain my assumptions for as long as I needed them. The second of these assumptions was that my return to a buried "near-death" experience had endured at least fifteen minutes or more.

For many minutes I could do no more than to utter things like, "Oh, my God," and "Wasn't that *amazing*?" I remember telling Lila that I wished I'd had the courage to travel further than I had, but cowardice had driven me out of the extraordinary. I told her that I had been terrified of disappearing from the couch, from the room, from the world altogether. Some unimaginable transformation had awaited me, and I knew no more than that I could not imagine it with any accuracy. Ultimate things really are ultimate, and what is ineffable cannot be described. One of the few things I did understand was that I was not supposed to be able to imagine or describe it. Nobody was. Whatever had been at the end of my journey toward what had irresistibly felt like the next step was too charged, too packed with contradictory emotions, for human comprehension. It was unbearable. What I had undergone, one had to die to see. To travel even the pathetically brief distance I had managed, one had to forgo the entire structure of the self and implode to the size of single cell. No, the size of an atom.

At the end of one of Ted Berrigan's sonnets, he wrote, "And I have seen what other men sometimes have thought they've seen." The first time I read that line, all I knew was that it had gone very deeply into me. The last time I read it, I knew why.

Eight or nine months later, I realized that Lila had no idea of what I had undergone. The experience had lasted no more than a couple of seconds. One moment I was saying "A child," and the next I began to babble of green fields. Lila swiftly managed to piece everything together and waited for me to realize that she had seen no more than an outsized middle-aged man lying supine, and for once silenced, on her couch. Long after, I thought I had fled that realm at the same half-second I had at the age of seven. Because I was going to live, I could go no further. Death would elude me until it eluded me no longer.

INVITATION TO THE DANCE

Sometime about thirteen years ago, my mother's brain began to shrink. The signs that something was wrong proliferated slowly, but as ominously as something out of a science-fiction movie. My mother became unaccountably restless and unable to concentrate. She complained constantly that Larry, my stepfather, didn't take her out anywhere, that they never did anything—although she could no longer follow the conversation at a dinner party and said things that other people found incomprehensible. She tried going back to work in some of the little tourist shops where she lived, in Rockport, Massachusetts. My mother worked most of her adult life, but now she couldn't figure out how to run a cash register or follow the simplest directions. Each time, she was fired after a few days, returning home baffled and indignant.

She was becoming indignant a lot. She began to fly into a rage at the smallest frustrations, cursing at herself and at other people in words we never heard her use before. She started to drink as well, something else she had never done much before. My mother had been a classic half-a-glass-of-champagne-on-New Year's-Eve drinker. Now she had to have wine every night, and even a little made her garrulous and belligerent.

It was as if every part of her personality was being slowly stripped away, layer by layer. The loving, gentle woman my sisters and I had known was being replaced by someone we did not recognize.

There were other things going on as well, physical changes. Her speech was often slurred, even when she was not drinking. Her movements became jerky and exaggerated, as if she could no longer fully control her limbs. She could not abide any restraints. During a drive one Christmas afternoon, I watched while she sat in the passenger's seat, compulsively buckling and unbuckling her seat belt, again and again, for over an hour. She kept complaining about how it stuck against her body, as if she had never seen or used a seat belt before.

My youngest sister, Pam, and I persuaded her to see a doctor. Her primary-care physician thought she knew what was wrong and sent her to a neurologist to confirm it—but at the last minute my mother refused to keep the appointment. Instead, she went on drinking and growing steadily more impatient with everything and everyone around her. She shoved a woman she thought was crowding her at an airport baggage carousel, swore at people over parking spaces. Mostly she fought with Larry. When he tried to stop her from drinking, she became incensed, threatening to burn down the house they owned together or to blacken over the paintings he sold at a local gallery. Their fights became wild and vituperative. She accused him of being the one with a problem, of being a depressive, of stifling her. A certain mania seemed to come over her during these arguments. Once she did a sort of Indian war dance around him, challenging him to fight.

"I told him, if you want to fight, my family knows how to fight!" she told me. "You ain't seen nothin' yet!"

Around that time, I went to Boston to try to intervene. I remember it was a beautiful spring day and we were walking around Beacon Hill. She seemed delighted to see me, but all I could notice was how strange she acted. She hadn't had a drink, but her gait was wobbly and her eyes looked glazed. She no longer seemed to understand how the stoplights worked. Repeatedly, I had to reach out and pull her back from walking straight into traffic. We strolled down into Boston Common, where a homeless guy on a bench made some innocuous passing comment to her. My mother, always the most private, the most dignified of people, stopped and twirled around, doing a little pirouette for the homeless man, beaming the whole time.

Soon afterward, Larry confronted her with an empty wine bottle she had secreted in their closet. She wrenched it from his hand and hit him across the face with it, cutting his nose. He needed stitches to close the wound, and while he didn't press charges, my mother had to appear in court under the domestic-abuse laws. I hired a defense lawyer, who got her off with a warning, and finally we prevailed on her to go to a neurologist. This was a full eight years after we first noticed dramatic changes in her behavior. The tests revealed what her primary-care doctor thought all along: my mother was suffering from Huntington's disease.

Huntington's (HD) is a hereditary disease, its most illustrious victim the folksinger Woody Guthrie. It's caused by a defective gene that produces a mutant "huntingtin" protein. The protein is necessary to human development, but its mutant version produces an excess of glutamines, amino acids that begin to stress, then eventually kill, the brain's neurons. Huntington's is also known as Huntington's chorea, or "dance," for the florid movements that are its most obvious symptom. But such movements do not afflict all sufferers, nor are they the illness's most destructive characteristic.

Huntington's is a "profound" disease, one of the few neurological disorders that attacks nearly every area of the brain, says Steven Hersch, an associate professor of neurology at Harvard Medical School and Massachusetts General Hospital, and my mother's neurologist. It affects the cerebral cortex, where thought, perception, and memory are stored. It also shrinks the basal ganglia, which serve as a sort of supercomputer for the rest of the brain, regulating almost everything from movement to the input and output of thoughts, feelings, emotions, behavior. The result is what Hersch terms a loss of "modulation" and "a coarsening" of how we do just about everything—move, think, react. Huntington's sufferers have trouble correctly reading emotions in others or even recognizing familiar faces. They no longer understand when their behavior is inappropriate, and have difficulty planning, organizing, and prioritizing. They can become both intensely angry, and apathetic and indecisive.

"They're losing possibilities," says Hersch. "They're losing the possibilities of things they could do, or think of, or want to do."

Not the least of Huntington's effects is what the knowledge of the disease does to its victims. There is no cure. Adult-onset Huntington's usually afflicts individuals sometime between thirty-five and fifty-five, although early-onset, or juvenile, Huntington's can manifest itself before the age of twenty. The disease commonly takes ten to thirty years to run its course, as body and mind slowly shut down and leave the sufferer all but inert. Before that happens, victims commonly die from major infections, pneumonia, choking, or "silent pneumonia," as food goes down the wrong pipe.

Suicides are not uncommon, even among "at-risk" patients who have yet to actually ascertain that they have the disease. Depression is also frequent among such individuals. If one is faced with such a fate, denial can be a survival strategy.

"Often the people who do best are those who can wall it off and go on with their lives," acknowledges Hersch. "It's a very good approach in a lot of ways. The trick for people sometimes is to figure out when it's in their best interest to drop the denial and gain knowledge that will help them."

The test results devastated my mother. Before long she reverted to denial. She insisted that her test had produced "a false positive." She told us that she had "the syndrome of the disease, but not the disease itself." She told us that, somehow, she was "the control" in the test. But as her brain continued to shrink, she began to lose even these words. It became a little joke between us.

"Dearest, I don't have this, you know," she would tell me, very seriously, out of the blue. "I'm the—the . . ."

"The control?"

"Yes, that's it!" she would say, delighted.

"Mom, you can't be the control if you can't remember the word 'control,'" I would tell her, and she would laugh, and I would laugh. But a few minutes later, she would tell me again that she didn't really have this, you know.

The fact that my mother had Huntington's meant that I had a fifty-fifty chance of inheriting the gene—and thus the disease—myself. I didn't like to look at this too directly. That was my own form of denial. I told friends and relatives that I would not take the genetic test that my mother had taken. What was the point, without a cure? It could only screw up my health insurance, and who wanted to live with such a fate hanging over their head?

But those fifty-fifty odds worked their own havoc. Eventually, I found that I couldn't help thinking about the disease whenever I had trouble coming up with a word or organizing an article. I noticed whenever my body flinched involuntarily. I became especially aware of how often I would drag one of my feet along the sidewalk, or how frequently my left arm would twitch. I took to holding my left hand out in front of me, trying to reassure myself by seeing how long I could keep it still— a better test for delirium tremens, I suppose, than Huntington's disease.

"Would you stop doing that? You don't have it!" Ellen, my wife, would tell me. Yet I was sure that I could feel something deep inside me, something that I came to think of, a little melodramatically, as a stirring. Sometimes, lying awake in bed late at night, I was sure that I was only holding it back by force of will. I was certain that if I let go, I would begin to move compulsively, uncontrollably, just as my mother did now. The dance.

"I think I might have this," I told Ellen.

"I don't think you do," she said.

But her assurance was based on wishful thinking, or the sort of baseless conception one often has about someone else's life. My wife didn't want me to have the disease, and she thought of me as a lucky person, somebody who just wouldn't get such a thing. Yet none of this mattered. In reality, unlike fiction, people's lives don't run according to some overarching narrative. We never suspected this disease was in my family before my mother was tested, we didn't think of ourselves as shadowed by some sort of gloomy, gothic fate. But nonetheless, here it was.

I kept surreptitiously doing my little tests. Should I forget me, may my left hand lose its cunning. . . .

Every step of the way, meanwhile, my mother's denial only made everything worse for her. It now meant the dissolution of the life she had made with Larry—the quiet days in retirement they loved to spend fishing or reading and watching the news together in the evening; going to their favorite bakery every Sunday morning. None of it was enough to appease what was going on inside her brain. She wouldn't stop sneaking drinks, wouldn't keep taking the medications the doctors prescribed to control her moods. We would have been happy to let her drink if that had helped her, but the alcohol only stressed the brain and served to dilute the effects of the drugs. My mother now demanded almost constant attention to keep her entertained, to keep her from wandering into disaster. Eventually, Larry told us he wanted out. They had been married for twenty-one years, and my mother had nursed him through a heart attack, cancer, and occasional bouts of epilepsy. But Larry, an émigré from Middle Europe, had seen both the Nazis and the Communists march into his life, and he knew when to head for cover. I couldn't blame him. It's an enormous burden for any one person to take care of a Huntington's victim, particularly someone who is a senior citizen himself, and he had been dealing with it for a decade. Pam and I hired more lawyers to negotiate the divorce, the sale of their neat little house, the overwhelming thicket of bureaucracy that determined where and how she might live now.

Pam managed to find her a nice studio apartment in an assisted-living facility in Beverly, Massachusetts: a converted high school with the pretentious name of Landmark at Ocean-view. (Just what was the "landmark"? The last leg of the voy-age before you ease into the good harbor of death?) There were big school windows that brought in lots of light, and bright, cheery carpeting, and a diligent staff to make sure that she took her pills and to cook her meals and do her laundry—all tasks that she was having increasing difficulty performing.

Personally, I wanted to shoot myself every time I set foot inside the place. My mother, on the other hand, thought it was unbelievably "posh," the sort of home where she had always dreamed of living.

Meanwhile, my father, whom she had divorced nearly thirty years ago, came east with cinematic notions of getting remar-ried and taking care of her. He disregarded almost everything we told him about Huntington's and instructed her that she should just try to concentrate on holding her limbs still. Before one ghastly family dinner in a restaurant, he let her have a drink, then tried to cut her off. When his back was turned for a moment, she calmly snatched up his full wineglass and downed the contents in one swallow. I saw his eyes widen. My mother spent the rest of the meal barely able to speak, rolling her head back to try to get food down, until we made her stop out of fear she would choke to death in front of our eyes. My father fled back to his apartment in Hollywood. Good-bye, Golden Pond.

I was determined by this time to face the disease head-on. If my mother had made everything worse for herself by remaining in denial, I would throw it off. I would take what-ever medications were necessary, volunteer for whatever exper-imental programs there must surely be. I convinced myself that this was a purely practical idea. Why go about looking for cures or ways to ameliorate the effects of the disease if I didn't have the gene? Looking back now, I think my decision may have been more emotional than anything else, a desire to know this and be done with the uncertainty. I told myself I would be stronger than my mom, and take whatever I was given. Early in 2007, I set up an appointment at Columbia University's HDSA Center of Excellence, located up in Washington Heights.

The Columbia center deals with every aspect of the disease, both for those already suffering from HD and for those at risk, and it endeavors to help patients through each stage. It's unique in that the care it offers is free, although there are nominal fees for some parts of the gene test. The center's testing protocol, established and refined over the fifteen years since the Huntington's gene was first identified, is actually an involved process, one that takes place over a few months—and is an infinitely better one than what my mother went through. One of its chief purposes was to slow me down—to let me think over what I was doing. As the center's genetic counselor warned me at the start, "Once you know, you can't not know."

There was the session with the genetic counselor, a visit to a psychiatrist, neurological and neuropsychological exams. If after all that I still wanted to know, they would draw my blood and tell me the result of the gene test. That result would be a number—the number of times a particular string of glutamine DNA, known as CAG, repeated itself at the beginning of my Huntington's gene. If that number was 27 or below, I was in the clear. If it was 36 to 39, I would fall into a tiny percentage of the population that might, or might not, develop the disease. If it was 40 or more, it meant that I had inherited the defective gene—and that I would get the disease.

I threw myself eagerly into the testing process, glad now to be doing this, to be confronting these phantom fears. The not-knowing by now had become as bad as knowing the worst could possibly be, I told myself. I disavowed everything I had told people before. Best to look this fate in the eye, to see if it really was waiting for me.

The initial exams went well. The doctor found no signs that I had the disease already (my twitching left arm promptly stopped twitching so much). But the doctor seemed less than pleased that I was taking the test at all. The genetic counselor had insisted that there was no right or wrong reason for want-ing to take the gene test, but it seemed clear that I had made the wrong choice.

Later, I found that I had misinterpreted the doctor's atti-tude. There really was no right or wrong reason to get the test; she was simply a little surprised by my motives. Most of the people they saw came because of some life trigger. They were making career decisions, getting married, thinking of having children—or wanting to spare their children, now marriage age, from having to take the test. Or they had just learned that Huntington's was in the family, or that a genetic test existed.

Getting tested so that you could see what you could do about the disease was unusual, in part because there is currently nothing you can do to cure the disease or even curb its progress.

Huntington's is what the Food and Drug Administration (FDA) officially calls an "orphan disease"—it affects too few people to make it worth the drug companies' while to develop a drug for it on their own. The official cutoff number is 200,000 people; Huntington's currently afflicts only 30,000 to 35,000 people in the United States, with perhaps another 200,000 to 250,000 at risk of getting the disease.

The National Institutes of Health (NIH) provide subsidies in such cases, but the total amount spent in the United States on finding a cure this year will probably be no more than $120 million to $130 million. A substantial sum, to be sure—but not so much when you consider that it can easily cost drug companies $1 billion to come up with an effective drug. As it stands now, a cure is not on the horizon. The most promising idea seems to be "turning off" the defective Huntington's gene, but discovering how to do that presents a host of technical problems that remain far from solved.

The doctor's surprise at my motives drew me up a little short—not a bad thing. Getting tested for the gene of a hereditary disease with no cure is and should be a hugely complicated decision, one with implications beyond one's own self. It can mean "outing" other family members, who may have no desire to learn if they will get the disease. It can mean any number of problems with one's health insurance (no doubt a big reason why fewer than 3 percent of at-risk Americans get tested for HD, as opposed to 20 percent of Canadians who might have the gene). It can mean dealing with unanticipated feelings of guilt, dread, despair. It all made me think again. Was I engaging in a reckless act of bravado, moving into a realm that I was not psychologically or emotionally prepared for, just to show that I could do it?

"No matter what the result is," my genetic counselor warned me, "nobody is the same person they were when they walked in here."

I was pretty sure that if the results were negative I would be the same person I was in about five minutes. On the other hand, the fifty-fifty chance that I had the gene had already begun to unravel any peace of mind about my future. Bravado or not, I had to know. I had them draw the blood. They told me it would take two to four weeks for a result, depending on how crowded the lab was. No matter what the verdict was, I would have to come back to the clinic for the counselor to tell me in person.

During my trips to the Columbia Center, Ellen and I would sit in the plain, institutional waiting room and watch other outpatients coming and going. Some displayed no outward signs of having the disease; others clearly had the telltale movements. Some of these people carried themselves with remarkable bravery; others were so young that it was almost unbearable to watch them. I knew that, in a very short time, I would either walk away and never see them, never see this place again, or that I would join their small fraternity.

The two to four weeks that I had to wait seemed to stretch out like a lifetime—in the best sense of the words. I put the possibility of having the gene out of my head again, and was more sanguine about my chances than I had been in months, still buoyed by the revelation that all my twitching had been, so to speak, in my head.

Only one afternoon, while I was working in a library, did the full understanding of what I was doing sneak up on me. "What if it really is positive?" I thought to myself, out of the blue, and I realized that I had no answer. I was stepping over a cliff, into a state of mind that I had no real way of even imagining. I quickly went back to my research, shutting this idea safely away again behind my own walls. But it was still there.

When the call came two weeks later to set up my appointment, I wished for more time. I had two days to wait. I joked with my wife that our appointment was on an auspicious day—the anniversary of Hitler's invasion of Russia. But I also couldn't help wondering, "If it's negative, wouldn't they tell you over the phone? I mean, even if they say they won't? Just to give you peace of mind as soon as they can?"

"No, they have a whole procedure," my wife insisted. "It's going to be fine, you don't have this."

"But I'm just saying. Wouldn't you tell the person? Wouldn't it be sadistic to let you wonder for the next two days if the news was good?"

"It's a procedure!"

We took the subway up to the Center and got there a little early, seating ourselves in the waiting room again. Almost as soon as we arrived, my genetic counselor came out to see us— and we had our answer. When she walked into the waiting room, we could both see that tears were welling up in her eyes and that her mouth was set in a tight little smile, like someone trying to pretend there's nothing wrong. It was like being on trial and having a jury come back that won't look you in the face. After that, it was all over very quickly. The counselor sat us down in her windowless office and told us at once that the number of my CAG repetitions was 41—one number higher than my mother's. I had the defective gene, and my brain too would begin to die.

I can't say that I was immediately stricken or horrified. I didn't even feel as upset as I have sometimes when an editor hasn't liked a manuscript. It felt, as bad news often does, as if I'd known what it was going to be all along. Outside, it was still a sunny early-summer day. We got back on the subway. Ellen tried to be consoling, but I wasn't in need of any, not just then. What was there to say? When we got home, I got a call from a podiatrist wanting to move up an appointment for a minor foot problem I was having. I hustled over to the East

Side and there I sat, in another doctor's waiting room, not an hour later. It all seemed unreal, like some weird simulation of what I had just been through. I thought about how giddy I would have been feeling if the results had been negative. I felt like blurting out the news to anyone I encountered, I just found out I will get a fatal disease. But I didn't. The doctor prescribed some egg cups for my shoes, and I went home.

A couple days later, the bottom fell out. I was working at my desk when I began to doubt every single thing that I was writing. I was certain that I was already losing my ability to think, to put together a simple sentence. Later that night, lying in bed, I was gripped by a terrible, souring sense of dread, a feeling that everything in my life was useless, meaningless. I had never experienced anything like it before. I am a person of faith and optimism, at least when it comes to my personal outlook, but all that gave way before this wrenching, physical sensation of despair. This feeling came over me several more times during the week after my test. Nothing, not even the most soothing and optimistic thoughts I mustered, could ameliorate it. I wondered if this was what true, clinical depression felt like.

Then it would fade away and I would feel strangely exhilarated, just as one does when a fever passes. I learned to ride these moods out, just try to get through them, and soon they largely disappeared. I was, I suppose, building a new wall. All that brave confrontation, just to escape behind a new layer of denial! Nonetheless, everything did seem more intense, more edged. My moods were more mercurial, I was angrier, more sympathetic, even more apathetic about things—always

aware that these very mood swings too were symptoms of
Huntington's.

I made predictable resolutions. I would live more in the
moment. I would hone my life to the essentials; read more
great books; stop wasting so much time on newspapers, the latest catastrophe from Africa or China, or the op-ed pages. Who
had time for it? Instead, I would write and write and write,
build a legacy of work.

Yet this soon created its own sense of panic. I had easily
twenty, thirty, maybe more good ideas for novels, histories,
screenplays—how would I ever get all that done? What I really
wanted was to live like I always did, taking little care of myself,
wasting time worrying over politics, or how the Yankees were
doing, or even the banality of other people's opinions. As a
novelist I learned long ago to pace myself, building something
day by day, rewarding myself along the way with all the sweet
distractions of modern, urban life. I wanted my trivialities. I
kept thinking of the title of that self-help book, something like
Don't Sweat the Small Stuff—and It's All Small Stuff. But of
course, it's the small stuff that we crave. That's what gives us
the illusion that life is infinite, the only thing that saves us from
the terror of consciousness, the root of which is that uniquely
human knowledge that we are going to die. My mother's denial
did indeed make everything worse for her, and at times it tor-
mented those of us who loved her. But now I found her stub-
bornness, her desire to cling to the life she had known,
understandable, even admirable.

I started to tell people about my test results, what they
meant. This made my wife uncomfortable, but I couldn't help
myself. I had some kind of compulsion to tell friends, family,
even professional acquaintances. I wasn't sure why I felt this

need. Was I trying to solicit their pity, their admiration? See how brave he's being!

Probably. But I think I was also doing it out of sheer incredulity, or even as a cry for help. Here I am, dying. Do something!

My friends duly praised my courage—as if I had any choice. They spoke about all the great things going on in medicine today. I nodded and smiled, told them yes, I would pursue every cure. But there are no cures, at least not yet, and I doubt that a nation bent on spending three or four trillion dollars on the grand task of making the Iraqi people learn to love one another is ever going to devote much more to solving my little brain ailment. For that matter, I can't honestly say that my disease should have any priority over the likes of breast cancer, strokes, heart disease, or any number of other maladies that affect many more people.

All things considered, I knew that I had already had a phenomenally good life. Even when it came to the Huntington's, I had been lucky enough not to live with the disease hanging over my head. I was never somebody who worried about death or thought about it much at all. My wife and I had fortunately decided not to have children, a decision we reached more or less by inertia over the years and which meant that, thank God, I didn't have to worry about having passed this on to someone else.

And yet, inevitably, I would find myself filled with rage at times. I thought maybe it was the knowing that made all the difference. I joked about the old Woody Allen lines, from *Love and Death*: "How I got into this predicament I'll never know. . . . To be executed for a crime I never committed. Of course, isn't all mankind in the same boat? Isn't all mankind ultimately executed for a crime it never committed? The difference is that all men go eventually. But I go at six o'clock tomorrow morning."

But I wasn't going tomorrow morning. No one is sure what triggers the onset of Huntington's. The gene's interaction with other genes, or environmental factors, or even aging itself may play a role. Heredity and especially gender seem to be very strong factors. The disease could begin to take its toll at almost any time, but because I inherited it from my mother instead of my father, it is more likely to manifest itself around the same age when she got it, at sixty-five or maybe even older—a very late onset.

"The brain copes, until it can't anymore" is the exquisite phrase with which Herminia Diana Rosas, professor of neurology at Mass General, describes the progress of the disease. Huntington's may well be active in the brain ten, even twenty, years before any symptoms begin to show up. We don't see its effects because the brain rallies to adjust. In a touchingly human response to this threat, the neurons compensate by trying to do less, or by sharing vital information among each other, squirreling away knowledge and memory where they can.

In other words, I had not received some fatal diagnosis, not really. All my Huntington's gene guaranteed was that I was going to start to die, most likely at the same age that many people start to die, from one thing or another, prostate or heart disease, stroke or diabetes or Alzheimer's—much as we are all dying, all the time. I might have another good sixteen years ahead of me, maybe even more. I joked that it was like being on death row, only with better company. I joked that it was like being on death row, only with better food. Coming out of my agent's building on yet another gorgeous summer day—and what a beautiful summer it was—I told myself, "You'll be doing this ten years from now, and you'll still have six years to go. Think of how long that is, how much will happen and how much you can do!"

What I really feared was not death but what would precede it. Dr. Hersch's "coarseness" meant a lack of nuance—a great prescription for a writer. I would be unable to work, to organize my thoughts or comprehend the world around me. I would forget friends, names, faces, facts, memories. I would be unable to control my moods, my movements, my urges, would become a living caricature of my former self—much like what I had seen happen to my mother.

Our efforts to get her to adjust to life at her assisted-living facility were breaking down. She became belligerent if she felt she was being mistreated or thwarted in any way. She kept insisting that she wanted to be married again, kept pursuing men of any age. When someone told her that a ninety-five-year-old fellow resident at Landmark had said she was nice, she harassed him to the point where she had to be forcibly removed from his room, slugging a female staff member in the process.

This time she was ejected from the facility. After a brief and volatile stay in a nearby nursing home, my mother was shipped out to a psychiatric ward, where she was drugged nearly to the point of being insensible. She couldn't speak, could barely move, and seemed to be experiencing hallucinations. My sister, noticing other inmates walking around dressed in some of her clothes, raised hell, cajoled doctors, and managed to get her transferred to a much better facility, a sprawling state hospital.

It was a place with light and space and a dedicated staff that adjusted her medication so that she was alert and talking again. She seemed much happier, the violent rages ebbing away, but all the transfers, and the progress of her disease, had taken its toll. She had trouble completing even a simple sentence, and her gait was so unsteady that she was confined permanently to a wheelchair.

There was no disguising that she was in an institution now. Her ward was all tile and linoleum, and she was surrounded by other inmates suffering from advanced neurological disorders, Huntington's and Parkinson's, multiple sclerosis, retardation, and dementia. There was one man, younger-looking than my mother, who just sat about with his head crooked permanently to one side, his tongue lolling out of his mouth. Another woman, all but immobile, told us how she had been a nurse for many years but was now suffering from Parkinson's. She seemed to be alert enough and in her right mind.

Which was better? To be past any awareness of your condition—or to be sinking slowly into it, still conscious? I wondered what the point was of trying to extend the longevity of the human body before we knew more about preserving the mind. How much would I understand when I was put in some institution like this? Ellen swore that she would take care of me at home, and I knew she meant it. But I also knew that in the end, she would not be able to do so, that this was my fate I saw here before me.

Visiting my mother was an ordeal to me now. And yet it also felt oddly soothing to just sit with her in silence while she patted my arm and smiled at me, saying little. It occurred to me that she was tracing the path I would follow. It reminded me of *The Vanishing*, that creepy European film in which a man is so guilt-stricken over not knowing what became of his lover that he allows her psychotic killer to kill him in the same extended, horrifying manner, just so he can know what she experienced. When my mother first went to live at Landmark, my sister persuaded her to give up her car; her deteriorating physical skills made her a menace to herself and to others on the road. But Pam gave her a few weeks first to get used to the idea, to ease her transition to living on her own, in a strange town, at the age of seventy-five. My mother would usually drive back to Rockport, a place she loved, a place where she had lived for nearly forty years, and where she no longer belonged. There she would just sit in her car, out on the town wharf, and watch the gulls circling and diving over the harbor. I often thought of her there, and now I understood that I would, one day, know what she was going through.

A Huntington's drug trial materialized late last year at a Mass General clinic up in Charlestown, Massachusetts—the first interventionary test ever, for at-risk subjects who as yet had displayed no symptoms of the disease. I volunteered immediately. The trial consisted mostly of taking daily supplements of creatine, the bodybuilding drug, which, it was thought, might strengthen and extend the life of neurons. It wouldn't "cure" the disease, but at my age, preserving as many brain cells as possible—buying time—might prove almost as beneficial.

The first step was another battery of tests, starting with an MRI. When it was over, I got to see a picture of my brain for the first time. Dr. Rosas, who runs the program with Dr. Hersch, her husband, told me that there were no visible signs of Huntington's yet and pointed out the caudate nuclei, the parts of my brain that were most likely to shrink first. They lay along the edges of the pool of cerebral-spinal fluid that separates the left and right hemispheres of the brain—an area that looks like a pair of dark wings on the MRI, delicate and beautiful. I stared at them for a long time, thinking of how someday the wings would lose their shape as my brain shrunk and they expanded, leaving only more of the blackness.

There was something else on the scan as well. A little white circle, maybe half the size of a dime. Dr. Rosas wanted to know if I'd had any headaches or violent seizures recently. I had not, but it seemed the suspicious little dot could be a tumor in the making. More tests would be required, through my primary-care physician in New York. Oh, and it also seemed that I had a cataract in each eye.

I left the clinic in Charlestown before they could diagnose me with malaria or dengue hemorrhagic fever. It took most of a month to get a more detailed CAT scan and learn the results. I didn't really think I had a brain tumor, since I didn't have any symptoms. I told myself, half-joking, "I cannot get two brain diseases in the same year." But I knew enough now not to try to outguess the tests, and the waiting began to drag on me. A few days into the new year, I went to get those cataracts looked at. They proved to be no real problem, so small now there was nothing to be done but wait for them to grow. Still, coming back from my ophthalmologist's, I could barely see through my dilated pupils; struggling to dial the number on my cell phone for the MRI results that were due back that same day. Staggering blindly up Riverside Drive on a blustery January day, the wind whipping at my face and hair, I had to laugh, thinking how my life was turning into a road production of *King Lear*.

This time, the news was good. I didn't have a brain tumor. The little white dot was nothing at all. One brain disease to a

customer. There was life, there was hope. There was the recognition that all I was going through—the torment of an
aging parent, the knowledge that I would likely follow in her
footsteps—was really nothing that unusual in our America of
aging seniors and genetic testing. What was to be done but to
make the most of it?

Back at home, I looked at the scan with my wife. "I'm going
to miss that brain," she said.

"I know," I told her. "I'm going to miss me too."

MARGO JEFFERSON

DEATH WISH IN NEGROLAND

The boys in Negroland learned early how to die. They started in their teens, dying in period rec rooms with wood paneling and pool tables, train sets, golf clubs, liquor cabinets. Did Father keep a rifle on the wall there, or did the son find his old army gun in the bedroom closet and sneak it downstairs? There, in the rec room, an amiable, well-mannered doctor's son shot himself. Motive, unknown; verdict, accidental death; time, not long after his father was arrested for assaulting his second wife. A few years later, in another rec room, a sweet-faced doctor's son with a soft voice did the same. Suspected motive: he feared going the way of his father, sweet-faced, soft-voiced, seductively effusive, and (suspiciously) no longer married.

Vietnam opened other routes to self-extinction. A Negro boy could drop out of college, enlist, and come home a junkie. He could drink, shoot up, steal for several years, pawn his grandmother's silver, asssault a homeless man, and evade a jail sentence because his parents, both doctors, knew the judge. He could retire to the family homestead in Virginia, decline steadily in health, and die of kidney failure.

Negroland was a small region of Negro America in which children were sheltered by privilege and plenty. They were warned by their parents that few Negroes enjoyed privilege or plenty, and that most non-Negro Americans would be glad to see them returned to indigence, deference, and subservience.

Their parents made sure to supply them with well-appointed homes and apartments, tasteful clothes and plenty of them, handsome cars, generous allowances, sailboats, summer camps, music and dance lessons, flying lessons, private schools, tutors, and an array of clubs where other children exactly like them met for splash parties, hayrides, ski trips, theater excursions, and Christmas visits to old people's homes to sing carols.

Nevertheless, life in Negroland meant that any conversation could be taken over by the White Man at any moment. He dominated army stories about the brown-skinned Negro officer who'd had to escort his angry unit to the shabby back cars of a segregated train; the light-skinned Negro officer who'd been given the last seat in the white section of a train until he said he was a Negro, whereupon a porter (another brown-skinned Negro) was sent to find a curtain that could separate him from the Caucasian in front and join him to the Negro behind.

When he's not lynching you, he's humiliating you, said the men at the dinner table. They leaned forward and raised their voices, then subsided into their chairs, shook their heads, let out a *hmmnnnn. He keeps us out of his hospitals, his law firms, his universities. Even his damn cemeteries. He never lets you forget you're a second-class citizen.*

Privilege and prosperity let you forget. Cocktail parties and dinner dances urged you to forget. So did season tickets to the opera, summer trips to the Caribbean and Mexico. The family together watching *Ed Sullivan*, watching *Gunsmoke* and *Maver-*

ick, watching *Playhouse 90* and outstanding cultural productions like *Peter Pan* and *The Nutcracker*. Suavely complicated marriages and urbane extramarital liaisons; hushed quarrels at the breakfast table. Fathers at the office, at the fraternity house, coming home late so many nights. Mothers picking the children up from school, shopping, planning meals, lunching with friends, working to safeguard their marriages.

La Vie Bourgeoisie.

Round up the usual Oedipal conflicts and divided loyalties. Fathers, insist that your sons become high-achieving Negroes, prepared, like you, to push their way manfully past every obstacle. How are they to do this? Force of will. You did.

But the boys had started dying.

Negroland girls couldn't die outright. We had to plot and circle our way toward death, pretend we were after something else, like being ladylike, being popular, being loved. Between the late 1940s to the mid-1960s, Good Negro Girls mastered the rigorous vocabulary of femininity. Gloves, handkerchiefs, pocketbooks, for each occasion. Good diction for all occasions; skin care (no ashy knees or elbows); hair cultivation (a ceaseless round of treatments to eradicate the bushy and nappy). Manners to please grandparents and quell the doubts of any white strangers loitering to observe our behavior in schools, stores, and restaurants.

We were busy being pert, chic, cool but not fast. Fast meant social extermination by degrees, because the boys who'd sampled a fast girl would tell another girl they'd taken up with (who was desirable but not fast) that the first girl was a slut. The

boys knew this because she'd made the mistake of being fast
with more than one boy, so they'd talked about her with one
another. And then her girlfriends talked about her with each
other. They were still cordial to her at parties. She wasn't put
out of her clubs. But if she weren't already in the Etta Quettes
or the Co-Ettes, she wasn't asked in.

Occasionally, a daughter who'd been silly enough to get
herself pregnant would actually drop out of college, have the
child, and marry its father. That meant she had disgraced herself
and her family. In fact, she had committed matricide: she had
destroyed the good reputation her mother, her grandmothers,
and her grandmothers' grandmothers had fought for since slav-
ery. Premature sexual activity and pregnancy out of wedlock?
She was just another statistic to be held against the race.

The world had to upend itself before shades of possibility
between decorum and disgrace could emerge. Suddenly, people like us were denouncing war and imperialism, discarding
the strategic protocol of Civil Rights for the combat aggression
of Black Power. We remade our pristine diction, unmade our
straightened hair, renounced our social niceties and snobberies.

The entitlements of Negroland were no longer relevant.

Good Negro Girls in search of lives their parents hadn't
lived had to seek men their parents didn't know and didn't care
to know. Naturally, errors were made. The doctor's daughter
studying architecture married a man with suspected ties to the
drug trade; within the year, she was shot in the head from
behind and left beside her murdered husband, a large pool of
blood widening in what *Jet* magazine called their "affluent
South Side home." The dark-skinned daughter of socially
responsible educators—who left her Paris career as a provoca-
tively keen-featured model with exorbitant long limbs to teach

early childhood education at an Illinois community college—
was stabbed multiple times in the head and neck by an estranged
husband who then drove her body to the police station and
turned himself in, telling the officer simply, "I just went crazy."

Average American women were killed like this every day.
But we weren't raised to be average women; we were raised to
be better than most women of either race. White women, our
mothers reminded us pointedly, could afford more of these
casualties. There were more of them, weren't there?

There were always more white people. There were so few of
us, and it had cost so much to construct us. Why were we
dying?

The first of the dying boys succumbed to the usual perils of
family life—the unkind, philandering father, the kind but
closeted father, the absent or insufficient mother. Then came
the boys who threw off privilege and lusted for street life, imi-
tating the slip-slide walks of the guys who lounged on street-
corners in caps and leather coats, practicing the raucous
five-stage laugh (clap, fold at the waist, run forward, arms in
loose boxing position, squat and return to loose standing position), working as hard as any white boy at a frat party to sound
like Bo Diddley and Otis Redding. Striving ardently to be
what they were and were not.

Behold the Race Flâneur: the bourgeois rebel who goes
slumming and finds not just adventure but the objective cor-
relative for his secret despair.

I won't absolve the girls. We played ghetto too, tried to jump
double Dutch as well as the dark-skinned girls from the other

end of the block who wore red nail polish by the age of nine and made fun of things they didn't like by loudly sneering *Ooo-oooo-OOO! Un-unn-UNNNH* . . . We rolled and cut our eyes to show disdain, flung putdowns like *You must be on dope!* But the boys ruled. We were just aspiring adornments, and how could it be otherwise? The Negro man was at the center of the culture's extravagant race obsessions. The Negro woman was on the shabby fringes. She had moments if she were in show business; of course, we craved the erotic command of Tina Turner, the arch insolence of Diana Ross, the melismatic authenticity of Aretha. But in life, when a Good Negro Girl attached herself to a ghetto boy hoping to go street and compensate for her bourgeois privilege, if she didn't get killed with or by him she lived to become a socially disdained, financially disabled black woman destined to produce at least one baby she would have to care for alone.

What was the matter with us? Were we plagued by some monstrous need, some vestigial longing to plunge back into the abyss Negroes had been consigned to for centuries? Was this some variant of survivor guilt? No, that phrase is too generic. I'd call it the guilty confusion of those who were raised to defiantly accept their entitlement, to be more than survivors, to be victors who knew that victory was as much a threat as failure, and could be turned against them at any moment.

In 1937, James Weldon Johnson wrote a diagnosis of this condition that reads like an epitaph. Johnson was a worldly stoic who, along with with W. E. B. Du Bois and Alain Locke, fathered the modern Negro as thinker, artist, political strategist, and cultural theorist. And I feel a shudder whenever I read this passage from his autobiography, *Along This Way*. Calm yet tense with restraint, Johnson describes the grave dilemma that faces all Negro parents.

Awaiting each colored child are cramping limitations and buttressed obstacles in addition to those that must be met by youth in general. How judicious he is. Yet, implacably, this dilemma approaches suffering, *in exact proprotion to the parent's knowledge of these conditions, and the child's ignorance of them. Some parents try to spare their children this bitter knowledge as long as possible. Less sensitive parents (those maimed by their own bitterness) drive it into the child from infancy on.*

At each turn, Johnson forgoes high rhetorical drama. He chooses "this dilemma" over "our burden," prefers our "condition" to our "fate," and comes at last, with stately tread, to *And no parent may definitely say which is the wiser course, for either of them may lead to spiritual disaster for the child.* Tragedy has arrived and is content to wait quietly. In time, it may be able to claim both parent and child.

Those of us who avoided disaster encountered life's usual rewards, pleasures, obstacles, and limitations. And if we were still marked by a longing for death, we had to make it compatible with this new pattern of living.

In the late 1970s, I began to experience and actively cultivate a desire to kill myself. I was, at that time, a successful professional in my chosen field of journalism. I was also a passionate feminist who refused to admit any contradiction between, on the one hand, my commitment to fighting the oppression of women and, on the other, my belief that feminism would let me draft a death commensurate with social achievement and political awareness.

A little background is needed here. The women's movement was controversial in the black community at this time. Many men and all too many women denounced feminism as a white woman's thing, an indulgence, even an assertion of privilege, since she was competing (and stridently) for the limited share of benefits white men had just begun to grant nonwhites. Black feminists responded that, thanks to sexism, women of color regularly got double blasts of discrimination and oppression. And, anyway, we had our own feminist history. Relations between white and black women had been wary, inequitable, or bluntly exploitative. Alliances between them had been scant and fraught.

Nevertheless, social and cultural progress through the decades had made interracial cooperation and friendship available to my generation. I'd had white friends since kindergarten. And I was willing to acknowledge this irony: the rituals of bourgeois femininity had given the girls of Negroland certain protections the boys lacked. A vision of feral, fascinating black manhood obsessed Americans of every race and class. There was no equivalent for black women. If you were a successful, upper-middle-class girl in the 1950s and '60s you were, in practice and imagination, a white Protestant upper-middle-class girl. Young, good-looking white women were the most desirable creatures in the world. It was hard not to want to imitate them; it was highly toxic too, as we would learn. Still, these rituals allowed girls the latitude to go about their studies while being pert and popular, to stay well mannered and socially adaptable, even as they joined the protests of the sixties and seventies.

So, when the black movement and the women's movement offered new social and cultural opportunities, we were ready to accept them.

But one white female privilege had always been withheld from the girls of Negroland. Aside from the privilege of actually being white, they had been denied the privilege of freely yielding to depression, of flaunting neurosis as a mark of social and psychic complexity. A privilege that was glorified in the literature of white female suffering and resistance. A privilege Good Negro Girls had been denied by our history of duty, obligation, and discipline. Because our people had endured horrors and prevailed, even triumphed, their descendants should be too strong and too proud for such behavior. We were to be ladies, responsible Negro women, and indomitably Strong Black Women.

I craved the right to turn my face to the wall, to create a death commensurate with bourgeois achievement, political awareness, and aesthetically compelling feminine despair. My first forays in this direction were petty. I conducted my own small battle of the books, purging my library of stalwart, valorous titles by black women and replacing them, wherever possible, with morbid, truculent ones. Out with *This Child's Gonna Live,* up with *There's Nothing I Own That I Want.* Goodbye *My Lord, What a Morning* by the virtuous Marian Anderson; hello *Everything and Nothing* by the wanton Dorothy Dandridge. As for Mari Evans's iconic sixties poem, *I Am a Black Woman* (impervious/indestructible), I tore it out of my black poets' anthology and set fire to it in the bathroom sink.

I found literary idols in Nella Larsen, Adrienne Kennedy, and Ntozake Shange, writers who'd dared to locate a sanctioned, forbidden space between white purity and black invincibility. A Negro girl could never be purely innocent. The vengeful Race Fairy always lurked nearby; your parents' best hope was that the fairy would show up at someone else's feast and punish *their* child. Parents had to protect themselves too, and protect you from knowing how much danger you were all in.

And so arose one variation on the classic Freudian primal scene in which the child sees or imagines her parents having sex and finds it stirringly violent; here the child sees and imagines her parents having fraught encounters with white people who invade their conversation and shadow their lives beyond the boundaries of home or neighborhood.

Work hard, child. Internalize the figures of your mother, your father, your parents (one omnipotent double-gendered personage). Internalize the Race. Internalize both races. Then internalize the contradictions. Teach your psyche to adapt its solo life to a group obbligato. Or else let it abandon any impulse toward independence and hurtle toward a feverishly perfect representation of your people.

The first unapologetic black female suicide took place in a small Off-Broadway theater in 1964, in a taut gothic play by a fiercely imaginative Negro woman playwright. I wasn't there, but I understood that Adrienne Kennedy's *Funnyhouse of a Negro* was as much a demand for freedom as the Civil Rights bill passed the same year. Kennedy's heroine, Negro-Sarah, was a young middle-class woman, *good-looking in a boring way; no glaring Negroid features, medium nose, medium mouth, and pale yellow skin. My one defect is that I have a head of frizzy hair, unmis-*

takably Negro kinky hair . . . She lives alone in an Upper West Side brownstone, longs to be bohemian and distinctive, fears she is merely drab and decorous. She mistrusts her white poet boyfriend: *He is very interested in Negroes.* She mistrusts her own passion for white culture. Its great works have no place for her; its great figures would deem her an insignificant cultural arriviste. One woman, one room, one anguished, polyphonic consciousness. Queen Victoria and the Duchess of Hapsburg prowl her psyche, lamenting the awful curse of blackness. Patrice Lumumba and a shadowy black father are there, too; they struggle and fail to lift that curse. At the play's end, the light goes black, then blazes white. *The poor bitch has hung herself,* says the landlady. *She was a funny little liar,* adds the boyfriend.

Negro-Sarah embodies our Negroland legacy of proscription and privilege, grief and achievement, a mingled love and shame for our people, a mingled love and terror of white culture. And then (as if the result of these others), despair and a furious will to extinguish the self. My people's enemies have done this to me. But so have my own loved ones. My enemies took too much. My loved ones asked too much. Let me say with care that the blame is not symmetrical: my enemies *forced* my loved ones to ask too much of me.

Nella Larsen's 1920s novels were republished in the late sixties and early seventies, part of an exuberant rush of books by women, by gays, by nonwhites of every hue, that the culture had contentedly left out of print for years. Some of these books appeared in pleasingly well-wrought editions. Larsen's were among those given the cheapest paper and crudest design publishers could get away with. Her own heroines would have disdained to buy them.

For they are touchy and proud, these Jazz Age heroines. They read widely, wear soignée frocks, give smart parties, and make clever remarks. They have keen minds, keen features, fair skin, and can be suitably ironic about *what called itself Negro society*. They cultivate the advantages of being New Negroes and New Women; sometimes they even indulge in being New Negroes who can pass for white. They pursue La Vie Bourgeoisie with too much anxiety or too much ambivalence. Their sexual allure trips them up; their sexual reserve holds them back. They are timid where they should be bold, reckless when diplomacy is needed. Secretly, they feel contempt for their own failure to imagine anything more for themselves. Each one finds death of some kind: a lethal marriage, a fatal accident. But their longing for death, the drive toward it, is never quite acknowledged. Larsen's women stumble into suicide by misadventure or miscalculation. They avoid premeditation, just as they avoid stringent self-reflection.

So, when Ntozake Shange stood on the stage of the Public Theater in 1975 and spoke the words *And this is for colored girls who have considered suicide*, my heart took flight. We were the same age. We were both doctors' daughters who'd attacked our girlhood gentility with the blunt weapons of black power and radical feminism. Now we colored could consider—toy with, ponder, contemplate—suicide. I tried to quash my envy by seeing the play two, three, and four times, taking friends and paying for their tickets. I told myself, *Ntozake is laying the groundwork for all black feminists. She's taken her stand as an artist, while you hide behind being a journalist. You must rid yourself of jealousy. You hate the second-raters who quibble with the brave ones.* I'd always derided Anne Sexton's suicide competitions with Sylvia Plath. *Thief,* Sexton wrote, *how did you crawl into, / crawl down alone / into the death I wanted so badly and for so long . . . ?* Maybe because Plath had more nerve and wrote better poetry, was my answer.

I channeled my envy into aesthetic dissatisfaction with the words that followed. *For colored girls who have considered suicide* when *the rainbow is enuf,* they went. *For colored girls who are moving to the ends of their personal rainbows.* I found the rainbow overused and trite, even if it was an honored symbol in every culture, an honored trope of lyric poetry. When I'd finished this spiteful formalist critique, I was left alone with my fury. Ntozake said we had found God in ourselves and loved her fiercely. I hadn't and I didn't.

I knew that unrequited death is as futile as unrequited love. *You must take hold,* I told myself. *You are suffering the long-term effects of profound fatigue. This is the result of all the work, the years of work required to be wholly normal and wholly exceptional. You must set an example for other Negroland girls who suffer the same way.*

You must give them a death they can live up to.

GREG BOTTOMS

GRACE STREET

> The world dies over and over again,
> but the skeleton always gets up and walks.
>
> —HENRY MILLER

DOG'S LIFE

My neighbor, the guy across the street, says, "Have you ever had it with a man?"

Fall, 1993. I'm twenty-two, broke, living on a poor block of Grace Street in Richmond, Virginia.

He's sitting on his stoop, identical to my blistered, gray stoop and all the other stoops along this street of row houses dating back to the late nineteenth century. His brown Pekinese curls on his lap like a big combed rat, as it has every morning for the two months I've lived here. His eyes are red and rimmed. His lipstick is smeared. He's wearing his usual green dress and white wig, and he looks like a chubby Andy Warhol on the wrong side of a bender. I smell him—faintly sour; stomach lining and citrus. But I drink as much as he does lately, maybe more; in recent weeks I've been trying to vacate discomfort with booze, which works only temporarily, if at all.

My neighbor's bare feet—very delicate, almost sickly—glow white, much like the feet of my dead father, which I looked at for almost an hour only weeks ago.

"No," I say. "I've never had sex with a man, if that's what you mean."

A sad come-on, I think. It's happened before, men gauging me, wanting a quick entwining of physical selves. But I'm hetero as far as I can tell from my fantasies. I'm also sick with death, as if sprayed by its mist. I want to say I was in bed with a man recently, and a dead one, I laid with him under covers, kissed his cool, waxy face, can still smell him if I concentrate.

I try to look calm, in a hurry, though I'm unemployed and there is nothing I need to do, nowhere I need to go.

"You like my dog," he says. Where is this going? "You look at her. You never pet her. You could pet her, you know. She is a lady. She is fine and wondrously gentle. She does not bite. You could come put your hand over here, just here, right behind her ear, and pet her."

I hesitate, look around: a couple of black teens in full hip-hop garb coming down the sidewalk; an old Asian woman in a frock and high-top basketball shoes across the street; the dirty brick of building faces; the yellow-striped stretch of weathered asphalt heading down the hill, toward the shallow, burbling James River. I take a few steps toward him and lean over and pet the dog on his lap. The dog licks my hand, a warm, wet touch.

After a moment, I smile and make as if to turn and cross the street in the direction of my place.

Shadows of old trees stretch out across the parked cars and

meters. Wet red and yellow leaves stick to the sidewalks and curbs. The hum and rumble of engines, the squeak of brakes. Faces passing by in bus windows.

"I bet you think I like men because I dress like this," he says. "Hold on. Don't walk away. What's your hurry? Where's the fire? Let me get my sunglasses out of my purse so I can look at you in this light." He puts on a pair of giant black glasses, the kind Jackie Kennedy used to get photographed in. "I'm telling you about my dog, how I got her, why I have her. And I'm telling you not to judge someone a fag." He flops his hand forward, mockingly.

The Pekinese sneezes and shifts, puts a paw over and then under her nose.

When he was a boy, he says, living in his momma's house outside of Greenville, South Carolina, he always had small dogs because his momma loved them. His momma also loved men. One of the men his momma loved did not love himself so therefore did not know how to love or show love and he beat on my neighbor's momma when he drank and he beat on my neighbor, just a boy then, when he drank and he beat on and kicked the little dogs in the house when he drank. The dogs hated him, hid under couches, scurried out dog doors when they heard his boots. *Clop-clop. Clop-clop.*

One late afternoon when my neighbor was a teenager, fourteen or fifteen, he can't exactly remember, and the man his momma loved even though he beat on her and beat on her son and beat on her dogs had moved away, one of the man's old friends came by to see if the man was there. My neighbor doesn't describe the friend of the man who beat his momma and beat the dogs and beat him, but I imagine, as I stand listening, a white man, a scruffy beard, an old baseball cap, a flannel shirt and jeans—maybe I'm stereotyping. No one was home but my neighbor. The dogs all ran. My neighbor told the friend no one was home and the man he had come looking for had not lived in that house for more than a year and his momma was at work on the night shift but would be home soon and if the visitor called back later on the phone—he stressed *on the phone*—she could tell the friend where the man who used to beat him and his momma and the dogs was.

The friend came into the house. He wanted in. Said something, was in.

He did not force my neighbor—my neighbor (sun shining, traffic whizzing by, dog almost purring) is clear to state and restate this as he tells the story; there was nothing illegal in what happened; he, my neighbor, participated and is not now making a complaint or offering an excuse for anything—but the friend did talk to him and walk into him and breathe on him and whisper softly and my neighbor, later, would decide that that was not what he had wanted, not at all, but at the time he was a teenager in a house in a hard life and the man's friend had walked out of his own hard life and into my neighbor's hard life—little dogs yelping out back, furious and scared— and was not, in that moment, rough but was in fact gentle, even kind, there was sweet talk, and my neighbor, back then, could not say what he wanted really, other than something different than what he had and all he had known his whole life.

This was different. This was new. He would be someone new.

Later, after the friend had left—he never called back and my neighbor never told his momma about any of this, and she died a long time ago, died of cancer like my father, without knowing the story I am hearing—he took a long hot bath to get the

sweat-smell of the man off of him and there was blood in the
water, and he felt a sharp, burning pain and there was swelling
and he thought he might be seriously hurt down there because
of all this pink water. I see an awkward teenage boy in a house
alone in pink bath water. He becomes my neighbor twenty
years later in a green dress and white wig and oversized sunglasses on a bright morning.

"What," he says, sliding his sunglasses down the bridge of
his nose, "does this have to do with a dog is what I bet you are
thinking. Well, that's what I'm going to tell you." He rubs the
dog's back. The dog stretches.

I wait. My hands are shaking.

"After that, after the bath," he says, "I took my momma's
dogs for a walk. I had a head full of new thoughts. It was dark.
It was hard to walk. The dogs were a comfort. The dogs could
be trusted. A dog loves you and is your best friend and if you
do right by it, it will do right by you. It will comfort you. That
is decency, neighbor. Aspiring to the life of a dog. We should
all be dogs, if you ask me."

I don't see the point of his story. But he's at the end of a
drunk, a real slurry bender, and language is an imperfect tool
in the best of circumstances.

"You look at me," he says. "Maybe you judge me—I mean,
look at you; you're young. I bet you miss your momma [I do].
I bet you miss your home [I do]. I bet you have a sad little story
[I do]. Maybe you know about being alone in a house [I do].
We all do. My story, your story. Who cares, really? Maybe you
think when you see me, 'Hey, there's the fag and his little faggy
dog again. I'll wave to the fag and his faggy dog as I walk past
because I'm a nice, decent person just passing through and I
even wave to fags, I'm so *enlightened* and all.'"

His eyes are just visible behind the lenses, blinking.

I nod. The dog stirs, settles. I begin to turn around.

"Don't think you know me, boy," he says. "You don't know a thing, not a damn thing. I don't even like men. I don't like men so much I didn't want to be one anymore. So I got rid of the part of me that wanted men and I got rid of the part of me that was a man. And all I had to do was get a wig and a cheap dress and move away once my momma died and left me a little money! Anyone can do it! Come on, you try!" He almost spits these last words. *"Ta-da!"*

I put up a hand, still shaking—some lame wave—and turn around and start walking back toward my new apartment across the street, where I have a mattress, some books, some CDs, and a roach problem.

"I didn't tell you why I have my dog," he yells.

"I think I understand," I say over my shoulder.

"No you don't!" he shouts, "No you don't! No you don't!" and I hear him laughing the whole way back to my place, and it only stops when I shut the humidity-swollen wooden door behind me like the lid of a heavy coffin.

SOMETHING SMALL

Another neighbor, a laid-off mechanic, digs up the bush in his narrow, gravelly side yard and places it at the end of the alley entrance between our buildings.

I walk over to inspect it. It's partially blocking my vehicle, a sputtering blue Dodge Raider parked back in the alley.

My neighbor walks out of his bottom-floor apartment, letting the hole-poked screen slam shut behind him, as if he's been waiting. He's forty, forty-five, wears beat-up work clothes and has an untrimmed mustache that makes me want to write the word "crustacean" in the little notebook I carry around. He's now working part-time as a skilled laborer for a plumbing company—digging trenches, clearing clogged toilets—is scraping by, but he hates the job, the little know-it-alls telling him what to do. He loves talking, though, is outright *loquacious*, and often stops me when I come home or go out. He's lonely—who isn't?—though he's married and I can usually see the back of his wife's head in their window as she watches TV for most of the day and into the evening. He says hello, like "yell-o," glances at the bush.

"What happened?" I ask.

"Bush was scaring the baby."

"The baby?"

"My grandbaby, a girl."

"A grandbaby?"

"Yeah," he says. "My son had a baby. His girlfriend, I mean. She had the baby."

"Didn't know you had a son."

"Long story."

What can I say? "Congratulations."

He makes an unsure grunting sound. I regret my comment. He tells me how he got the baby, why he dug up the bush.

He received a call from his son's girlfriend's grandmother. That's how it started. The grandmother of the girlfriend, who had raised the girlfriend because the mother was gone, or dead, or something—I can't quite understand this part because he seems to have some of the details mixed up and he's talking fast—called my neighbor to deliver the news that she (the grandmother of the girlfriend, the great-grandmother of the baby) and he and his wife were going to need to take care of the baby in the short term, until something could be worked out with either social services or, possibly, the parents. There was a baby. It needed taking care of. They could take turns. The grandmother, he says, had gone to her granddaughter's trailer because the granddaughter and my neighbor's son, who is eighteen, were fighting almost constantly since bringing the baby home from the hospital. The grandmother "got a bad feeling" after getting off the phone with them, the baby screaming in the background the whole time, and went over to the trailer in the morning to see how things were going, if she could help. When she arrived, she found the infant in a battery-operated baby swing in the small kitchen, sitting in her own waste, which was spilling out of her diaper and onto the floor. The granddaughter and my neighbor's son were sleeping in the bedroom with the door shut and the stereo up loud enough so they couldn't hear the child's crying. The child, too young to hold her head up, too small to fit properly in the plastic seat, had been in the swing all night and had badly rashed legs from the sitting. She was slumped sideways and exhausted. The grandmother thought of calling the cops, to show her granddaughter a lesson, but just yelled at the parents, packed a bag, and took the baby home instead, with no objection from the young couple, who stood chastened and bewildered and wondering what to do as the baby slept in her great-grandmother's arms.

"A couple of *children*," he says. "Two kids leaving a baby in a swing all night in a cold kitchen." He shakes his head. "We have her for now. She's a beautiful child. My son—he hasn't come to see her. Hasn't called. He wants her to be someone else's problem, my problem, his mom's problem. He wants to get some pussy, that's all, just a little pussy. He needs an ass whooping, that boy. If he was here right now, I'd beat his damn ass. I'd beat his goddamn ass." He smacks his hands together, says, "God*damn*it, boy" and a little clapping echo bounces off the row houses across the street.

There are questions. But what am I, some kind of reporter? I can't ask them. Really, I should get away from a person this emotional. I'm a little too close to the fire as it is. I look back at the bush.

"Last night, when the wind was going," he says, "the branches were scratching the screen of the baby's room and keeping her up. I went out and kicked it down. I hope you didn't hear all that. If you did, I'm sorry. She was screaming for a while. I lost my thinking cap, you know. I was ready to do whatever it took." He grimaces, embarrassed. "I beat the hell out of the bush. Broke every bone in its body." Shakes his head. "I went out this morning and dug it up because it was crushed. Pretty well smashed to bits. Looked awful. I'm going to tell the landlord it was dying of some kind of disease or something, or that it had poison ivy on it, choking it. So if he asks . . ."

"Sure," I say. "Not to worry."

After a long stare at the bush, he says his son's girlfriend's grandmother will probably take the baby. "She had to work a double shift this week, though, so we've got her for now. Lot of work to have a baby around. Twenty-four seven. You forget. I think she can get a pretty good check from the state if she goes to court and gets custody. Best if the baby goes with her, I think. A great-grandmother raising a baby? My son ain't worth a damn, is he?"

I ignore the question. "Good luck," I say.

"Before she goes," he says, stopping me before I turn, "we're going to get her baptized at our church. I don't go to church

but my wife does and I'm going to go for this, you know. It's
the right thing to do."

I nod.

"That way," he says, and his voice almost cracks, "no matter
what happens to her from here on out, I mean no matter what
goes on in her life, even when she's grown up, you know, she'll
be protected."

A siren blares as lights doppler by and keep going.

"Anyway," he says, "my buddy's coming over with his truck
and we're going to take this bush and some scrap wood I have
out back to the landfill. If you got anything needs dumping,
anything small, I can take it."

Thanks, I say, but I don't have anything small that needs
dumping.

IT'S LIKE

Near my place is a halfway house, where a couple of schizo-
phrenics live. One, a big black guy, calls himself Adolph. The
other is a small South Asian girl, Indian or Pakistani. She's
maybe seventeen, named Chan, short for Chandra. I know
they are schizophrenic, or supposedly schizophrenic, and I
know their names because a social worker stopped me on the
sidewalk one day to tell me. He said if they acted a little strange,
that's okay, that's normal—or not normal, but, you know, to be
expected. They are on strict medical regiments with antipsy-
chotic prescriptions, and part of his job is to police their drug-
taking. Sometimes the mentally ill get the idea the meds they
are forced to take are not good for them, are making them
sicker than they already are, or sick in different and equally bad
ways—like maybe you take Haldol and stop hearing voices but

you can't go to the bathroom for a week or sleep, or you get really fat and your hands twitch as you try to get your cigarette to your mouth, or you get tortured by an unquenchable thirst and your tongue is just this leathery, swollen thing in the way of your breath and cottony residue collects around your lips. I told the social worker fine by me, I didn't mind mentally ill people. I said I acted a little strange too, especially if you considered talking to yourself and gesticulating to a room full of imagined people, an invisible audience of rapt listeners, strange, which I do all the time. He stared, realizing, probably, that he needn't have bothered talking to me, I didn't live next door and I had no power, no will to file a complaint, and thus no relevance to any of this, to anything at all.

ADOLPH

"So why do you call yourself Adolph?" I ask. The social worker told me his real name is Terrence. It's raining. He's wearing a gray trash bag over his dirty clothes, arms sticking out of two jagged, knife-cut holes. Big, brown-rimmed, rain-dropped glasses enlarge his eyes. I have mental illness in my family. Schizophrenia, bipolar disorder, depression. I get it better than most. I read a lot. I write. I can speak in metaphor. I want to say, It's like falling down a dark hole, isn't it, and then staring back up at everyone's tiny little leering face, so terribly far away. Or: It's like being on stage and having a heavy velvet curtain drop between you and everything you care about and you can't figure out how to get off this dark fucking stage and back to the part of the world where the people who *aren't* actors are. Or: It's like standing on the edge of a building and looking down, isn't it, and getting stuck in the moment just before your

heart jerks and every cell claps and gravity eats the space
between you and your thudding death, only it never quite happens, you just wait and wait and wait with skipping eyes and
teeth like diamond crushers too close to that big, dry tongue.
Who can function—what superhero could function—while
stuck in a moment like that?

"It's my name," he says.

"Okay."

"Yeah."

"That's a German name."

"I'm German."

"Oh."

"You don't believe me?" He pauses, looks right into my
eyes. "Who you calling black?" His fists close and open.

"Nobody," I say. Hands up, palms open. "I didn't say
anything."

"I'm German," he says. "Look around this place, man. If I
was black, I wouldn't take this. I'd burn some stuff down, dude.
This place, this city, is *racist*. When I was in jail, it was filled
with blacks. There are like ten white people out of a hundred
in city lockup. Think about it: are you telling me ninety out of
a hundred crimes are committed by black men? *Sheeeeit*."

"No," I say. "Of course."

"Before I lived here, I lived down in South America, in
Argentina. Beautiful, beautiful country, dude. And before that
the motherland, the rolling meadows of Germany. My father
was an Australian Austrian." He starts laughing.

"Where will you go when you leave here?"

"Why would I leave here? I mean, look around you, dude.
I got ideas. I got vision. There is money to be made here.
Green."

"I just mean the house," I say. "When you leave the house."

"Who said I had to leave the house? Who you been talking to, dude? What is this all about? What's with all these questions? You a cop? You talking to that social worker again? He can't kick me out of here long as I'm behaving. That guy is trying to *poison* me just like they did in *prison*."

CHAN

"What are you listening to?" I ask Chan as I walk by.

She's on the halfway's porch, smoking as usual, headphones on her ears, which she removes. She's looking down at me on the sidewalk. She often waves to people. She's small, like a black-haired doll almost, with delicate features. If she took a shower, washed the nervous sweat from her body, and untangled her hair, she might be beautiful. As it is, she's too busy with something going on inside her to tie her shoes.

She says, "My father. He's dead."

"You have a tape of him?"

"No. He speaks between the words of Stevie Wonder."

"What does he say?"

"I can't tell. It's the sound of his voice, but far away, and in the old language. These things, me and him, it's just impossible. He was a doctor, so you don't know where to place your trust, inside or outside, in the body or the mind. What pocket is the right pocket, you want to know. And what, what, what are you going to put in there? If you get a chance."

"Is it always there, his voice?"

"No. His voice lives near Stevie Wonder and is a thin whistling cloud and anyone can see the dark wind is almost always blowing in here."

CAR FOR SALE

I get on the bus one afternoon.

I walked out into the west end of the city, through the sun-speckled shadows of statues and old trees, out past the last row houses, through the boutiquey part of town—past mannequins dressed for the evening, past BUY ONE GET SECOND FOR HALF cigarette specials, past a homeless man in a ragged topcoat and newspaper hat shuffling by a McDonald's drive-thru window, a line of cars waiting for him to *move out of the way*—one foot in the front of the other, trying not to think about my dead father, thinking about nothing else—death all around me, embedded in every symbol and scene, pushing me constantly toward the narcissism of grief, some tiny little room at the center of self—and then, hours later, I was in the suburbs, among tract houses and half-empty strip malls, the soles of my feet numb. A thunderstorm rose up gray-purple out of the south like a mood. I couldn't walk back in this wind and beating rain, so I took cover in a shed-sized box with a metal sign of a bus screwed into the side of it. The bus came, tires separating puddles as if tearing dark fabric.

I sit beside an elderly white man. He has thin gray hair, wears a plaid, short-sleeve shirt. I say hello. He smiles. Pink gums where teeth used to be. Brown splotches on white skin like Alaska and the Aleutian Islands.

Track lighting and the dark day tint everything green, and I feel not so much as if I'm bumping along on the bus as watching an amateur film for which the camera hasn't been held steadily.

All the other passengers—maybe fifteen people, and all several seats away from the old white man and me, behind us—are black, as is the driver, the only person up front. I feel self-conscious, even before I'm settled in the seat, about how I seem to have chosen, without thinking, a place beside the one other white person here.

The old white man says, "I lost my car."

I say, "I don't want to walk in the rain."

We need to say why we're on the bus with all the poor people.

"Boy stole it," he says.

"Your car?"

"Yessir." There is a faint whistle when his tongue hits his gums over the *s* sound.

"Sorry to hear that."

He parked his car, an old Ford sedan, on the lawn of a friend's house, near the highway. He put a FOR SALE sign in the window. "That way," he says, "lots of folks saw it as they drove by. Good way to advertise."

"Sure," I say. "Makes sense." I look out the window at the wet city blocks gliding by, not feeling up to talking.

His friend called one day and said a "colored fella" had been coming around, looking in the windows of the car. Just walking right into the yard. "A black boy," he says, "walking right into a white man's yard. How 'bout that?"

The temperature rises in my face. I don't want the other riders to hear him, to associate me with someone who says "boy" to describe black men.

The engine sends a loud humming noise through the gray metal around us. I look back. No one seems to hear us. Everyone sits quietly, stares ahead or out the windows.

"So I go out there to my friend's one afternoon 'cause the black boy's around again," he says.

He met the man, shook hands, asked if he was interested in the car.

The black man wanted to test-drive it. The old white man didn't feel good about letting a "colored boy" drive the car, so he asked if he could see his license, hold onto it during the drive, "like they do at car lots." Afterward, the black man could either buy the car or take his license back and decide not to.

He looks around the bus. He leans forward with his elbows on his knees and clasps his hands together. Quieter now, he says, "But the boy didn't have his license on him, see."

The black man asked the old white man to drive him to his house so he could get his wallet, which had all his money and his license in it. "I didn't know about that," he says. "That seemed fishy. Why would he look at a car he might want to buy without his wallet?" But he wanted to sell the car, which his friend had been nice enough to let sit in his yard for over a month, killing a tan spot in the shape of a rectangle. And his friend was "particular" about his yard.

"So I drove on down a road, and then another road, and then another road," he says. They came to a house, a big house set back among trees, and the black man said this was it, this was the house, his house, but his wife was not home—he forgot she had to work today, sorry. The black man asked if maybe they could drive to where the wife worked at a factory not too far away and then he could get the key from her to get into the house, to get his wallet and license and money. So the old white man would have to drive the black man even farther—to now get a key, to then come back to the house, to then get his wallet and license, to then drive the car, to then possibly decide to buy the car. Or not. Hours would be involved.

"Once we got another thirty minutes down the road, toward some factory I'd never heard of, I get ornery," says the old white man as we bump along, rain beating against the rain-dark windows, "I don't want to deal with this anymore. And he's acting real fishy now, you know, getting kind of fidgety." He says he politely asked the black man where would be a good place to drop him off nearby, because now going back to where the black man said he lived was way out of his way in relation to getting back to his own home. He says he wanted to drop the black man off near a pay phone, so he could call someone. The black man became furious then, he says, "just crazy," like he was frightened of something, and started cursing as they were driving, and he, the black man, said he was going to, according to the old white man, cut some "white ass." He pulled out a little Bowie pocketknife and opened it and showed it to the old white man, said, "You ain't leaving me out here!"

The old white man swerved the car over to the side of the road, into some gravel, way back among fields and a few small patches of woods. He jumped out. "I pulled my own damn knife and I says, 'Come on. Cut me if you can.'" They began swinging their respective pocketknives around in the air, neither of which had more than a three- or four-inch blade, cursing one another, saying, "You old white bastard" and "You old black sombitch. I'm going to cut you to bits!" Bugs swarmed in the sweat of the old white man's ears, he says. The car was still running, and the driver's door was open, and the black man, says the old white man, got the idea to jump in and leave the old white man curs- ing and swinging his knife and swatting bugs from around his ears way out on an old country road. I wonder, of course, about the black man's version of this story. I wonder if there is a real villain, or two villains, or if the villain has been mixed up in the telling. I wonder if maybe there are no villains at all, only two people confused and afraid about the other because of forces neither thinks about. I wonder, but I'll never know.

"I never saw that car again," he says.

"Did you report it?"

He says he did, but it was gone. Gone.

I'm suddenly chilled, aware of the cold, damp shoulders of my T-shirt sticking to me. I look around and take note again of all the black people sitting toward the back of the bus, and sitting quietly.

I look at the old white man. And I don't feel like I'm in a film anymore but rather in a dream. I ask, "When did this happen?"

"While ago," he says.

"When?" I insist.

"Seventy-three."

"1973?"

"That's right."

"Twenty years ago?"

He doesn't answer. He looks at me as if my question is ridiculous.

I don't ask anything else. I didn't want to talk in the first place.

I get up at the first stop I recognize, twenty or thirty blocks from my apartment. I step out of the bus into blister-bright sun as if stepping out of a dark moment traveling, unchanged, through time.

YOU KNOW HOW IT IS

"What are you writing?" says the man from behind the counter.

I look around the empty pizza shop, to make sure he's talking to me. "Notes," I say.

He's twenty-five maybe. Dark hair, short beard, thick accent I can't quite place. He stands by the pickup sign and cash register. Behind him, a couple teenage pizza-makers drink sodas from Styrofoam cups.

"Are you writing about my pizza parlor?" he asks.

"No," I say. "Someone told me a story."

"A writer?"

"Not really."

"I knew a writer," he says. "In the army. He looked a little bit like you. Writers—they have a funny way. They look at you and they talk to you and they are doing things but they are somewhere else, you know. The writer I knew in the army, he lived in his head." He points at his ear.

"Where were you in the army?"

"Russia."

"Russia?"

"Yeah. That's right. *Russia*. Right next to Miami Beach." He smiles.

"What did he write?"

"Poems and stories," he says. "Maybe a play too, I forget. I didn't read that one. But the poems were songs. He would write on napkins, on cardboard."

He looks at his palm. I wonder about the poems.

Then he says, "He would talk, my friend the writer, and he was saying war is like this, or the people, you know, were like this, but the way he said it, it all made sense. He could use words and give you a very clear picture. Make you think differently about what was happening."

"He must have been a good writer."

"He was." He leans on the counter. He raises one hand and waves it in the air, a triumphant gesture, like "all this" or "everything" or "the whole world." He says, "He would have maybe become great." He shakes his head.

"What happened to him?"

The front doorbell mechanism *dings* as a few teenagers come in from the bright day. He stands straight up, looks at them, ready to go to work, looks back at me. "Afghanistan. He was talking, you know," he says, "and looking at the world. He was making sense of everything to tell people about it later. He was being a writer. You know how it is. Living up here." He points at his ear again. "So someone shot him."

THE FINAL PLOT

Some writers believe they control their fictional worlds, and nothing else; others that they are conduits for a story—words arrive, characters write themselves. (Few believe they have no control at all over what or how they write.) But even if one can imagine dying or being dead, one can't represent it autobiographically. The impressions and scenes that can be imagined will have been nourished by others' deaths—those witnessed, heard, or read about. (Duchamp's tombstone epitaph, "After all, it's always the other one who dies," means it's always the other's story too.) The way being dead actually feels, a lack of all sensation, supposedly, can't be described, depriving human beings certainty about life's afterlife; but, conversely, fomenting, with death's partner sexual curiosity, a drive for knowledge.

Ones who know they are dying, those physiologically at death's door, and also those who pathologically fear death, might want to rush life's conclusion and kill themselves. Suicides, or self-murderers, as the Dutch put it, can select the method, day, and hour, and direct the last narrative, up to a point. Despair, significantly and regularly, overrides choice and strips it of volition. And, how being dead feels will also elude a suicide's capacity to know. (Virginia Woolf wrote in her diary that it was "the one experience I shall not describe.")

When death progresses naturally, which can be slow-going, over days or months, unless from a high-impact, head-on car crash, when organs fail fast, depleted of blood and oxygen, there comes a stunning withdrawal: people, like other animals, remove themselves psychically and physically from the known world. A person goes elsewhere, while the body works hard to shut itself down. One is "actively dying," hospice workers say. Death is oxymoronic until it finishes its work.

On ordinary days, a depressive has her funeral to fantasize, an activity that reassures with sad, cozy comfort. When required in actuality, planning it will probably be discomforting. A dying person may type, scrawl, or dictate a list of demands or wishes for a service or memorial, exerting a sort of posthumous control. (The list can also be a preemptive strike against the omissions or excesses of fond others). A funeral might be plain as a pine coffin or theatrical. One who is dying might have specified songs, musicians, speakers, and kinds and colors of flowers, or, if possessed of minimalist inclinations, wanted no displays or eulogies, just a plaintively beautiful song. (Both may have designated worthy charities.)

For a writer's funeral, words could seem superfluous, though there can never be enough, also. Selecting speakers raises unique problems. Most particularly, eulogizers script themselves. Some will mumble, overcome or shy, while others will improvise on humiliating episodes in the dead person's life. All jokes will be on the dead. (Most people will speak primarily about themselves.) In fantasy, a depressive mourns herself and watches the abstract procession, loving the inconsolation of others; but soon her morbid pleasures are jolted by the awkwardness of social situations, pre- and postdeath. Inclusions, exclusions, who speaks first, last? (Funeral rites survive, and have changed historically, for the living.) Planning an actual funeral might allay worry or generate more.

For writers and nonwriters, other kinds of writing than suicide notes can be left behind. A letter might confess secret loves and hates, with recuperative gestures of remorse and forgiveness. Or, it could be a screed against the living. A death essay could be an *avant-fin* manifesto, raving mad, or setting out rational principles for existence. (A treatise on melancholy risks mawkishness and unoriginality.) The essay could haltingly document one's protracted departure (exquisitely incomplete).

Any of these compositions might supply a reason to live fully while dying, but inciting, for writers, a specific anxiety. The final text could cause a cascade of revisionist views of the individual and the body of work, staining both, and lasting until everyone who knew the writer had died (considered in Buddhism an individual's "second death").

Most likely, one will have scant energy for planning and writing in the final stages of life. (There are exceptions, who prove the rule.) Meeting death, sometimes called "the maker," though really the unmaker, is essentially debilitating, so its specific conditions dominate and alter the living. A dying person may have no ambition or desire to control anything during the process (in itself unburdening). One's death, though, will likely be written about by someone else or, even more likely, no one. Most deaths go unremarked. So-called "ordinary people" get thousands of hits on YouTube when killed by a usually docile lion on an ecological safari or pushed in front of a train. (The living identify with the pathos and meaninglessness of random, final endings like these.)

An ignominious death recasts an entire life as unintelligent and witless. A relatively healthy person moves an old, huge TV set or a five-drawer steel file cabinet, which, unbalanced, leans, starts falling, its weight unbelievable, gains velocity, collapses, and crushes one beneath it. (Domestic deaths invariably make foolish last impressions.) An ignominious end is beyond prediction. But the great majority of deaths will be common, following a predictable course indicated by one of several illnesses, resulting in complete organ failure. Sherwin Nuland, in his book *How We Die*, refutes the contemporary delusion of living forever by defeating the ageing process. He insists, almost too vociferously, that human beings will die sooner or later, because of the wear and tear on the body, also known as old age, which is not a disease. But if one believes people are dying as soon as they are born, then living itself is an illness overcome only by dying.

Near to death, people usually don't speak or have last words, hospice workers say, especially not those profound or pithy final utterances compiled in books.

Thomas Carlyle: "So this is Death—Well!"

Aleister Crowley: "I'm perplexed."

Ulysses S. Grant: "Water!"

Emily Dickinson: "Let us go in. The fog is rising."

Goethe: "More light!"

Edgar Allan Poe: "Lord help my poor soul . . ."

Washington Irving: "Well, I must arrange my pillows for another weary night! When will this end?"

Gertrude Stein: "What is the question?"

Ludwig Wittgenstein: "Tell them I've had a wonderful life."

If a dying person had her wits about her and enough bodily function—swallowing becomes impossible—she might be able to come up with a line or two. But this also can't be plotted. (Spoken and written communications not close to death are technically not deathbed statements.) Withdrawing from life for days or weeks, one is expected to be silent and uncommunicative, or will communicate but be misunderstood. (The writing of Ivan Ilych's death, hospice workers say, is eerily close to how dying people feel; they wonder at Tolstoy's prescience.)

Since what death feels like is unknowable, most people fear it, and dying, particularly in great pain. In this time, as no other before, unless wishing to suffer mentally and physically, a patient can receive palliative care and medicines that make the "transition," a hospice term, from life to death painless or nearly painless. (Many believe hospice speeds death along, but often it prolongs what life is left.) Against all reason, which death conquers easily, a few want to feel pain, not to remain as lucid as possible and say their good-byes, but as self-punishment for past bad acts and guilty consciences.

Hardly anyone wishes "to die badly." In the Late Middle Ages, when the concept of *artes moriendi* was formulated, the ideal of "a beautiful death" emerged, and it thrived through the nineteenth century. "Dying well" has replaced "dying beautifully" and is rigorously enforced by postmortem judgments. People aren't supposed to struggle at the end, people should be "ready to go" and "accepting," and opprobrium is cast on those who aren't ready and willing, on those who "died badly."

This ultimate indictment glosses and assesses a human being's last trial. (To die smiling makes it easier for the living.)

But in the matter of dying and death, mortal judgments, like most received wisdoms concocted of exasperating pieties and galling stupidity, should be eliminated. Only death's uninitiated would espouse these moralisms.

Of death, mortals are absolutely ignorant. The dead, fortunately, are beyond caring.

LANCE OLSEN

LESSNESS

A little less of us every day.

  Seven words, nine syllables, twenty-three letters.

That's all that is the case, precisely what we really know about ourselves, sans irony, sans wit, sans posturing, sans philosophy, sans desperate belief: how it is impossible to reason with our own bodies.

There is hope, Franz Kafka once wrote, but not for us.

Blessed is he who expects nothing, Alexander Pope once wrote, for he shall never be disappointed.

An e-mail from a friend, her lung cancer having recently metastasized to the brain: "They have me on this experimental chemo pill, long-term, which is supposed to reduce the risk of recurrence greatly. The problem is it made my face break out in this horrendous acne-like rash. So I've cut back to half a dose and begun taking antibiotics as well as using all sorts of creams. My dermatologist's assistant spent nearly an hour with me showing me how to use makeup to cover the rash. I've never used makeup in my life, and really hadn't planned on starting now, but it does seem to make a difference."

Grenz-Situationen, was Karl Jaspers's term.

We seem to believe it possible to ward off death by following rules of good grooming, Don DeLillo once wrote.

How we keep writing anyway.

Grenz-Situationen: Limit Situations.

How we keep writing anyway until we don't keep writing anyway.

The bioengineered replicant Roy Batty to his creator, Tyrell, in *Blade Runner*, a moment before Roy crushes Tyrell's skull, drives his thumbs into Tyrell's eyes: *I want more life, fucker.*

How I saw the writer Ronald Sukenick for the last time one humid rainy April afternoon in his Battery Park City apartment two months before he died of inclusion body myositis, a muscle-wasting disease that eventually makes it impossible for one to swallow, then to breathe.

Jaspers's philosophy being an extended effort to explore and describe the margins of human experience, an effort to confront what he thought of, beautifully, as the Unconditioned.

Death is so terrifying, Susan Cheever once wrote, because it is so ordinary.

Ron couldn't use his fingers anymore, so he bought a voice-recognition program and wrote by means of that.

Ridley Scott re-editing the scene so that in the final cut Batty says: *I want more life, father*—thereby draining the life out of the line, making it into mere Frankensteinian, mere Oedipal, cliché.

How my wife and I strolled along the banks of the Bagmati River in Kathmandu among myriad cloth-wrapped bodies burning on funeral pyres.

How Ron and I both knew this was it, how there would be no future meetings. How we both understood there were no social conventions to cover such an event. How the unsettling result was that each of our simple declarative sentences seemed anything but.

When we speak of "seriousness" in art, Thomas Pynchon once wrote, ultimately we are talking about an attitude toward death.

How, shortly before his in 1631, John Donne obtained an urn, his own burial shroud, and the services of an artist. He wrapped himself in said shroud, posed atop said urn, and had said artist render a charcoal sketch of him, which the poet kept by his bedside throughout his final illness.

The distance between the real and the ideal.

Two large framed photographs hang on the walls of my writing studio, both by Joel-Peter Witkin. They are the only ones by an established artist my wife and I have ever felt a need to purchase. Each is a still life, a *nature morte*, constructed from corpse parts the photographer found and posed in morgues in Mexico and France.

Families of the dead in prim circles around the pyres along the river.

Holy men spattering butter on the fires to help them burn faster.

How, to pass time on the Paris Metro once between stops, I asked my sister, with whom I was riding during a visit, how old she wanted to live to be, and, instead of answering, she began to cry.

Jaspers referred to the ultimate boundaries of being as *Das Umgreifende*—The Encompassing: the indefinite horizon in which all subjective and objective experience is possible, but which can itself never be apprehended rationally.

How, after fifty, your face becomes an accomplishment.

Eighty-three, less than a year before he died, Kurt Vonnegut: "I've written books. Lots of them. Please, I've done everything I'm supposed to do. Can I go home now?"

One only becoming authentically human, in other words, according to Jaspers, at the instant one allows oneself awareness of the Encompassing by confronting such unimaginables as universal contingency and the loss of the human, the loss of the body—the latter otherwise known as death.

Everything else refusal, fear, repression.

How the last words Roy Batty speaks, huddled on a dark rainy L.A. rooftop in 2019, are some of the saddest, the most powerful, in the entire film: "I've seen things you people wouldn't believe. Attack ships on fire off the shoulder of Orion. I've watched C-beams glitter in the dark near the Tannhauser Gate. All those moments will be lost in time, like tears in the rain. Time to die."

How it is the case, precisely, that life can be defined as a slow dying.

A terminal illness.

Birth, Beckett once wrote, was the death of him.

The goal of all life, Freud once wrote, is death.

How it is the case, precisely, that death is a protracted amnesia visited upon those who live beyond the lost one's passing.

Ernest Becker: The irony of man's condition is that the deepest need is to be free of the anxiety of death and annihilation; but it is life itself which awakens it, and so we must shrink from being fully alive.

Remembering, Milan Kundera once wrote, is a form of forgetting.

My dying friend: A lot of the brain motor difficulties that I was expecting after the first surgery seem to be appearing now. My left hand feels more or less like a stroke patient's, unable to

do very much except spill a glass of water on a computer key-
board or leave A. walking two blocks behind me because I had
no sensation that I let go of his hand. For about two weeks
there I was having some real palsy tremors, what they're calling
mini-seizures.

On a large enough time line, Chuck Palahniuk once wrote,
the survival rate for everyone will drop to zero.

That's it. That's all.

How, as I was working on my novel about Friedrich
Nietzsche's last mad night on earth, I couldn't shake off the
abrupt uncanny realization that inside always becomes outside
in the end.

The simple, brutal notion: how that which separates us
from the world—our sphincterial control, our skin, our existential deep-sea suit—gradually goes away.

We are always becoming something other than we are,
something other than we want to be.

Traveling.

Every once in a while, Ron stopped talking, shifted in his
electric wheelchair, looked out his picture window at the Hudson, then drifted back to what we were saying, and we would
pick up where we had left off. I drank bourbon, Ron tea
through a straw. He was having trouble swallowing. He was
becoming tired very quickly. You could see it.

Every parting gives a foretaste of death, Schopenhauer once
wrote.

How I could hear steam building in the skulls of the corpses
as I moved along the banks of the Bagmati.

How Hemingway turned himself into a character in one of
his books and shot himself in the head. How Hunter Thomp-
son turned himself into a character in one of his books and shot

himself in the head. How Yukio Mishima turned himself into a character in one of his books and committed seppuku. Publicly. In 1970.

Outside, people not cheering him on, but heckling him, jeering, as he disemboweled himself.

Gradually, or not so gradually. It depends.

I lost all my hair two weeks ago, my dying friend wrote. One of the things they talked about was the need to keep the head covered at all times and I ended up buying a large assortment of what they call chemo turbans, some of them reasonably stylish, to wear around the house. I mean, it's a perfectly good wig, and I'm sure was once a very nice beaver or groundhog or whatever it was, but I hate it. The hair of my nightmares.

The head. Not *my* head.

As if she had already begun to become something other than her own body.

My sister-in-law was in town, my dying friend wrote, and her comment was it looks okay, it just looks nothing like me. I'll use it for teaching, since it still masks hair loss, and there's no need to impose my limitations on the students. Then I decided to say screw the chemo turbans and looked at some hats. I ended up buying three outrageously exquisite retro-style felt fedoras which cover the whole head and are marvelously comfortable. You won't believe these. I've never been so stylish in my life.

Roy Batty, a replicant, virtually identical to humans in every way except for the fact that the memories he believes are his own are really someone else's, except for the fact that he has a four-year lifespan, is more human than the other so-called humans around him.

A ball will bounce, Richard Wilbur once wrote, but less and less.

How the sadhus, Hindu holy men who live by begging, cook bread by burying it among shards of smoking human bones.

I want to enjoy my death, Beckett once wrote.

Presumably with some irony.

In that race which daily hastens us toward death, Camus once wrote, the body maintains its irreparable lead.

But how Tennessee Williams accidentally swallowed the cap of his nasal spray and suffocated alone in his hotel room.

How Sherwood Anderson choked on a toothpick at a party in Panama.

How Maupassant tried killing himself by slicing his own throat, failed, was declared insane, spent the last eighteen months of his life in an asylum, dying from syphilis he contracted in his youth, as did Manet, as did Gauguin, as did Schubert, as did Nietzsche, as did Scott Joplin.

How, after a little more than an hour, I realized I should take my leave of Ron. How I don't believe I ever experienced more difficulty closing a door behind me.

How that door both shut and remained wide open.

How the only real closures come in mimetic fiction and memoir, redemption and faux wisdom hardened into commodity. Like an order of Arby's Cheesecake Poppers.

How a group of children stood knee-deep in the river, oblivious, in the black oily water that used to be strangers, throwing a red rubber ball through gusts of coppery haze.

Charles Sanders Pierce: If man were immortal he could be perfectly sure of seeing the day when everything in which he had trusted should betray his trust, and, in short, of coming eventually to hopeless misery. He would break down, at last, as every good fortune, as every dynasty, as every civilization does. In place of this we have death.

The graveyards are full of indispensable men, Charles de Gaulle once wrote.

Death is not an event in life, Wittgenstein once wrote: we do not live to experience death.

Yes, I want to say, and no.

My mother waiting primly in her living room in suburban Dallas, also dying, also of cancer, this time breast metastasized to the spine, the liver, the brain, inventorying the clutter that took her nearly seventy-four years to quilt around herself, noting out of the blue, almost casually, to no one in particular: *All these things will forget their stories the moment I'm gone.*

A little less, and then a little less.

The first Witkin photograph on my wall: a plump old woman, the top of her head missing, her skin blotched, her body supported by wires, sitting at a chair next to a table in a sparse room. On the table is a book. Her finger holds her place, although the arm to which the finger is attached isn't itself attached to her torso. *Interrupted Reading*, the photograph is entitled.

Anna Karenina throws herself under a train.

His books are questions of survival of personality, Carole Maso once wrote of the narrator's former lover in *Ava*.

Yes, and no.

My cousin entered the hospital for routine hip-replacement surgery to fix his fullback years in college. The operation went off without a hitch—until an infection flowered within him, one of those virulent bacterial strains that chew through a patient's every prospect. One week my cousin was perfectly fine, minus the limp and a certain throbby stiffness. The next he was on a ventilator. The next his wife was e-mailing what amounted to acquaintances like me in an attempt to drum up something that looked like an acceptable audience for the memorial service I had absolutely no intention of attending.

Emma Bovary eats arsenic, Eva Braun cyanide, Alan Turing cyanide, Abbie Hoffman phenobarbital.

> *There is no boat in Hades, no ferryman Charon,*
> *No caretaker Aiakos, no dog Cerberus.*
> *All we who are dead below*
> *Have become bones and ashes, but nothing else.*

Someone once carved on a Roman tombstone. Two thousand years ago.

The second Witkin photograph: a woman's untorsoed head, eyes closed, atilt on some dark surface (let's call it a table), next to which a stuffed monkey is posed.

Patrik Ouředník recounts how, during the first months Buchenwald was open for business, those in charge gave the inmates postcards that said: *Accommodation is wonderful, we are working here, we receive decent treatment and are well looked after.* The inmates were made to sign them and address them to relatives, some of whom apparently believed what they read. One Greek prisoner mailed his postcard to his father in Pyrgos. Three months later, his father arrived for a visit.

At the railroad platform, the son leaping on him and strangling him to death before the Germans could get their hands on the man.

My wife's grandmother refused to be buried, insisting on

being entombed in a mausoleum instead because, she said, she didn't want to get dirty.

The distance between the real and the ideal.

Whatever opinion we may be pleased to hold on the subject of death, Proust once wrote, we may be sure that it is meaningless and valueless.

How it would be a perfect misreading of his work to suggest that Witkin's intent is to shock, disgust, exploit his subjects, his viewer's vision.

My uncle had a heart attack on a beach while feeding pigeons. A good Scandinavian, he was too embarrassed to draw attention to himself, reported his wife, who had been sitting beside him at the time, and so he expired, sotto voce, on the spot.

Diane Arbus swallows barbiturates and slashes her wrists, as does Mark Rothko.

The living being is only a species of the dead, Nietzsche once wrote, and a very rare species.

Death is the mother of—

No, that's not it.

Another dying friend. Another e-mail. Another cancer. Another metastasis to the brain. Sorry not to have updated you sooner, but the fog is settling in so even this will have to be short. Not much news. I wish I could write something light and cheerful, at least something light and pomo-ish, but, fact is, cancer does suck. Or, rather, it's the treatment that sucks: makes me want to do nothing but sleep all day (and night). Not much pain—occasional headaches, joint aches. What's most scary is the felt deterioration of my mental abilities (such as they were)—each day, I get dumber and dumber, and know it. Memory loss, inability to follow conversations, inability to

find words. B. finds it inevitably frustrating, seeing me standing in the middle of a room, clearly without a clue what I'm
doing there; and never sure if I understand or will remember
two minutes later something she asked me to do. Frustrating
for me, too—feeling like a retard who needs to have notes
pinned to his shirt, reminding him what he's supposed to be
doing.

Every plot being an education, ultimately, about how everything ends.

Jerzy Kosinski swallows barbiturates and puts a bag over his
head, as does Michael Dorris.

While I thought that I was learning how to live, Leonardo
da Vinci once wrote, I have been learning how to die.

Witkin's work performing an act of reminding.

This is how to say it.

Every narrative being, ultimately, a study in death.

Freud overdoses on morphine.

How, as one gets older, deaths begin arriving closer and
closer, like mortar shells zeroing in on their target.

Death being the one idea you can't deconstruct, David
Lodge once wrote.

How I was reading to my mother from Eliot's *Four Quartets*
when she died. My wife was holding her hand. We were at her
bedside, talking to her, trying to comfort her, even though
she was already unconscious, even though she had been for
more than a day. After a while, I began reading to her, to us, a
little from her favorite book, the Bhagavad Gita, a little from
late Eliot. She suddenly flinched and stopped breathing.

She was herself and then she wasn't.

One thousand and one things change the meaning of any
book on any given reading.

Witkin's goal slant-rhyming with Viktor Shklovsky's: the technique of art being to make objects *unfamiliar*, to make forms difficult, to increase the difficulty and length of perception.

Alice Bradley Sheldon, aka James Tiptree, Jr., mercy-kills her terminally ill husband and then shoots herself.

Near death and incoherent, Nietzsche lay in his narrow bed in a small room on the top floor of the archives his sister Lisbeth had had built in Weimar. The people Lisbeth had brought in with the hope of establishing a lucrative cult around her brother were talking about literature. Nietzsche roused, opened his eyes briefly, said *I too have written some good books*, then faded back into silence.

Gregor Samsa starves himself, as does the Hunger Artist, as does Kurt Gödel.

And I have come to relinquish that most modern of stances: uncertainty, Carole Maso once wrote. I am certain now of what will happen.

How my mother changed tenses before my eyes.

They said the side effects of these last two chemo sessions would be the hardest, my dying friend wrote. The latest development is that I'll suddenly pass out for a few minutes. Yesterday I was teaching and woke up as they were loading me into an ambulance. They checked my vitals, did a quick EKG, I signed a waiver stating that I didn't want to be taken to the hospital, and I went back to teach without incident.

Witkin's goal slant-rhyming with Gaston Bachelard's: art, then, is an increase of life, a sort of competition of surprises that stimulates our consciousness and keeps it from becoming somnolent.

Edwin Armstrong, inventor of FM radio, jumps out a window, as does Gilles Deleuze, as does F. O. Matthiessen.

In heaven all the interesting people are missing, Nietzsche once wrote.

Witkin asking his viewers to sympathize with the fragility of the human flesh, the human heart, the act of lessening that we call ourselves.

Birth was the—

The head. Not *my* head.

Everything else refusal.

Grenz-Situationen.

Everything else fear and repression.

Yes, I want to say, and—

It happened on a Sunday when my mother was escorting my twin brother and me down the steps of the tenement where we lived, Joel-Peter Witkin once told an interviewer, recounting a pivotal moment from his childhood. We were going to church. While walking down the hallway to the entrance of the building, we heard an incredible crash mixed with screaming and cries for help. The accident involved three cars, all with families in them. Somehow, in the confusion, I was no longer holding my mother's hand. At the place where I stood at the curb, I could see something rolling from one of the overturned cars. It stopped at the curb where I stood. It was the head of a little girl. I bent down to touch the face, to speak to it, but before I could touch it someone carried me away.

Remember that we are what we are.

How the angelic four-voice vocal texture of Guillaume Dufay's masses make the day on which you hear them feel thoroughly lived. How your consciousness arranges the entire piece of theater called living into a series of remarkable paintings called recollection.

A *polyptych.*

How each morning, as you rise from your bed, the belief hums through your head that you are going to die, going to die, going to die, yes, surely, no doubt about it, but not today— an observation that will remain correct every morning of your life, except one, because—

Because—

To hope, E. M. Cioran once wrote, is to contradict the future.

MARK DOTY

BIJOU

The movie I'm watching—I'm hesitant to call it porn, since its intentions are less obvious than that—was made in 1972, and couldn't have been produced in any other era. A construction worker is walking home from work in Manhattan when he sees a woman in a short fake fur coat knocked over by a car when she's crossing an intersection. The driver leaps out to help her up, but the construction worker—played by an actor named Bill—picks up her purse and tucks it in his jacket. He takes the subway to a banged-up-looking block, maybe in Hell's Kitchen, climbs up to his tiny, soiled apartment, nothing on the walls but a few pin-ups, women torn from magazines. On his bed, he opens the purse, looks at its spare contents, keys and a few dollars. He opens a lipstick and touches it to his tongue, tastes it, does it again, something about his extended tongue touching the extended lipstick . . . Then he's lying back, stroking himself through his jeans, getting out of his clothes; he's an arche-typal seventies porn guy, lean, with thick red hair and a thick red mustache, a little trail of hair on his wiry belly. Then he's in the shower, continuing his solo scene, and he begins to flash on images of women, quick jump cuts, but just as he's about to come, he sees the woman in fur falling when the bumper of the car strikes her. That's the end of that; the erotic moment is over, for him and for the viewer, once that image returns.

Chastened, toweling off, he's back in the bedroom, looking again at what spilled from her purse. There's an invitation, something telling her about—a party? an event? someplace called Bijou at 7 P.M.

Then he's walking in Soho—the old Soho, long before the art glamour and even longer before the Euro-tourist-meets-North-Jersey shopping district: garbage in the streets, cardboard boxes in front of shuttered cast-iron façades without windows. He finds the address, goes in and up, and the movie shifts from the gritty Warholian vocabulary it's trafficked in thus far to another cinematic tongue. An indifferent woman in a lot of eye makeup sits in a glass booth; Bill proffers the invite; she gestures toward a door and utters the movie's only line of dialogue: *Right through there.*

"There" turns out to be a hallucinatory space, its dominant hue a solarized, acidy green. Within that color, Bill moves forward. He confronts the image of his own body in one mirror and then in many, reaches out to touch his own form with pleasure. Time dilates, each gesture extended, no rush to get anywhere, only a little sense of forwardness. In a while, there's another body—man or woman?—prone, facedown, and Bill's on top of him or her, they're fucking in a sea of all that green. In a while, we can see the person beneath Bill is definitely a man. Then, much later, Bill's alone, lying prone on the floor as if now he's let go, all his boundaries relinquished, and one man comes to him and begins to blow him. Bill lies there and accepts it. In a while, another man enters the scene, and begins to touch and cradle Bill's head, and then—no hurry here, no hurry in all the world—there's another. Now the pattern is clear, one man after another enters the liquid field of green that sometimes frames and sometimes obscures—and they are all reverently, calmly touching Bill. They have no end save to give him pleasure, to make Bill's body entirely, attentively, completely loved.

This is the spiritualized eroticism of 1972 made flesh, more sensuous and diffuse than pointedly hot, a brotherhood of eros, a Whitmanian democracy. It makes the viewer feel suspended in a sort of erotic haze, but whatever arousal I feel in imagining Bill's complete submission to pleasure suddenly comes to a halt, as surely as if I'd seen that woman struck down in the crosswalk again, because I realize that all the men in the scene I'm watching are dead. Every one of them, and the vision they embodied, the idea they incarnated gone up in the smoke and ashes of the crematoriums, scattered now in the dunes of Provincetown and Fire Island.

Or that's one version of what I felt, watching *Bijou,* Wakefield Poole's weird period piece of art porn. Of course, it is not news that the players are all gone now. How beautiful they look, the guys in the movie, or the men in the documentary *Gay Sex in the 70s,* posing on the decks in the Pines or on the porches of houses in San Francisco, eager for brotherhood and for knowledge of one another. That is a phrase I would like to revive: to *have knowledge* of someone. It suggests that sex is, or can be, a process of inquiry, an idea that Poole would certainly have embraced.

Watching the movie is just one of countless experiences in which the fact of the AIDS epidemic is accommodated somehow. "Accommodated" doesn't mean understood, assimilated, digested, interpreted, or integrated. Accommodated: We just make room for it because it won't go away.

I don't know what else I expect. What could lend meaning to the AIDS crisis in America? Hundreds of thousands perished because there was no medical model for understanding what was wrong with them, and no money or concerted effort offered soon enough to change the course of things in time to save their lives. They died of a virus, and they died of homophobia. But this understanding is an entirely social one, and it doesn't do much to help the soul make meaning of it all. I have no answer to this problem save to suggest that a kind of doubling of perspective—an embracing of the layered nature of the world—is one thing one could carry, or be forced to carry, from such a shattering encounter. AIDS makes the experience of the body, a locus of pleasure and satisfaction, almost simultaneously the site of destruction and limit. What if, from here on out, for those burned in that fire, the knowledge of another body is always a way of acknowledging mortal beauty, and any moment of mutual vivacity understood as existing against an absence to come? Presence made more poignant, and more desirable, even sexier by that void, intensified by it.

Maybe the viewer's involuntary gasp, when Bill thinks of the woman hit by the car as he's jerking off, is twofold—first, the shock of the inappropriateness of it, and then the secondary, deeper shock—that the particular fact of her body is differently understood, differently longed for, when it is seen where it really is, in the world of danger—and that such a perception shakes the desirer out of simple lust and into some larger, more profound realm of eros.

I used to like to go to a sex club in the East Village, a place now closed through some combination of pressures from the Health Department, the police, the IRS, and the real estate developers who are remaking Manhattan as a squeaky-clean retail zone. A combination Whole Foods/condo development has opened right down the block.

Beyond a nearly invisible doorway (shades of the one Bill entered in Soho, long ago), there was a bouncer inside the door, a flirty man who loved jazz music, and then an attendant in the ticket booth ("Right through there . . ."), and then a sort of living room where you could check your clothes with the two attendant angels, one black and startlingly shapely, one blond and ethereally thin. They were loving, kind, and funny boys; they looked at the goings-on before them with a sly combination of blessing and good humor, which is just what you'd want in an angel.

Then, beyond a black vinyl curtain shredded so that you could part it dramatically with a swipe of the hand, were two floors, with a kind of stripped industrial look to them—bare brick and cement, a certain rawness, and structures of wood and metal in which to wander or hide, all very plain the first year I went there, and later redone with branches and dried leaves everywhere, as if an autumn forest had sprouted in the ruins of a factory.

Sometimes it was a palace of pleasure, sometimes it was a hall of doom. Sometimes when you thought you wanted to be there, you'd discover you just couldn't get into the swing of it. Sometimes you weren't sure you'd wanted to go and it was marvelous. Often it felt as if whatever transpired had little to do with any individual state of mind, but rather with the tone of the collective life, whatever kind of spirit was or wasn't generated by the men in attendance that night, or by the city outside busily thinking through the poem of this particular evening. There were regulars who became acquaintances and comrades. There were visitors who became dear friends. There was a world of people I never saw again, once the doors closed.

Whoever made the decisions about what music to play preferred a kind of sludgy, druggy trance, often with classical or operatic flourishes about it. The tune I'll never forget was a remixed version of Dido's great aria from Purcell's *Dido and Aeneas*. It's the scene where the Queen of Carthage, having been abandoned by the man she's allowed to wreck her kingdom, watches his sails disappear out to sea and resolves to end her life. As she prepares to bury a knife in her breast, she sings, unforgettably: *Remember me, but— ah!—forget my fate.*

It seems, in my memory, that they would play this song every night I attended, always late, as the evening's brighter promises dimmed. There was a bit of a backbeat thrown in that would come and go, in between the soprano's great controlled heaves of farewell and resignation, but the music always had the same effect. I'd take myself off to the sidelines, to one of the benches poised on the edges of the room for this purpose, lean back into the swelling melancholy of the score, and watch the men moving to it as though they'd been choreographed, in some dance of longing held up, for a moment, to the light of examination, the perennial hungry quest for whatever deliverance or release it is that sex brings us. It was both sad and astonishingly beautiful and now it seems to me something like the fusing of those layers I mentioned above: the experience of desire and the awareness of death become contiguous—*remember me*—one not-quite-differentiated experience.

My partner Paul's mother has Alzheimer's, or senile dementia. The first sign of it he saw was one morning when, for about a forty-five-minute period, she didn't know who he was. Now she doesn't know who anyone is, or if she does it's for seconds at a time. I was sitting beside the condo pool with her—the Intracoastal Waterway behind us, so that we sat on delicate chairs on a small strand of concrete between two moving bodies of water—along with one of her other sons. *Who are you,* she said to him. *I'm Michael, your son,* he said. She laughed, the kind of humorless snort that means, *As if . . .* Then he said back to her, *Who are you?* And she answered, *I watch.*

That's what's left for her, the subjectivity that looks out at the world without clear attachments or defined relations. She is completely obsessed with who everyone is; she is always asking. I wonder if this has to do with her character, or if it's simple human need; do we need to know, before we can do or say anything else, who people are to us?

Not in *Bijou;* abstracted subjectivities meet one another in the sheer iridescent green space of sex. They morph together in patterns, they lose boundary; they go at it so long, in such fluid ways, that the viewer does too.

Paul's mother's state is not, plainly, ecstatic; she wants to know where she ends and others begin. The desire to merge is only erotic to the bound.

The other day my friend Luis asked me if I thought there was anything spiritual about sex. We happened to be walking in Soho at the time, on our way back from some stores in the Bowery, so we might have passed the very door through which Bill long ago entered into his acidulated paradise. That prompted me to tell my friend about the movie, and my description prompted Luis's question. Luis has a way of asking questions that seems to say, *You really think that?*

I am not ready to give up on Whitman's vision of erotic communion, or its more recent incarnation in Wakefield Poole's pornographic urban utopia. But the oddest thing about Poole's film, finally, is that woman knocked down by the car; why on earth was she necessary to the tale? I suspect it's because even in the imagined paradise of limitless eros, there must be room for death; otherwise the endlessness of it, the lack of limit or of boundary, finally drains things of their tension, removes all edges. Poole can almost do this—create a floating, diffuse, subject- and objectless field of eros. But not quite; the same body that strains toward freedom and escape also has outer edges, also exists in time, and it's that doubling that makes the body the sexy and troubling thing it is. *O taste and see.* Isn't the flesh a way to drink of the fountain of otherhood, a way to taste the not-I, a way to blur the edges and thus feel the fact of them? Cue the aria here: *Remember me,* sings Dido, *but—ah—forget my fate!* That is, she counsels, you need to both remember where love leads and love anyway; you can both see the end of desire and be consumed by it all at once. The ecstatic body's a place to feel timelessness and to hear, ear held close to the chest of another, the wind that blows in there, hurrying us ahead and away, and to understand that this awareness does not put an end to longing but lends to it a shadow that is, in the late hour, beautiful.

Shadows, of course, lend objects gravity, attaching them to earth.

Luis is right, sex isn't spiritual. The spirit wants to go up and out; it rises above, transcends, flies on dove wings up to the rafters and spies below it the formbound world. Who was that peculiar French saint who died briefly, returned to life, and then could not bear the smell of human flesh? She used to soar up to the rafters in church, just to get away from the stench of it. Sex is soulful; sex wants the soul-rich communion of other bodies. The sex of *Bijou* isn't really erotic because what it wants is to slip the body's harness and merge in the light show of play, the slippery forms of radiance. That's the aspect of the film that's more dated than its hairstyles, as if it were desirable for sex to take us up out of our bodies, rather than further in. That distance is a removal from knowledge; the guys who are pleasuring Bill aren't anyone in particular, and do not need to be individuated. But that's not soul's interest. Back in the sex club in the East Village, soul wants to know this body and this, to seek the embodied essence of one man after another, to touch and mouth the world's astonishing variety of forms. Spirit says, I watch. Soul says, Time enough to be out of the body later on, the veil of flesh won't be set aside, not tonight; better to feel the heat shining through the veil.

CÉZANNE'S COLORS

My second husband is writing an obituary of my first husband for the UC Berkeley English Department archives. Rain runs past spiky succulents and roses into storm drains near where we all stood together once, laughing and chatting by the gate. Lenny thinks this is hilarious and is telling jokes in heaven. Whatever heaven is for him. Or us.

I have been thinking about the nature of abstraction, about rivers in California, and the way water molecules attach themselves in a completely generous fashion. I've been thinking about Cézanne going back to fetch the paints he'd left on Mont Saint-Victoire. Some say this trip back up the mountain made the painter ill. He had by then combined shapes that could withstand the retreat of color—cylinder, cone, and sphere. Perhaps the people standing before his paintings helped them breathe at night.

Shortly after the Iraq War began, we lost three loved ones in our circle of family and friends. Each death seemed the opposite of the previous death yet they are connected somehow. Each person died in a way that made no sense. Our friend Carol Thigpen Milosz had come from Poland with an undiagnosed blood disorder. We stood next to her bed daily at UCSF Medical Center for a few weeks, watching her body be inhabited by a spreading of red. I fixated on the monitors and her medication schedules, on things she said and scrawled on her paper, on the cycles of relief from Ativan. I came to hate the morphine drip, the thought of all the opium fields controlled by the CIA. The morphine drip, like the Internet, protecting the traveler from the other senses.

Hemoccult. Tubes with their entrances.

Rainer Maria Rilke took a great interest in Cézanne's work and process, and for several weeks in 1907 while living in Paris wrote a series of impressionistic letters to his wife about the painter. The letters are remarkable for their accuracy about existence and the suffering of the soul. Rilke was not interested so much in the technique of the paintings—though craft was always of interest to him—as he was in the approach of the materials to the brink of being. As usual, Rilke wanted to see artists demonstrate an ability to live in an absolutely uncompromised manner; he looked to visual artists—particularly to Cézanne and the late impressionists—to help him on his way: "Here, all of reality is on his side in this dense quilted blue of his, in his red and his shadowless green and the reddish black of his wine bottles." The letters track Rilke's quest for pushing language through to the edge; he studies the paintings in which Cézanne foregrounds shapes and volume over luminescent color. Cézanne is not like other painters who are trying to perfect the drop of water, the virgin's smile, the slain rabbit beside a cornucopia of autumn vegetables, or (after all of these things) the release of light into impression. Cézanne is trying to release color from shape, and then to give shape abstract volume—and Rilke tries to track Cézanne's unmanageable blue from its sources.

Referring in contemporary conversations to the busyness of a spirit in afterlife does almost nothing but send horror and nervous panic onto the faces of what used to be called "the intelligentsia." When I start talking about the spirit on a bardo journey, friends want to know if I "really" "mean it." I have never thought my belief in the animating spirit world does any harm whatsoever to my daily life. I do not try to convert others to my belief, and it does not stop me from being a fairly high-functioning, occasionally rational adult. I haven't ceased to be interested in the facts of daily existence, in the well-being of family and friends, in poetry, in politics. The notion of a highly populated, invisible world seems one of the best metaphors for meaning-beside-the-meaningless. *Do you believe that with a straight face,* asked another friend. *I mean, do you believe she is floating around in some invisible world?* Let me say I refuse to limit my experience by not including this possible reality.

Carol Milosz suffered her death in a way that emptied the world of meaning and color. She bargained and pled with her loved ones to stay all night. We were not allowed to stay as long as she would have preferred us to stay. The doctors were unable to diagnose her blood disorder, and when her elderly poet husband arrived from Kraków to see her, she was about to be transported "upstairs to hospice," we were told one day. At the end of an illness when the body is undergoing radical change, its transfer of color is, at the very least, amazing. Her legs filled with red as they changed and swelled and became streaked. We ceased to understand color as a form of familiar experience; the varieties of red in her legs were in a realm between familiarity and terror. We could not contact Carol, a somewhat religious person, but kept her company by her bed, as a stay against the utter meaningless of her torment. "The new drugs are helping," she reported to us, for the dying are some of the best reporters. I think we stood there as much from duty and curiosity as from love, though it is shameful to admit. Each night we went back to our bed across the bay, to sleep and to wake in torpor. My husband's mammal body, turned away from me in the dark, kept meaninglessness away.

A spider bundles up a blond caterpillar, hanging deftly outside our kitchen window in the rain, and it is placed against the dewy morning as a constellation stands against the void; the caterpillar continues to squirm back and forth for hours, and when it is no longer mobile, is poised in relief, an inch-and-a-half pellet of matter with knobs protruding from other knobs, head facing down. Is its death just part of nature as a mere event in the morning? For maybe it has a grand meaning somehow, traced in some other realm.

Using an image system from trance work, I envisioned white figures at the edges of the field. One day when we went back to the hospital, I felt the figures waiting for Carol across a river while resting my chin on the bed rail; I couldn't see them exactly, I simply experienced them at the periphery of the scene and supposed someone had extended a hand. I said to the spirits, "Take her with no clothes; the clothes are bothering her." I stood on this side of the river; they stood on the other. I knew it was my brain but our river.

In the late eighties, I worked on a series of pastoral elegies I called "Tractates," after some Gnostic Christian texts I was reading at the time; in my poems, a grieving person seeks to contact the mourned presence by looking sideways, rather than up or down, into death. What lived/lived on both sides. The loved one's soul floated next to me, in bushes, in streams. The diagnosis for everyone is death, yet even in times of thinking about the afterlife, I've thought of being part of an endless system of metaphors, and imagine consciousness as something like a very large state-run park near our home, next to a petite lake called "Jewel" in which turtles are lined up like shallow helmets, and where beneficent rangers are in charge. A phoebe; a blue heron stimulates its oil glands with its long beak; and even

in the driest time, murky green water is full of infinitely interesting wildlife, inch-long minnows, frogs about to be ingested
by the heron. But not just being that, a part of that, but being
conscious of being that. Of its being all right.

About half a year after Carol's death, we received news of the
suicide of a friend, J. J and I had lunch the year before, and she
had told me she felt incurably depressed. J had a very good support network and plenty of resources for medical care, and I
always felt reassured by the fact that she could get the care she
needed. She was leading a vital, useful life, full of activity, and
was much loved by her husband and friends. So it was with
horror that we learned of her suicide outside her home. I imagined on the leaves that had breathed in and out with her daily,
an inappropriate, unmanageable red. On the backs of them,
intricate veins, having evolved . . . not *toward* anything, exactly.
Suicide removes "the plan."

A *life plan.* In the Greek pantheon, the Fates trumped Zeus.
Even as the sky gods win out over the earth gods, and Zeus
becomes the head of the Eumenides, the Furies, what trumps
them all is the unknown that seems to be based on a series of
whims of unknown origins. I shall consult the Fates, says Zeus.
Having a life plan might be a lottery ticket scratched off by the
desperate being who stands at the checkout counter of the convenience store.

For months the first thing I thought of each day was bright

red among the green plants. I kept saying to J in the bright red: "You have misunderstood. We had a contract. We stay here for each other till fate removes us. You don't get to do this." I said it in my selfishness—the selfishness of the living.

I refuse to rule out the opening of the senses, which can make of death an entrance—not in any happy American way, but an entrance that might fill the dying brain with unmatchable awe. This sense of irrational commerce between living and dead— something that began when I was a child in the desert—derives from an energy experienced in dirt and plants and energy, an energy that is in itself the greatest thing, and is absolutely outside of anyone's control. Our senses are simply not tuned enough to perceive all there is to perceive, as William Blake observed ("If the doors of perception . . ."). If the mapping of knowledge includes a panoply of physical facts that have not been completely accounted for, based on laws of nature that are ceaselessly revised, if dogs and elephants have a larger range of senses than we, if certain forms of life are able to exist at temperatures that would make our blood boil, why is it not possible that there are other forms of matter in which consciousness, as puffs of otherness, carries on beside bodies enclosed in skin?

One of Rilke's most intense letters to Clara about Cézanne concerns the painter's late years when he is working, old and sick, nearly exhausted, by himself, yet attending mass and trying to find redemption by driving himself to work. Rilke writes: "Beginning with the darkest tones, he would cover their depth with a layer of color that led a little beyond them, and keep going, expanding outward from color to color, until gradually he reached another, contrasting pictorial element, where, beginning at a new center, he would proceed in a similar way." He writes of Cézanne's struggle to make the most of what is perceived, as if it is all, always, a process. This has reminded me also of Rilke's search in his own poetry for the relationship between the symbolic figure and the general matrix of the search, the background of the search, as it were. It is in this hall between being and nonbeing that both poetry and art have always been of most interest. Dying people are some of the best reporters.

I know little about J's last days except that it seems she left many writings. She and I had had many arguments about whether modernist poetry in fragmentary form can address suffering. I argued that the sentence is not a requirement for thought, and in fact, sometimes the brief spurts, the more abstract or difficult fragments, can speak to conditions of human suffering in ways that are useful to the average person because they are brief and pure. Floating shards of a wreck that are whole. (Microsoft Word's squiggly green line recognizes I have written a fragment—it calls on me to complete it.) In the mystery of suffering, that tiny biochemical ability of either not being able to look forward to living a day, or being able to. Even if meaning is not a net, the search for meaning is something like a net; the suicide forcibly withdraws it. It is unfair to say, but suicide changes the possibility of grief in the same way that sudden death by unwillingness allows. In that hall between being and nonbeing, there is neither ignorance nor knowledge. The splatter of red in the garden. The degree to which living from moment to moment can both sabotage and save . . . Our friend's husband said at the memorial that J was only able to hold on to herself for a minute at a time. I think of this quite often now: the idea that suffering of a particular kind is about finding a momentary accommodation to one's ego deficiencies. I will never get over thinking I should have done more for J. . . .

Here is a poem I wrote for a suicide some years later:

> DECEMBER MOON
> *Suppose you are the secret*
> *of the shore—a strong wave*
> *lying on its side—*
>
> *you'd come to earth again*
>
> *(as if joy's understudy*
> *would appear) & you*
> *could live one more bold*
> *day without meaning to,*
> *afresh, on winter's piney floor;*
>
> *you say, I've been*
> *to the door & wept;*
> *it says, what door*

Cézanne's suffering seems to have interested Rilke in part for the overlapping ways complex emotions inform abstract decisions in an art. Rilke admired the sacrifice of the artist and the suffering when faced with the unknown, having absorbed Nietzsche's fierce *Übermensch* philosophy in an odd way. In October of 1907, he writes to Clara about Cézanne's days: "To achieve the conviction and substantiality of things, a reality intensified and potentiated to the point of indestructibility by his experience of the object, this seems to him to be the purpose of his innermost work: old, sick, exhausted every evening to the edge of collapse by the regular course of the day's work (often he would go to bed at six, before dark, after a senselessly ingested meal), angry, mistrustful, ridiculed, and mocked and mistreated each time he went to his studio— . . . hoping nevertheless from day to day that he might reach that achievement which he felt was the only thing that mattered."

In the spring of 2003, my first husband, Lenny Michaels—in a somewhat similar manner as Carol Milosz—came back from Europe with cancer of the blood. He had been diagnosed with lymphoma, although doctors were not sure what sort. Those of us who loved him—and who lived with his particular brilliance and craziness—know that he did not always "embrace death," as many people learn to do; when I lived with him, he feared death absolutely and thought the death of any individual human was an outrage. With little warning about his own, he had fought death in his life and writings. And when he was in the hospital, his body, like Carol's, exchanged colors with the world's colors. He made jokes under the morphine, and laughed. We tried to laugh back because it was Lenny. Our daughter stood at the door daily, waiting for reports from the doctors, and the doctors went in and out. His children and his wife, Katharine, and friends stayed beside him day and night.

When he was moved to Intensive Care, several of us slept in the waiting room, and when we were told he would die that day, we gathered. Many were called to his side: his wife, children, ex-wife, former lovers—we held his feet and hands and begged him to stay. We told him it wasn't time yet. I can almost compose a Lenny sentence about this, even now: "They held Ickstein's feet." Not only did he not die that day, he rallied. He lived several days after that, as if he would be able to fight what was absolutely not negotiable. We were almost powerful enough to hold him, and Lenny knew this. When his mother arrived a few days after the rally, he was able to say good-bye.

Not a day goes by that I don't think of Lenny being here in some form still, laughing over something ridiculous. There are aspects of the physical universe we do not understand; far from imposing the notion of the spirit world on civilization, my own confusion carries me into places in the afterlife that do not seem forward or backward, nor do they seem like personal memories of the dead, of Carol or J or Lenny. In culture after culture in which such a fringe of entities have access to another reality, our great dead help us, and they are far more numerous than are our present bodies. This makes sense, for the world of the dead is very populated and they are helping us be wise; those extra realms have far more cumulative consciousness than just my own.

My husband, Bob, and I have experienced several other

deaths since then, and in all the states between consciousness and unconsciousness—these states in which one is loved, but in which one must go to the great sea, not to be particular. We want unbearably much for these loved ones to feel at peace with their fate. I do not think human memory is the only form of "theoretical immortality"; works of art and aspen trees are other forms.

Years later, I dream my second husband and I are taking my first husband to the Louvre. Eager as a nuthatch, packed and solid, Lenny looks for the things he agrees with, or that his body might be comforted by—the colors of Cézanne, for example.

When I see Cézanne's last paintings, I think of the bodies standing before them during the so-called Great War, and the way the warmth of bodies met the warmth of the colors. As people stood admiring them, the heat of bodies entered the paintings. Their edges did not beat antique drums for the coming violence, yet the edges accompany whirlwinds in the terrible war. The paintings are free and do not grasp; their abstract logic, hovering at the boundaries of meaning, never eclipses the reason of atoms.

GEOFF DYER

WHAT WILL SURVIVE OF US

The first one I saw was on the corner of West 36th St and Sixth Avenue: a racing bicycle, painted completely white (tyres, saddle, spokes—everything) and chained to a street sign ("Left Lane Must Turn Left"). Plastic flowers had been threaded through the wheels and around the cross bar. New York, that week, was hosting a clutch of art events so I assumed that the white bike was a spin-off from the PULSE or Armory art fairs; either that or a harmless bit of street art. Or maybe it was a prop belonging to one of those irritating mimes, like the ones you get in Covent Garden, presumably painted in matching white and performing nearby. But no, there was no human accompaniment, just this white bike with—I could see as I drew close—cards attached to the sign and to the crossbar:

DAVID SMITH

63 Years Old

Killed by Car

December 5, 2007

A memorial, then, but unlike any I had ever seen before.

The habit of placing flowers or other tributes at the scene of a murder or fatal accident is well established in Britain and America. Two new novels offer vivid essays in contrast between the default style of commemoration in London and New York respectively. For the East End–based narrator of Emily Perkins's *Novel About My Wife*, these "tawdry plastic sheathes of flowers in memory of a loving colour-photocopied mum or restless young chav who's got in the way of somebody's else's crack-fuelled Stanley knife" are "a new form of urban decoration, mawkish post-Diana grief." The Lower East Side equivalent, as seen in Richard Price's *Lush Life,* is altogether more extravagant: "There were dozens of lit botanica candles, a scattering of coins on a velvet cloth, a red cross laid flat on a large round stone, a CD player running Jeff Buckley's 'Hallelujah' on an endless loop, a videocassette of Mel Gibson's *The Passion* still sealed in its box, a paperback of *Black Elk Speaks*, some kind of unidentifiable white pelt, a few petrified-looking joints, bags of assorted herbs, coils of still-smouldering incense that gave off competing scents, and a jar of olive oil." Just four nights later, this wild, neo-Kienholzian shrine is on its way to becoming visual compost. Already it seems "all wrong, sodden and charred, sardonic and vaguely threatening; as if to say, this is what time does, what becomes of us mere hours after the tears and flowers."

This bike, though, had advanced the practice to a far higher level of commemoration and artistic expression. With its poignantly flat tires, the white bike was unmissable and yet, even in the crowded streets of Midtown Manhattan, it didn't get in anyone's way. Robert Musil writes somewhere that nothing is as invisible as a monument; this unmonumental memorial was distinctly visible and yet so discreet as to be *almost not there*. As they waited to cross the street, several people touched the bike: a casual version of the gesture made by Catholics, of crossing themselves when they pass over a threshold. By virtue of the white bike, a completely innocuous corner of Manhattan—one of thousands—had been imbued with a uniquely gentle aura. Perhaps I am being sentimental, but it felt as if this was the safest intersection in the whole of the city.

I had no idea how the white bike came to be there or how it was regarded by the authorities. After a few more months, would the chain be cut and the bicycle discreetly removed? Or would it be allowed to remain perpetually in the sun and rain, like the cars and bikes that have been left to fade, rust, and rot at Oradour-sur-Glane in France since the massacre that took place there on June 10, 1944? I assumed it was a one-off guerrilla action but, in the course of a week in the city, I noticed two more of these white bikes: at Houston and Lafayette, and on the Hudson bike path (in memory of Eric Ng, aged twenty-two), right by the PULSE art fair:

ERIC NG

22 Years Old

Killed By

Drunk Driver

December 1, 2006

Love & Rage

So these bikes *were* part of an organized if unofficial campaign of remembrance. As far as I can work out the first so-called ghost bike appeared in St. Louis, Missouri, in 2003. The ongoing initiative is now part of a loose alliance of websites and organizations such as Visual Resistance and the NYC Street Memorial Project (another strand of which commemorates pedestrian fatalities). According to ghostbikes.org, there are now similar memorials in more than thirty cities across the world. I've never seen one in London, but there are, apparently, ghost bikes in Manchester, Oxford, and Brighton. On the ghost bike website, Ryan, a volunteer, had written about the creation of the bike I had seen outside the PULSE art fair:

> I started making ghost bikes for strangers in June 2005. A year and a half later, my friend Eric Ng was killed by a drunk driver while riding on the West Side bike path. Eric was 22 and had just started teaching math in a Brooklyn high school. He was the kind of person that made you want to live a little more. A year later I still expect to see him when I show up somewhere. His death ripped a hole in my heart.
>
> When we make ghost bikes we tap into the hurt of the world. Each person is part of the soul of their city. These stories can make headlines one day and are forgotten the next—we try to make the city remember. We choose to honor that stranger we know could just as easily be our friend, our sister, our own self. That choice makes us whole.

As well as being part of a web of activist organizations, the ghost bikes can be seen in the context of the ad hoc accumulation of street art generally, from loutish graffiti litter to Banksy's ironic—now ironically iconic and commodified—stencils, to community-based murals. In civic ambition, the ghost bikes

are like a quiet and respectful aspect of the old Reclaim the
Streets initiatives—except they proceed from the premise that
the streets do not need to be reclaimed by confrontation, that
they are *already* ours. But the bikes also throw into relief something about the inadequacy of much public art in general and
"official" memorial art in particular.

At its worst, public art in Britain typically defaults to the
level of the Norman Wisdom sculpture outside Edgware Road
tube station or the justly derided couple kissing good-bye at St.
Pancras. The fact that the latest round of proposals for the
fourth plinth at Trafalgar Square included Tracey Emin's idea
for a little group of sculpted meerkats as "a symbol of unity and
safety" reconfirms what everyone already knows: that it is possible to gain a reputation as a serious and important artist on
the basis of work devoid of seriousness or importance. With the
odd honorable exception—Antony Gormley's *Angel of the
North,* for example—most contemporary public sculpture
prompts the viewer to echo the question posed fifty years ago
by Randall Jarrell in *Pictures from an Institution*: well, it's ugly,
but is it Art?

Rituals of remembrance now come freighted with worries
about whether they will be properly observed. As the singing
stops and the players find their spot "around the ten-yard circle
that until tonight seemed redundant" (Paul Farley, "A Minute's
Silence"), the possibility that homage will turn to insult hangs
over football stadiums like a threat of terror. State-sponsored
memorials like the Diana Fountain in the Serpentine are distinguished by their failure to give voice to the sum of individual feelings they are designed to articulate. In Britain one has
to go back to the numbed aftermath of the First World War, to
Charles Sargeant Jagger's statue of a soldier reading a letter at

Paddington Station (by platform 1) or to the Cenotaph (designed by Sir Edwin Lutyens) on Whitehall to find memorials of high aesthetic quality that are also in step with the needs of a grieving populace.

Most deaths, of course, cannot be expected to be recorded and memorialized on the official monuments of a large city. Nor should artists be required to devote themselves to creating anything other than exactly what they feel like making at any given time. But the hope that the larger needs of society might coincide with the deepest, uncoerced urges of the best artists is never to be entirely extinguished. Perhaps it is a sign not only of the solipsism of the contemporary art world but of a wider social failing, that it is on the margins—and beyond—of the competitive, hedge-fund-powered art market that one finds evidence that art, rather than being an amusing diversion or a profitable investment, might be integrated with a broader goal of social progress. The flip side of the art boom of recent years has been that one notion of value—cash—has become so engorged as to have caused other ones to wilt. This is not to hark back to the earnest early 1960s when John Berger, then art critic of the *New Statesman*, was content to ask a single simple question of any piece of art: "Does this work help or encourage men to know and claim their social rights?" Nor does it date back to the heady days of the Bolshevik Revolution when artists eagerly put their shoulder to the Soviet wheel which would eventually break them. No, this takes us much further back, to the prehistoric dawn of art and of human consciousness, to the realization that, as Lewis Mumford famously expressed it in *The City in History*, "the performance of art itself added something just as essential to primitive man's life as the carnal rewards of the hunt."

The Temple of Tears and the Temple of Joy were created by David Best at Burning Man, Nevada, in 2001 and 2002 respectively. Made out of the wooden offcuts from a toy factory, these huge, Balinese-style structures were constructed by changing teams of volunteers in the course of the weeklong festival. As the temples were being built, people left photographs and keepsakes, or wrote prayers and messages on the wood to loved ones who had died. On the understanding that suicide places the greatest burden on the ones who are left behind to mourn, the altar of the Temple of Tears was dedicated to those who had died by their own hand. Needless to say, there were no notices or guards stipulating appropriate behavior. (Solemnity, it is worth remembering, is usually a form of decorum, a way of behaving that is entirely compatible with a *lack* of feeling.) The boom of sound systems could be heard in the distance; people wandered through in their wild, sex-crazed costumes, but the atmosphere of compassion and kindness was palpable—overwhelming, in fact. In scale and intensity of effect, these Temples were comparable to Lutyens's Memorial to the Missing of the Somme at Thiepval. The difference, of course, is that whereas Lutyens's monument was built to last, the temples were built in order to be ceremoniously burned within days of their completion. In a postreligious culture that lacks appropriate rituals of grieving and mourning—and the solace that is provided by such rites—there was something perfectly appropriate about this: a memorial predicated on transience, a work of art that was absolutely inseparable from the temporary city and the community it was designed to help and to please.

In their less spectacular, more modest—and, already, more lasting—way, the ghost bikes do the same thing: honoring the dead, delighting the living, making the world a safer, nicer place. If that is too humble a definition of art, then one wonders why it is so rarely achieved elsewhere.

POSTSCRIPT: A few days after this essay was published in the *Guardian*, a reader who had been in New York about a month after me sent a picture of the first ghost bike I'd seen, the one on 36th and Sixth. It had been completely vandalized: wheels buckled, signs and tyres torn off. This was sad but, in a way, the mangled bike looked even more poignant than it did in its original pristine condition.

ANNIE DILLARD

THIS IS THE LIFE

Any culture tells you how to live your one and only life: to wit as everyone else does. Probably most cultures prize, as ours rightly does, making a contribution by working hard at work that you love; being in the know, and intelligent; gathering a surplus; and loving your family above all, and your dog, your boat, bird-watching. Beyond those things our culture might specialize in money, and celebrity, and natural beauty. These are not universal. You enjoy work and will love your grandchildren, and somewhere in there you die.

Another contemporary consensus might be: you wear the best shoes you can afford, you seek to know Rome's best restaurants and their staffs, drive the best car, and vacation on Tenerife. And what a cook you are!

Or you take the next tribe's pigs in thrilling raids; you grill yams; you trade for televisions and hunt white-plumed birds. Everyone you know agrees: this is the life. Perhaps you burn captives. You set fire to a drunk. Yours is the human struggle, or the elite one, to achieve . . . whatever your own culture tells you: to publish the paper that proves the point; to progress in the firm and gain high title and salary, stock options, benefits;

to get the loan to store the beans till their price rises; to elude
capture, to feed your children or educate them to a feather
edge; or to count coup or perfect your calligraphy; to eat the
king's deer or catch the poacher; to spear the seal, intimidate
the enemy, and be a big man or beloved woman and die
respected for the pigs or the title or the shoes. Not a funeral.
Forget funeral. A big birthday party. Since everyone around
you agrees.

Since everyone around you agrees ever since there were
people on earth that land is value, or labor is value, or learning
is value, or title, necklaces, degree, murex shells, or ownership
of slaves. Everyone knows bees sting and ghosts haunt and giving your robes away humiliates your rivals. That the enemies
are barbarians. That wise men swim through the rock of the
earth; that houses breed filth, airstrips attract airplanes, torna-
does punish, ancestors watch, and you can buy a shorter stay in
purgatory. The black rock is holy, or the scroll; or the pangolin
is holy, the quetzal is holy, this tree, water, rock, stone, cow,
cross, or mountain, and it's all true. The Red Sox. Or nothing
at all is holy, as everyone intelligent knows.

Who is your "everyone"? Chess masters scarcely surround
themselves with motocross racers. Do you want aborigines at
your birthday party? Or are you serving yak-butter tea? Popular culture deals not in its distant past, or any other past, or any
other culture. You know no one who longs to buy a mule or
be named to court or thrown into a volcano.

So the illusion, like the visual field, is complete. It has no
holes except books you read and soon forget. And death takes
us by storm. What was that, that life? What else offered? If for
him it was contract bridge, if for her it was copyright law, if for
everyone it was and is an optimal mix of family and friends,

learning, contribution, and joy of making and ameliorating
what else is there, or was there, or will there ever be?

What else is a vision or fact of time and the peoples it bears
issuing from the mouth of the cosmos, from the round mouth
of eternity, in a wide and parti-colored utterance. In the complex weave of this utterance like fabric, in its infinite domestic
interstices, the centuries and continents and classes dwell. Each
people knows only its own squares in the weave, its wars and
instruments and arts, and also the starry sky.

Okay, and then what? Say you scale your own weft and see
time's breadth and the length of space. You see the way the
fabric both passes among the stars and encloses them. You see
in the weave nearby, and aslant farther off, the peoples variously scandalized or exalted in their squares. They work on
their projects: they flake spear points, hoe, plant; they kill
aurochs or one another; they prepare sacrifices as we here and
now work on our projects. What, seeing this spread multiply
infinitely in every direction, would you do differently? No one
could love your children more; would you love them less?
Would you change your project? To what? Whatever you do,
it has likely brought delight to fewer people than either contract bridge or the Red Sox.

However hypnotized you and your people are, you will be
just as dead in their war, our war. However dead you are, more
people will come. However many more people come, your
time and its passions, and yourself and your passions, weigh
equally in the balance with those of any dead who pulled
waterwheel poles by the Nile or Yellow rivers, or painted their
foreheads black, or starved in the wilderness, or wasted from
disease then or now. Our lives and our deaths count equally, or
we must abandon one-man-one-vote, dismantle democracy,

and assign six billion people an importance-of-life ranking from one to six billion whose number decreases, like gravity, with the square of the distance between us and them.

What would you do differently, you up on your beanstalk looking at scenes of all peoples at all times in all places? When you climb down, would you dance any less to the music you love, knowing that music to be as provisional as a bug? Somebody has to make jugs and shoes, to turn the soil, fish. If you descend the long rope-ladders back to your people and time in the fabric, if you tell them what you have seen, and even if someone cares to listen, then what? Everyone knows times and cultures are plural. If you come back a shrugging relativist or tongue-tied absolutist, then what? If you spend hours a day looking around, high astraddle the warp or woof of your people's wall, then what new wisdom can you take to your grave for worms to untangle? Well, maybe you will not go into advertising.

Then you would know your own death better but perhaps not dread it less. Try to bring people up the wall, carry children to see it to what end? Fewer golf courses? What is wrong with golf? Nothing at all. Equality of wealth? Sure; how?

The woman watching sheep over there, the man who carries embers in a pierced clay ball, the engineer, the girl who spins wool into yarn as she climbs, the smelter, the babies learning to recognize speech in their own languages, the man whipping a slave's flayed back, the man digging roots, the woman digging roots, the child digging roots, what would you tell them? And the future people, what are they doing? What excitements sweep peoples here and there from time to time? Into the muddy river they go, into the trenches, into the caves, into the mines, into the granary, into the sea in boats. Most humans who were ever alive lived inside one single culture that never changed for hundreds of thousands of years; archaeologists scratch their heads at so conservative and static a culture.

Over here the rains fail; they are starving. There the caribou fail; they are starving. Corrupt leaders take the wealth. Not only there but here. Rust and smut spoil the rye. When pigs and cattle starve or freeze, people die soon after. Disease empties a sector, a billion sectors.

People look at the sky and at the other animals. They make beautiful objects, beautiful sounds, beautiful motions of their bodies beating drums in lines. They pray; they toss people in peat bogs; they help the sick and injured; they pierce their lips, their noses, ears; they make the same mistakes despite religion, written language, philosophy, and science; they build, they kill, they preserve, they count and figure, they boil the pot, they keep the embers alive; they tell their stories and gird themselves.

Will knowledge you experience directly make you a Buddhist? Must you forfeit excitement per se? To what end?

Say you have seen something. You have seen an ordinary bit of what is real, the infinite fabric of time that eternity shoots through, and time's soft-skinned people working and dying under slowly shifting stars. Then what?

ACKNOWLEDGMENTS

The idea for this anthology arose during a conversation the two of us had on a train returning from Bard College to New York City. During the twenty-five years we'd known each other, we had never discussed the subject of death. As the Hudson River glinted in the late afternoon sun out the window, we realized there was no subject more interesting, nor one more difficult to address. Following our talk, we decided to approach a number of fellow writers, asking for meditations on the subject of mortality. We would like to thank all those who contributed to *Conjunctions:51, The Death Issue: Meditations on the Inevitable* (Fall 2008) and to *Seattle Review, Issues with Death* (Winter 2010 and Summer 2010), in which many of these essays originally appeared. We are especially grateful to Jill Bialosky, Arne Christensen, Elizabeth Cooperman, Henry Dunow, Alison Liss, Cara Schlesinger, and Pat Sims for their help along the way.

PERMISSIONS

David Shields is the author of ten previous books, including *Reality Hunger*; *The Thing About Life Is That One Day You'll Be Dead*, a *New York Times* bestseller; *Black Planet*, a finalist for the National Book Critics Circle Award; *Remote*, winner of the PEN/Revson Award; and *Dead Languages*, winner of the PEN Syndicated Fiction Award. His work has been translated into fifteen languages. He lives with his wife and daughter in Seattle, where he is the Milliman Distinguished Writer-in-Residence at the University of Washington.

Bradford Morrow is the author of the novels *Come Sunday*, *The Almanac Branch*, *Trinity Fields*, *Giovanni's Gift*, *Ariel's Crossing*, and *The Diviner's Tale*. His first collection of short stories, *Lush and Other Stories*, is forthcoming in the fall of 2011 from Pegasus Books. He has been the recipient of numerous awards, including the Academy Award in Fiction from the American Academy of Arts and Letters and a 2007 Guggenheim Fellowship. He is the founding editor of the widely acclaimed literary journal *Conjunctions*, for which he received the 2007 PEN/Nora Magid Award, and is a professor of literature and Bard Center Fellow at Bard College. He divides his time between New York City and an old farmhouse in upstate New York.